Birth of a Culture

SIMON &
SCHUSTER

London · New York · Amsterdam/Antwerp · Sydney/Melbourne · Toronto · New Delhi

First published in the United States by Amistad, an imprint of HarperCollins Publishers, 2026
First published in Great Britain by Simon & Schuster UK Ltd, 2026

All photographs and the drawing on p. vii are courtesy of the author.

1 3 5 7 9 10 8 6 4 2

Simon & Schuster UK Ltd, 7th Floor,
199 Bishopsgate, London, EC2M 3TY

www.simonandschuster.co.uk
www.simonandschuster.com.au
www.simonandschuster.co.in

Simon & Schuster Australia, Sydney
Simon & Schuster India, New Delhi

The authorised representative in the EEA is Simon & Schuster Netherlands BV, Herculesplein 96, 3584 AA Utrecht, Netherlands. info@simonandschuster.nl

A CIP catalogue record for this book
is available from the British Library

Hardback ISBN: 978-1-3985-6751-1
eBook ISBN: 978-1-3985-6752-8

Designed by Yvonne Chan

Illustrations © alex_bond/stock.adobe.com

Printed and Bound in the UK using 100% Renewable Electricity at CPI Group (UK) Ltd

FSC
www.fsc.org
MIX
Paper | Supporting responsible forestry
FSC® C013604

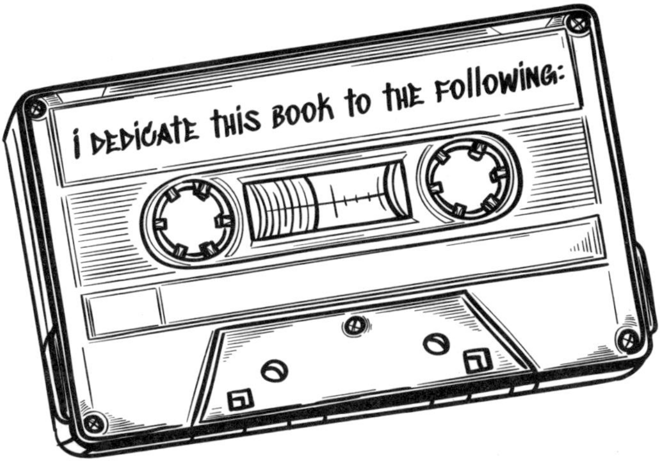

The mothers of my children: Paulette Dawson, Jean Sanders (Rest in Peace), Pamela Howell (Rest in Peace), and Angelique Jester—thank you for holding it down when I couldn't be there.

My children: Tawana, Lallanie, Joe Joe, Kareem, Keith, Christina, and Latoya—I apologize for not being there as much as I wanted to be.

My grandkids: Jakaya, Joe Joe Jr., Bishme, Brynia, Nas, Ling Ling, Laishelle—the coolest grandkids ever.

My cousins, nieces, and nephews, Leah, Salanesa, Cincerie, Takoda, Demetrius, Moycee, Venescha, Kalima, Ramel, Little Ramel, Kendell, Ayden, Ayala, Janay, Anaya, the Mavens family, Bullock family, Uncle Eddie, Uncle Rufi, Auntie Doris, and Uncle Phare—thank you for being there.

Sal Abbatiello, for giving me the opportunity to execute my Quik Mix Theory at Disco Fever on Tuesdays, which allowed me to expand my horizons.

Charlie Ahearn, Fab 5 Freddy, and Baz Luhrmann—thank you for choosing my city, the Bronx, as the template to make movies for all the world to see.

The Graffiti Writers: Ray-B 954, Super Kool 223, Phase II, and Riff—some of the Godfathers of the Graffiti culture.

The breakdancers that loyally supported my parties every weekend—Black Jerry, Bumpy Face Melvin, Avery, Flippin' Mike, Mean Jean (who eventually became my DJ partner), Sister Boo, Janice, and Mother Earth.

QUIK MIXTHEORY//QMT
4BF = 6CCR = FULL LOOP EXTRACTION
MC/RAPPER
DJ
MIXER
SAMPLING
CLOCKWISE
COUNTER CLOCKWISE
4 BARS FORWARD ARE EQUAL TO 6 COUNTERCLOCKWISE TO A FULL LOOP EXTRACTION
©
1972-2025

Contents

Part I
The Saddlers (Throggs Neck: 1957–1970)

1 **"Tramp"**
Otis Redding and Carla Thomas (1967)

2 **"The Champ"**
The Mohawks (1968)

3 **"Think"**
Aretha Franklin (1968)

4 **"I Can't Get Next to You"**
The Temptations (1969)

5 **"Thank You"**
Sly and the Family Stone (1970)

6 **"Ike's Mood"**
Isaac Hayes (1970)

7 **"Chicken Strut"**
The Meters (1970)

8 **"Funky Drummer"**
James Brown (1970)

9 **"Reach Out of the Darkness"**
Friend and Lover (1968)

Chapter 1

My dad, Joesph Saddler Sr., born in Boston, was a big collector of jazz music: Miles, Sinatra, the Glenn Miller Orchestra, Artie Shaw. My dad loved it so much he probably spent more time with his music than he did us kids. There was no interrupting him at night when he came home from work and listened to his music on 2730 Dewey Ave., Apt. 2C. For a living he was a railroad-track repair guy—worked for New York City Transit, Penn Station—a track worker for the subways. His routine when he came home from work was: get his dinner from my mom, choose his alcoholic beverage of choice for the evening, eat dinner, then he would go to his closet in the living room. And in this closet, he would pull out these square things that had pictures on them. I was a child so I had no idea what they were, but I would watch him and say, "What is he going to do with that?"

Now this is the mid-sixties, 1965, 1966, I was born in 1957. And all I knew was on these square things there were pictures. Pictures of a choo choo train, sometimes a person, sometimes flowers, sometimes it was just the sky, sometimes it was just words, writing. I was very confused and curious as to what he was going to do with them. Then he'd pull these black circular things out of the square art thing. Now I'm really wondering, *what the hell is going on? What is that?!? What is he going to do with that?* My baby sister, Lilly, and I would just watch. At the same time, me and Lilly were banned from going into the living room without an adult. Caught in the living room without an adult: ass whoopin'.

So my dad would take this black circular thing and go over to this brown box and continue with this procedure. Open the door to where the brown box was, lift up the cover on the top of the brown box, put the circular thing inside of the brown box, then place the black circular thing on the silver stick, put that arm thing that went up and down on the circular thing that magically started spinning, and sound would come out. It was amazing. "Oh. My. God! My dad is a magician!" I'm perplexed as hell. But I'd sit and watch until he was finished. When he'd pull the stick thing off the black disc, the sound would stop, and then he'd take the black disc off the brown box and put it back into the square thing that had the art on it, and he'd put the square thing back into the closet.

And it wasn't too long before I stopped paying attention and watching him when he came home from work and began paying attention and watching when he *left to go* to work. Early in the mornings. And I knew when he'd leave because he had this pouch of tools that he took with him every morning. And I'd wait to hear the *clinks* for when he'd put the pouch on his shoulder. Then I'd hear the door slam. That's how I knew. At this point I say to myself, as a toddler, "Hmmm, I'm going to time Dad. Wait for the tools to make noise, wait for the door to slam, wait for a period of time. . . ." Because once he went to work it gave me the chance to physically figure out his routine for myself. So I'd go into the kitchen, drag a chair over to the closet where these square things were. Get up on the chair, and turn the closet knob.

I remember the first time I got on that chair and opened that closet. I'd seen it from afar, from the other side of the room. I'd peeked at it, but never really seen it for myself. Not up close. When I first opened that door, standing on that chair, I was overwhelmed, my breathing shifted. Like "Wow!" My eyes kept going side to side and up and down. All the way to the ceiling, it was too much. I was amazed. "Dad has a whole lotta these square things with the round black circles inside." And because he wasn't home and because there were so many of those square cardboard things and because I knew and had studied his routine, I did the unthinkable.

To put the whole thing in perspective, two things must be understood: One, my mother, Regina Saddler, was a seamstress. She worked from home. And she warned me. Two, my uncle, my father's younger brother, was the featherweight and junior lightweight boxing champion of the world in the late forties and early fifties, Sandy Saddler. Ranked #5 on *The Ring* magazine's "100 Greatest Punchers of All Time." He beat the great Willie Pep three times. My uncle got his hands from my father. My father worked down on the tracks at Penn Station in New York. He used his hands for a living. If you touched them they felt hard as the railroads he worked on. My father had hands of stone. Getting a beating by him was almost like getting hit by a car—you tried everything to avoid it.

Back to the chair, as I stood on it, with my father's routine stuck in my head, I grabbed the nearest square thing according to my height, pulled it away from all of the other square things, don't remember the name that was written on it, took it over to the brown box, and followed my father's procedure of what I watched him do every night. When my mother, who was home, working, heard music playing, she ran over to me and said, "If your dad caught you in those records you're gonna get your fuckin' ass killed." All I heard was "whooped." When she told me that, I immediately, in fear, took the record off the spinning thing, put it back into the square thing, and put it back in the closest.

Dad comes home from work. Goes through his pre–square thing/round disc ritual. Notices something's not right and calls everyone out. "Violet!" "Carmetta!" "Penny!" "Little Joe!" "Lilly!" "Who was messing with my records?" Violet, who was my dad's favorite: "You know doggone well I don't mess with your stuff." Carmetta: "Nope. It wasn't me." Penny: "I don't even go near your records." By the time he got to me I was shaking. Me: "It wasn't me." And Lilly was too young. Once he figured out it was me, my shaking brought on by fear gave me away, I got my hind fried. Got the spanking of life from those hard-ass hands. Told to go eat dinner and straight to bed. I'm crying, Mom and Dad are arguing, she's protecting me. We all eventually go to sleep. Dad gets up in the morning, I get up too. Dad gets ready for work, I wait for the door to slam. Hear the tool bag. *Slam!* I wait. I go in the kitchen, grab the chair, same chair, drag it to the closet, back at it. Grab the square thing, nearest one according to my height, pull out the black circle, repeat the procedure, Mom heard music again. Let's just say: I took those ass beatings over and over. It was Dad and me. That was *our* routine. I was so fascinated with the discovery of that sound that I almost became immune to the butt whoopings. At this point my Dad and I were going at it, and my mom protected me from him. And this is why part of me believes I'm one of the reasons Dad left.

Time passed. Dad's gone. He was abusive to Mom, and she's now left to fend for us. Living on public assistance, we had to wait for that check to come on the first and the fifteenth of every month to live. Still in the midst of that, I'll use the word *change* instead of *trauma*, with Dad being gone I am even more fascinated with anything that has a switch to it or has an "on" button. Because as a child what really intrigued me from the brown box that lived in the living room was when Dad would turn that thing on there was a red light at the bottom and a picture of a dog that had these words along with it: RCA Victor. As I'd got older, I dove deeper into what this was. What made sound come out of this box? So I unscrewed the back of it. Keep in mind, this was Mom's box now, she'd bought another one, since Dad took his box with him. And when I unscrewed the back of this box I saw that it had a glass lightbulb-like thing, and I'm asking myself, *What do they do?* I'm also asking: *What are these colored things?* They looked like candy. Red, blue, yellow, green, silver. All markings on these parts. Later, I learned it was called the resistor color code.

Now I'm buggin'. I'm into it and want to know everything. I'm listening to the radio and wondering how is sound coming out of that, so I'm unscrewing everything electrical in the house; the table radio, the stereo, the television, my sisters' hair curlers and hair dryers. Anything that's electrical, I'm unscrewing and unknowingly destroying in our house. In our family circle, the unit that was still together, I became public enemy number one. And it got really bad because as I was unscrewing things, unfortunately, I didn't know how to put them back together. My sisters would get on me, which I thought was them hating on me: "Lil' Joe [my nickname], you have to stop doing this because Mom spends a lot of money on these things and you are ruining them." And around that time, it was decided by the whole family that because I was fascinated by this, I'd go to a school that could make clarity of how these objects and appliances worked. This was my family's way of saving me.

The school was Samuel Gompers Vocational and Technical High School. I began ninth grade there in 1971. I was fourteen years old. Once there, I began to get a better picture of what these things were and what they did and what made them work. I learned about alternating current (AC) and direct current (DC), and I learned about amplitude modulation (AM) and frequency modulation (FM), and both radio frequencies needed what's called the "carrier wave." I learned answers to questions that I didn't even know to ask: What was a solid-state versus vacuum tubes, what are resistors, what is a resistor color code, what are capacitors, what are transformers? I remember for one of the first projects we had to learn how to build an amplifier from scratch. It was a tiny one, but for me just understanding what an amplifier was and how it worked and functioned gave me a picture of what I was destroying as a toddler and preteenager in my mom's house. At school I began to get a better picture of how everything functioned, what colored items and parts were and what they did and what these electrical appliances did and what made them work. Diodes, transformers, amplifiers. How they work and how to technically repair stuff that I would eventually find in junk yards: stereos, rear car speakers, TVs. Samuel Gompers High School gave me a road map of how to build my own stuff.

Because I grew up poor, living in the projects—Throggs Neck Projects, in the Bronx, then moved to 927 Fox Street also in the Bronx—my mom couldn't afford to replace the stuff that I destroyed. But I was fascinated with how the amplifier worked; how the turntable worked; how the cartridge worked, whether it was ceramic or magnetic cartridges, even sapphire or diamond needles, which was called the stylus—elliptical verses conical—worked. It wasn't until I got a clear understanding of how the turntable functioned—belt drive then, direct drive later—that I was able to double back and make sense of how vinyl worked. I *finally* understood that on that black disc that was inside of the square thing, called a cover, was the identifier of each artist that made these songs. Back then for me, more intriguing than the music that the artists made was where the music was coming from. "Where is this music coming from?" haunted me.

One day, because Mom was a seamstress, I decided to try something. I went to the stereo, put the vinyl on, took one of my mom's sewing needles, turned on the turntable platter, and put her needle down on the vinyl record while the turntable platter was spinning clockwise. While it was spinning I noticed that I was getting a vibration in my thumb and forefinger. I'm like, "Oh wow! The music lives in the black tunnels of the vinyl! That's where the music is coming from!" Once I got that understanding I went deep into the cartridge, deep into the needle, deep into the vinyl, deep into the turntable—and all of their separate purposes.

* * *

Lil' Joe, again, was what my sisters, mom, dad, aunties, uncles, cousins all called me. And because my mother's mother—my grandmother—was from Barbados, we have Bajan roots and blood in our DNA. Even though my mother was born in New York. As was I. Before my father left, my parents and my older sisters used to throw parties. I would sneak out of my bed to watch them in the living room. I'll never forget hearing a very popular song they'd play during those parties called "Move On

Up" by Curtis Mayfield. It's 1970 and this is when I started paying scientific attention to the drum beat. That song had the world's longest drum break—it had to be two minutes or more. I would get lost in that drum break, trapped. So when I started listening to other records, I'd notice that when the drum break came in, the backsides of my mom and dad's friends would move more. Their behinds gyrated with more purpose; their dancing seemed to become more intense and serious. So, in my toddler mind, *the best part of the record has to be when the least of the band members were playing in accompaniment with the drummer.* They called it "the drum solo"—whether it be the drummer and the bass player, the drummer and the cellist, or the drummer and the trumpet, to any other instrument in connection with the drummer. This was very exciting for me. My thought was that all records had this long drum solo like Curtis Mayfield's record. As I was listening to other artists, to my disappointment, the drum solo on other records was over as soon as I blinked my eyes.

Because of this, 2730 Dewey Ave., Apt. 2C, in the Throggs Neck Projects in the Bronx was the home and birthplace of some groundbreaking elements of what would one day be called the "Quik Mix Theory" and "hip-hop."

As I got older and listened to the radio, the big music at that time was Mom and Dad's jazz or my big sisters' disco, funk, R&B, pop, and Latin music. I noticed that in some of the songs my big sisters listened to on the stereo, they had very short drum solos. And that upset me too. There was a song called "The Meditation," and the drum solo was amazing but very short. I was so disappointed. And I was slowly realizing during this time that the drum solo was always disappointingly short. As I was listening and learning the different genres of songs my sisters were playing on the stereo, anger was festering inside of me, wishing the drum solo was longer.

I became deeply interested in the DJs and the way they played this big music called disco. And in listening to disco DJs, I'm learning that they are playing vinyl on these two machines called *turntables* with this machine in the middle called a *mixer*. But I'm still perplexed on how they are going from one song to another flawlessly. I didn't necessarily know the names, titles, and artists of the songs, but I could hear one song departing while another song was slowly arriving. This was mind-blowing. I was extremely excited about this, very curious. As curious as I was about how the brown box worked. Even though I don't necessarily like the music they are playing—it's nothing like the music that was being played in Mom's house, at Mom's parties and the music my older sisters listened to—I was amazed at how those DJs were playing this music.

So, of course, with no money but a lot of innovation and knowledge of "how," with the things I was learning at Samuel Gompers, I built my own DJ set. It was a piece of shit, but I loved it. My oldest sister Violet's husband, Percy, was the superintendent where we lived with Mom at 927 Fox Street, where the only friend I had was Gordon Upshaw, who lived on the same block. (Gordon would later give me the name "Flash" because I could run fast.) Percy would allow us to have parties in the vacant apartments or block parties in front of the building.

I'm becoming friendly with my friends' parents. I'm becoming friendly with a few fans from my block parties. And I would ask them if they had any records that they don't want anymore. Some were glad to do it because the records were taking up space in their closets. Some parents had so many records I had to run home to get my mother's shopping cart to go back and get the records that they were giving to me. This was the early beginning of the building of my vinyl collection.

The big DJs during that time were Maboya, Pete DJ Jones (who I called "the King of Disco" in New York), DJ Plummer, David Rodriguez, Larry Levan. And by the time I'd built my own little sound system, I wasn't trying to do what they did, but I was trying to master a part of what they did by blending the records together without making it seem like there were two different songs playing at the same time. Little did I know I was about to change the way DJs played music, but I was hated for the style that I was about to invent. My best friend, EZ Mike, and another friend of ours named Dwyane told me, "We gotta take you somewhere to listen to this guy who has this very loud sound system, and he's playing these records that are not disco."

We all walk over to the west side of the Bronx, to Sedgwick Avenue, to the park. As we approach the park, there are tons of people. Approximately five hundred. And through all of that, there's this light-skinned guy, tall, not playing the songs that I hear from the disco DJs. He's playing soul songs, funk, and R&B, he'd throw a little pop in sometimes. Everything from James Brown to Rufus Thomas. His sound system was amazing, at my age, around fifteen or sixteen years old. I thought, *This guy must be a millionaire or something.* The sound was clean: bass, midrange, treble, all perfect. Plus he had dudes, goons standing next to him so no one could get near or next to him or, more important, his turntables.

He was playing the music my big sisters played on the stereo at home—but he was playing them on this big-ass sound system, and I'm hearing those same songs like I'd never heard them before. Lots of bass. People are dancing, people are breaking, he's king. But—and there's a major "but" in my little brain—

he's not doing it like the disco DJs that I was watching and listening to. His sound when he went from one song to the next would train wreck. His transitions were inconsiderate of timing or beats per minute (BPMs). I was very puzzled, *Why is he DJing like this?* The music he was playing was beautiful. I walked away confused. He's damn-near letting the whole record play before getting to the drum solo. I'm hearing this wonderful music sounding amazing coming out of his speakers, but it sounds like the songs are fighting each other when he ended one and played another.

His name was Kool Herc, and I knew that because he kept saying his name on the microphone. "Herc, Herc!" "Kool Herc!" "Herc, Herc, y'all!" To me his music was difficult to dance to especially when it came to transitions from one song to the next. Nonetheless, he was King of the Sounds. Although my sound system would not be able to compete with his, my newly invented style of DJing was untouchable. Every DJ who'd seen or heard about it wanted to learn it. I knew I would never play music the way Kool Herc did. In my head I called it, Disarray and Unison. A musical oxymoron. I learned, there was "the what" (being a DJ) and there was "the how" (how you DJ)—when it came to this, in my opinion, there's a big difference. As I walked home from watching Kool Herc play, I continued working on my new DJing invention.

So I began doing with DJs what I did with my father: I watched them. I studied the disco DJs and the nondisco DJs and learned their procedures and the law of transitions. I realized the disco and nondisco DJs' styles were based heavily on using the tonearm repeatedly and putting it down on the vinyl. They'd go into their crates to select the next record; they'd wipe each record off carefully with a velvet brush to clean it every time before they put it on the turntable, and they'd use the fader in a one-time slow manner to mix into the next selection. But me being very impatient I used the paniometer, which is another way of saying "the crossfader." And I'd play the crossfader like I was playing the guitar or a keyboard. Quick movement left to right, as I was opening and closing the crossfader. I came up with terms, words, that were unpopular to describe what I was doing: *punch phase*, *fake phase*, *front door*, *back door*. DJ purists hated it, but it was all part of the innovation.

The tonearm became 99.9 percent insignificant except for when I was changing the record. This also allowed me to move the fader into a very quick open and close manner while moving the vinyl backward and forward or in a counterclockwise way. This was my revenge to percussively extend a ten-second drum solo to two-minute drum break seamlessly by using duplicate copies of the same song placed on turntable one and turntable two.

I was in the dark musically; I needed a musical bridge between the dancer or rapper and myself. This is where God came in again. I discovered that I had to use the turntable and mixer the wrong way to make it right. It was paramount that I returned to the intro of songs with very short drum solos without the listener/dancer/rapper knowing what I was doing. I dug deeper into this understanding, and the tonearm became more useless when God said, "You're almost there."

I was desperately trying to find a way to keep that ten-second piece of music on time like everyone else with the tonearm, but it was too sloppy, too off beat. And I just couldn't accept it. The defining moment is when I said to myself, "What if I could touch it?" I slowly hovered my hand over the spinning vinyl, and then for the first time ever, a finger touched the wax.

I hadn't given this style of DJing a name yet, but I experimented in the parks, and the fans came to hear the music and this new style of DJing which was never seen or heard before. I remember saying to myself, "I'm playing the drum solos of the biggest pop, rock, jazz, blues, funk, disco, R&B, Latin, alternative songs." In my warped mind I was very excited, playing the best part of all of these songs back-to-back, seamlessly, perfectly timed, perfect BPMs.

So I continued my studies: How can I take the James Brown break of "Funky Drummer" and unify it with the intro break of Barry White's "I'm Gonna Love You Just a Little More Baby," Billy Squier's "The Big Beat," Cat Stevens's "Was Dog a Doughnut?" or the first four beats of the Honey Drippers' "Impeach the President." This became the most difficult time of my young life. I *literally* could not figure this out. How can I keep the unison going *endlessly*? How can I *do* that? How can I *create* that?

* * *

Of my crew, I was the corny one. The geek, the uncool guy. I wasn't hip, didn't know the latest sayings and slang, I didn't know how to rap to girls . . . yet. Truman, the first guy of the crew I met, was more like the swaggy kinda guy. He wasn't the flyest of the crew, but he was the swaggiest. Then I met Darnell, aka OJ. OJ was the good-looking one. Kinda shy too. Then it was EZ Mike, who of the crew was the fly guy, the bad boy of the crew. He had the baddest chicks, major street respect, and many women chasing him for many years. And he investigated that thoroughly.

The four of us in the beginning were like superglue. And we all ended up dating the Dawson sisters, who stayed on Faile Street in the Bronx. Because of that we'd always see one another and we became close, you could never separate us. Now Truman's father was the super of a building on Faile Street, across the street from PS 75. One block south from the Dawson sisters. He noticed how much we were hanging together and gave us a place to hang out in the vacant basement apartment of that building. I already knew EZ Mike was beginning to scheme on the skins (girls). Truman, like Mike, was probably scheming on the skins. OJ was the innocent one. Me, at seventeen years old, I was scheming on how I could wire the basement up and get sound and a setup. It became our clubhouse. Snow, rain, get some girls, smoke some weed, or drink Swiss Up or Mad Dog 20/20 just to not be on the streets. Somewhere we could go after school. Our compound. That was our hangout.

This was really the start for me. Of all the things I was doing, all of the things I was building from used equipment and parts I gathered from junkyards and other random places, money I was getting from a messenger job I had to buy decent turntables, the old speakers and car stereos, old amp equipment, wires, etc. Of everything I was hauling down into the basement to build my sound system, it was on Faile Street where I really began getting into wiring sound, bringing in turntables, and turning our hangout/clubhouse into a workshop/party spot. My system: two turntables, a homemade mixer, a tube guitar amplifier by Plush, and speakers that I'd built by hand. Mike used to crack on my speakers because they had plexiglass with Christmas lights on the top and white pleather wallpaper around the outside of them. About five feet tall, all midrange, no bass, no subwoofer. It was wack, but it was all I had. Because at this point I'm at the experimental point of developing my "theory" of sound, amplified by what the disco DJs were doing. My excitement for DJing increased and became more important to me.

* * *

The root of everything I was trying to discover was based on science and math. I didn't realize that at the time, but what was driving me were the same subject matters that drove Einstein, Tesla, and Edison—science and math—when it came to them inventing. Banneker, Westinghouse, Marconi. They were my electrical, technology heroes. I was a nerd, but I wasn't a "science" nerd in school. I was a nerdy, bothersome kid, especially to my sisters, but I wasn't a "nerdy" math-type of kid who walked around with a pocket protector or anything like that. I was a typical Black kid from the projects in the Bronx, who lived with an abusive father, still had fun despite surviving that, had friends, but also had an acute, almost obsessive interest in electronics and how they functioned. At the same time I was that kid—very much like the inventors I was reading about in school, who all had this "thing" for making something out of the ideas they had in their heads.

A scientist's desire to make mind and machine work together. I wasn't making something out of nothing; I was trying to make something *greater* out of something. Making something better that didn't exist out of something that already existed. That's what was in my teenage head, and it stayed there until I was grown.

All of this was pre-Herc in 1973, when he was given credit for throwing the first ever hip-hop party. But after seeing Herc in the park, when EZ Mike and Dwayne took me that day, I even went back to see him a few more times. I was a breakdancer for a very short period of time; I found it difficult to dance to the style he was playing even though he had the dopest style of the era. I watched the crowd, I watched the disco and nondisco DJs and my anger with the too-short drum solos, I knew I had to complete the process. I listened to how the music was being played, I knew what I was hearing in my head. I just had to incorporate math and science into what I was sonically hearing. Listening to it mathematically allowed me to listen to music without race, creed, color, or location. Math and science were the equalizers. White break, the black break, the foreign break, the American break. Music was colorless in my head.

Math ("the bars") and science ("kinetic energy") became the mixtures that gave me the freedom to listen to music without prejudice. I had to count the bars during the drum solos and named this the "Clock Theory," like a kindergartener learning how to count, and like a kindergartener I used crayons. The records represented my coloring books. I also had to count the beats-per-minute. The stylus became my best friend. It generated the kinetic energy that later became the kinetic energy of the speakers. Counting and listening. I had to be absolutely sure that the drummer actually playing was *perfectly* in time with the next drummer and the next drummer had to be in time with the next drummer. The main objective was to have the drummers play their separate styles but stay in unison with everyone's style. I watched my audience walk into block parties and go from a calm two-step to a frenzy, little did they know they were dancing to drum solos from all around the world. So while my stylus on the vinyl generates the kinetic energy that becomes sound, which is the science, I'm counting the bars to the next record, and that's the math.

The science, the math, and my fingertips are the pillars to what I call the "Quik Mix Theory." Using the tonearm as little as possible. The science and math generate a bed of music for the rapper. This was years before postmodern, big-business hip-hop comes into play. And then there's the secret weapon: a gentleman who lives in the Jackson Avenue projects. A drummer named

Stanley who practices his skills on this box. This electronic drum box. I can remember purposely walking through the Jackson Avenue Projects to track this man down. To discover the beats inside of this box.

As one of the inventors—as the architect—of this culture it sometimes scares me when a fan walks up to me and calls me a legend. It took me many years to accept that my ideas, concepts, and techniques are a major reason this thing is what it's become. I can only say that I think God chose me to bring this thing to the world.

* * *

In a weird way, this is where my mom comes in. She was part two of the person who inspired me to experiment with this appliance that had a needle. She was a seamstress, and she made my sisters' clothing and some of mine. Mom was a genius with all fabrics—polyester, rayon, silk, cotton, leather, suede, denim. Staring at a metal platter of a turntable with that rubber mat thing on top was my way of studying, and that's how an idea struck me. I grabbed my albums and I ran to the nearest fabric store. I remember walking through the aisles of the fabric store, touching every fabric I could get my hands on. When I touched the felt, I almost zoned out as it took me back to grade school.

A person who worked in the store walked up to me. "Can I help you with anything little boy?"

"I need two pieces of this felt the same size as this album, please."

The man looked at me very strangely. I said, "That's what I need, sir."

He grabbed the yardstick, scissors, and grease pencil to cut out two squares of felt that were slightly larger than the albums. I remember going home, grabbing scissors, putting them in the center of the felt, poking a hole in the center, and opening the scissors up to cut the edges off so I could get it precisely the size of the albums. I had a problem: the felt was circular and the same size as the albums and limp. I needed to stiffen the two pieces of felt. I got the spray starch when my mom wasn't looking, I turned the iron up to high and pressed the iron to the round felt on both sides. Going back to the turntable that rubber mat piece created drag friction and when I was trying to go clockwise on the turntable with the album, the whole platter would go clockwise using that nasty rubber piece. That was a huge problem. I removed the rubber mat and replaced it with the heavily starched felt that was stiffer.

Then I placed the felt on the metal platter and placed the album on the felt. Turned on the turntable and gently placed my fingertips on the vinyl, gently pushing the vinyl with my fingertips in a backward and forward motion, then with a fully clockwise motion I'm watching the metal platter. The key thing is to have the platter go in a clockwise motion perfectly while I go either backward or forward or counterclockwise. This procedure allowed me to check the metal platter to make sure that it was going comfortably in a clockwise motion while I was going clockwise back and forth, counterclockwise. I noticed that there was a degree of friction with the platter slowing down as I was doing these moves with the vinyl. It was pretty bad with the rubber mat, but *much better* with the felt on the metal platter. I needed one more piece of material to make the platter move comfortably in a clockwise motion.

I remember the days when my mom or someone in the family made chocolate chip cookies; sometimes because of grades or other times for no reason. When my Mom was unaware, I would go into the kitchen and take the wax paper she used to make chocolate chip cookies. I would cut the wax paper to the exact same size as the album. Two pieces, just like the felt. I would take the wax paper, place it on the metal platter and then the spray-starched felt that I called "the wafer" would go on top of the wax paper. And then I'd take the vinyl album and place it on top of the felt, press play on the turntable, and once again go backward and forward and counterclockwise with my fingertips on the record. I could feel and see that the platter was happy. It was going in a steady clockwise motion. Allowing me to go backward and forward and counterclockwise, backward and forward and counterclockwise. Problem solved.

The biggest problem with the Theory was trying to use the same fundamentals that every disco and nondisco DJ was doing; I struggled with this—the fundamentals, the mechanics of these DJs—a lot of them super-DJs. I had to do something that was considered vinyl blasphemy. I also had to figure out how to use the crossfader in a very different way. The way I had to use the mixer would definitely wear out the crossfader's life expectancy.

With the vinyl, I was hated. Where most DJs and music enthusiasts used the velvet brush to clean the vinyl, holding it gently by its sides while placing it on the turntable, with much fear and focus I needed duplicate copies of every song in my collection. And I needed them in one jacket. No velvet brush, no white liner paper that came inside of the jacket. The biggest and most hated thing I had to do was use a bright colored crayon or grease pencil to mark the drum solo area of each song. Marking vinyl anywhere was an absolute hell no! But I had to do this so I could see the bright crayon mark in a dark venue as I DJed.

I called the first marking "the circular." I would turn on the turntable, place the crayon precisely in the area, and press down to make a white mark that was bright enough for me to see. The next marking I called "the intersector." And this mark would go from the center hole of the record all of the way up to where it would meet the circular mark. The intersector mark was the math. And that line would tell me how many times I would have to spin the record back counterclockwise to arrive to the top of the break. I didn't need the tonearm, the circular mark was the area where the break lived. These two markings would be on all of my records so I could find the desired area *quickly*, using the tonearm on each side only one time apiece to put it on, one time to take it off.

Many DJs, especially the nondisco DJs, had to change the way they played. This style that I invented allowed me to create a music bed of drum solos so the rapper now had a bed of music to speak on. I was under the impression back then that I created the greatest DJ technique ever. I can remember trying to get weekday jobs, but rumors had already gotten around to club owners of how I disrespected vinyl. The word caught fire that I created this new style but that it consisted of me marking up records and putting my fingertips on the vinyl and putting pressure on the mixer. I can remember going to clubs and not being able to get in even at places where some of the DJs were my friends. It was sad and a rough time.

Today thank goodness for the DJs that I taught and for all who made it their own, every hip-hop DJ in the world uses this theory I invented. My objective was to make the vinyl play two roles: Be the sound source and controller. My intersector and circular points are today called cue points. The beatbox that I would later discover is now called the "human beatbox." Then there's the system I created so a DJ could hear the record in their ear before mixing it out to the public, which I called my "peek-a-boo" system and is now called the cueing system.

My problem back in the seventies was that the type of mixers hip-hop DJs needed were crossfaders or called "up and down" faders, but most of those mixers did not come with a built-in pre-hear system. And this is where Samuel Gompers High played a major role again for me. When I went to Radio Shack, I knew exactly the part I needed, and I knew exactly how to wire it. The key thing for me was in order to keep all of the breaks perfectly in line, on time, to the beat, seamlessly, over and over all night, I needed an amplified system with a headphone where I could hear the song I wanted to play in advance. That's how I came up with the peek-a-boo system. It consisted of two solo preamps, one single-pole double-throw switch or single-pole single-throw switch, two RCA splitters—one for the left turntable, one for the right turntable. For every turntable there is a left channel and a right channel, so what I did was split the signal on one side of the left channel per turntable with one signal going into the external preamp "in" and then "out" of the external preamp. I went through the single-pole double-throw switch on the left two points, then I split the signal on the right turntable where I broke into the left side of that wire, and I split that wire and it went into the other preamp which went into the right side of the switch. Then I soldered the wires together and crazy-glued the switch to the backside of the mixer. So in my headphones, when I click it to the left I hear the left turntable and when I click it to the right I hear the right turntable. So now on the output of the switch I was able to run it to a low-wattage amplifier with just enough to drive headphones.

When I switched the toggle switch to the left I could hear the next record before anyone in the crowd, and I could line the next record up. And once I lined it up, I was able to line up the next record in advance. As they are hearing one song playing, I'm preparing the next song, and I'm switching to the next song by clicking the switch to the right then preparing the next song, and when I have it ready clicking the switch to the left. I'm able to do this all night. I can preview whatever song I want to play, line it up so that no one hears me lining it up until I push the fader. If you are dancing to James Brown, Thin Lizzy, Sly and the Family Stone, the people dancing are staying on beat, all night. Whether the rappers want to say their rhymes, I had, again, a bed of music lined up that kept them on time, all night.

This is the essence of what's now called the "cue system." We didn't have this in the seventies. I had to build it.

So with the peek-a-boo system, the beatbox, the cue points and cue system, and the theory I would name later, I was an innovator. And now my upbringing of music having no color, I can play a white drummer's drum break, a Black drummer's drum break, a foreign drum break, or an America drum break, all on time to the beat. No train wrecks. A term I got from Pete DJ Jones, "The King of Disco DJing." He'd say "DJs who can't mix are train wreckers." Once I heard him say that I knew for me: No train wrecks allowed.

While DJs have taken my foundation and done extraordinary things with it, no one has changed the mechanics of what I started over fifty years ago. Quik Mix, record touching, the peek-a-boo (pre-hearing songs before the crowd in the headphones through the mixer), and seamless beat matching of your favorite records.

These are my contributions to the culture—these four inventions.

In this book you will hear from some of the most important, most powerful, and most impactful people who will share their stories and tell how they contributed to the culture. This is why this book is called the *Birth of a Culture*.

CHAPTER 2

In my early years on the roof of 927 Fox Street, when I was taking apart abandoned electrical devices that I may have gotten from some junkyard, the big sport or thing to do was kite fighting or flying pigeons. Me? I was a kite fighter. We would be on the roofs of our apartment or on some close by on other people's apartment roofs fighting with our kites against people whose roofs were very far away.

We would build our kites out of bamboo stick, tissue paper, ribbon, and glue. The ribbon we'd get from the arts and crafts store—we'd call them "sneakies." But in order for the kites to fight, we had to buy the shaving razors to put on the tails of the kite. The objective was to fly your kite as close as possible to another person's kite, lower your kite's tail on the opponent's kite string, and pull in your string with your razor-imbedded tail, making your kite's tail rub against the other kite's string and cut his string, which forced the opponent's kite to be gone with the wind. The winner would now say "hootah," and then go looking for other kites to cut out of the sky.

I remember a specific black kite that was handmade and had a white skull and crossbones on the canopy. It also had an additional weapon—we later found out his formula. This dude would not only cut his Gillette razor blades in half, he'd soak his kite cord in glue then smash fluorescent bulbs and grind them into a fine glass powder. Then he would take the glue-soaked cord—before the glue dried—and gently dust the fine glass powder lightly to the cord. Then he'd let it dry for a couple hours. Then he'd go back on the roof and sail his kite out to start slaying other kites. He had a few of them.

This guy—we never found out who he was even though we figured out his formula—had two weapons working for him: the blades on his extremely long tail embedded with razors and his glass kite cord. He would navigate his kite underneath the opponent's kite and allow his cord to rub on their cord. Killing their kite. Always another victory for the skull and crossbones. It got to a point that as soon as anyone fighting saw that skull and crossbones kite in the air people quickly started pulling their kites out of the sky. We were all afraid of the one we ended up just calling "Hoooooooooootah."

There was so much going on in the Bronx, I just gravitated to being a part of what was growing as a kid. Along with kite fighting, I did graffiti. "Flash 163" was my tag. I was a graphic artist—or thought I was—again, as a kid. I was a wack break-dancer. And it was the dance part that made me fall in love with music outside of just hearing it. I directly connected to the music and what it did when it connected to people. Music made people move. Music brought people together. Music created humans moving in unison. Dancing helped me curate how I played music. I was always thinking when I DJed about dancing, always thinking about the dancer.

Most of the guys I was hanging out with who became my best friends at the time all danced. That was their thing. B-boys. Breakin'. Mean Gene was part of this neighborhood b-boy crew, EZ Mike was one of the best b-boys I'd ever seen. On the other hand, I met this guy Arthur Haywood, aka "Disco Bee," through EZ Mike. He would come to the crib quite a bit but not to necessarily hang out, but for another reason. "I kept hearing about those parties at this place called 'The Hole,'" Bee reminded me. "I had to come see that shit." Bee ended up being my first real DJ partner.

And if it weren't for Bee, I'm not sure my whole DJ plan would have fallen into place.

Most of us lived in the projects; Bee's family lived in a private house. With a garage. Now, Bee's father was kind of a mean person. But he was also very understanding if you talked to him in the right way. His mom was just a sweetheart of a lady. And I remember asking her about what they were doing with the space in their garage. "Mrs. Haywood, could we . . . could I . . . could we [gulp] please put the sound system in the garage?" Just to see if we could have a place to house it when we weren't using it. She looked at me like I was half crazy and said, "I'm going to get back to you. I'm gonna go talk to my husband."

I remember a few days later Mr. Haywood wanted to talk to me. I was scared as shit of him. Deep voice, always serious, mean. He was like, "Alright, I'm going to let you guys keep your sound system in the garage. When you come in late at night don't make any noise. If you all disturb the peace in the house, the sound system goes out." And Bee was the one in charge making sure the system got in there safely and that no peace was disrupted in his family's house.

His parents, whom I later began to call Mama and Dad Haywood, by giving us space in their garage so that we didn't have to lift and carry "the Gladiator" system along with twenty crates of records up five flights of stairs, literally saved us.

Back to the whole "The Hole" thing. See, when my girlfriend first moved into this apartment on Brown Place in the Bronx,

I can remember I looked around. It was nice. It was new. As I looked around through all of the bedrooms, I came across this closet. I opened the door and something very strange was there. It was a square cut in the floor, like a hatch with a ring. But it was still an actual floor. I bent down, grabbed hold of the ring, pulled it upward, and heat rose from the opening.

I laid down on the floor, looked down into this hole. It was pitch dark. I got up, ran to get a flashlight. As I am looking down into the hole with the flashlight I notice that this is an unfinished space. I go get a ladder that I'd seen earlier that I was pretty sure belonged to some construction workers because, like I said, the apartment building was new. As I go down in the hole, I look around. There's dust everywhere. It's hot. So fucking hot. Almost "can't breathe" hot. No ventilation. No windows. No sockets to plug anything in. But I had a vision.

I said to myself, "This is perfect. I'm going to call this place 'The Hole.' And this is where I'm going to do my parties." It worked. People would literally climb down the ladder to come down to my parties in The Hole while my family was upstairs. EZ Mike came through The Hole. Disco Bee would come almost every time I had something down there. Even when I was still going to the parks to perfect the Theory, to find someone to speak on the mic to what I was doing, Bee was always there. That's how he became my official DJ partner.

Mean Gene, even though he was a b-boy, first became my DJ partner but eventually we parted. He created a crew called the L Brothers. Me? I was still in deep into the Theory. I go out to the parks to test it. I pick a guy who would speak on the microphone to my new style of DJing. His name was Cowboy. EZ Mike would still come around but he became somewhat unreliable. But, not Bee. He, again, was always there. And when it came to DJing he had a different style than mine.

Bee was a disco DJ. The beauty of Bee was he wasn't trying to do the same thing I was doing on the turntables. While I was getting most of the attention, Bee would relieve me and balance out the sets.

A lot of people would ask Bee, "You was with Flash, why you not as good as Flash?"

And he'd always say to them: "Why do I need to be as good as Flash? What sense does it make to go to a party and hear the same thing all night?" He'd tell people to their faces: "You didn't come to a party to hear Flash get off of the turntables and another DJ come on doing the *exact same* thing!"

Bee was Bee. He never tried or ever wanted to be a copy. Bee was comfortable being who he was as a DJ. R&B and disco songs I wouldn't touch, Bee would play and rock them. I was concentrating on finding and playing beats and breaks. "Got to Be Real" by Cheryl Lynn, he'd play that. "Do You Like It" by B.T. Express and "Rock Creek Park" by The Blackbyrds, he'd play those. "Music, Harmony and Rhythm" by Brooklyn Dreams, he'd play that. Those were Bee's type of records. When we'd go record shopping, he'd always look for remixes of popular disco songs because most of them had long breaks in the middle of the records that no one really knew about. (Which is a whole other story, us record shopping.) And he'd play R&B and disco records, blending one song after the other.

He would switch things up, throwing on Etta James's "Out on the Street Again" or "All the Way Down" for the hustlers (dancers who did the dance "the hustle") or "Let's Do the Latin Hustle" by Eddie Drennon and B.B.S. Unlimited or El Coco's "Let's Get It Together" and not lose the crowd, never kill the party. He was the one who played the melodies, the grooves. Kinda like the "ladies music." And that was the music that I really didn't play, so when I got off of the turntables and handed Bee the headphones he was going for the ladies music. When he handed the headphones to me, I was going for the music that took the crowd to the ceiling. So it was an even balance with Bee and me.

Bee's role, and he'll be the first to say this, was to "make Flash look better. To make him grow as fast as the ideas that were coming out of his damn head."

But the real brilliance in Bee and in this whole thing came after listening to Herc. "Apache" was Herc's go-to song, always played it. (Bob James's "Take Me to the Mardi Gras" was our song.)

I can't remember the exact day but Bee said to me, "Flash, why don't you try cutting a different record with 'Apache'?"

I was like, "What do you mean?"

He says, "Try cutting in a different record with 'Apache!'"

Ohhhh. I got it. So when I found "Heaven and Hell Is on Earth" by 20th Century Steel Band with the "Children growing . . ." part, I was able to cut that into the "Apache" beat on the turntables. I'd go back and forth with those two records. *Boom*. Drums. *Boom*. "Children growing . . ." lyrics. *Boom*. Drums. *Boom*. Repeat lyrics. I called it "the one and one." Bee originally gave me the idea.

EZ Mike, Bee, and me, that's how we got down. We knew how to play off one another. Most of the time it was Bee and me. When it was time for R&B I'd hand the headphones to Bee; when it was time to get crazy, he'd hand the headphones back to me. And these were at parties where we weren't playing for an hour, hour and a half, no, we're talking about from 9 p.m. to 4 in the morning. And of those seven hours, Bee and I would play for about six, and the MCs would come on every now and then and do their routines before leaving the stage. The rest of the party was pretty much all Bee and me.

And this is where the circular mark and the intersector really became important but at the same time impossible to explain to people. While it was discouraging when people didn't understand what I was doing, it made me realize that what I was doing was more science than DJing. Songs like "Harlem" by Bill Withers, "Give It Up or Turnit a Loose" by James Brown, clean drum breaks. Songs like "Catch a Groove" by Juice, which is basically all drums, "It's Just Begun" by the Jimmy Castor Bunch with all its clean grooves. While people weren't accustomed to anyone putting their hands or fingers on records, no one understood putting crayons or grease pencil marks on records. That's where the math came in. The counting of the rotations. I never understood why it was so hard for everyone to understand.

To locate that perfect spot, I'd drop the tonearm in the area where the break lived and I would make sure I was at the beginning of the break, and that tonearm was sitting on the vinyl. So while the platter was spinning clockwise, I would have my hand on the vinyl to pause it and have the crayon in my other hand. Then I would let it go while the record was playing, then I would paint the record up to the whack part.

Then I would draw a line from the center hole that intersects where the drum break begins. That is how I was able to count the bars in reverse. For every four bars forward, I would have to take the intersector back six times counterclockwise.

Moving the record back and forth was essential to cueing precisely. That small movement back and forth made a strange sound, but I liked it, got used to it because it let me know whether or not I was in the right spot. I called that sound, that back and forth, the "zukka-zukka." Which became the precursor to scratching. It was a technique that they'd give all of these different names and new subtechniques. Years later they'd be called "cuttin'," "backspinnin'," "rubbin'," "scratchin'," "transformin'," "crabbin'," and all types of other names are made possible by rubbing/juggling while opening and closing the fader. These mechanics and this style of DJing are the fundamentals of what I invented. The record was already moving back and forth because of my fingertips. The vinyl was already going counterclockwise because I did it with my fingertips—1972, 1973. I'm fifteen, sixteen years old. Now what they can claim is that they added a different sound to it while they were doing it, especially when they open and close the fader on the mixer, but they're still moving the record backward or forward or counterclockwise, which is a theory. One that I originated. Still, for years people continue saying to me, "Well, this person said he invented this and this other person said they invented that." To which, I always say to them, "How can they invent something that I already invented?"

The Square Things.
Album covers of some of the music I ended up building that became the universal sound of hip-hop. All genres of music were a part of creating the sound.

Chapter 3

While I was in the thick of shaping the Theory, Afrika Bambaataa was in Bronx River building a reputation for how he made gang members turn to peace, converting them into members of his Zulu Nation (now the Universal Zulu Nation), and his infamous record collection. This was a year or two after seeing Herc and about two years before I got the chance to meet Bam—late '74, early '75. We were all kids, still teenagers, doing this. We didn't realize that we were actually young entrepreneurs creating our own businesses, creating an ecosystem and culture. Organizing people, getting the parties, paying for the parties, paying for equipment, renting out spaces that we knew we couldn't rent out so we had to get adults to get the spots for us. It was entrepreneurship at a young age that was a gift from God Himself.

Back then all DJs had sets. People would run from DJ to DJ, set to set, at different places to see what the other DJ was playing and what records they had. Asking us, "What was that song you just played?" We'd soak our records in water to get the labels off so spies—or anyone—wouldn't know what we were playing. But we knew. If we didn't put white labels in place of the original labels, we would memorize the color left on the record—whether it was a Polydor record or an Arista record. Bam was a master of that.

He was like a historian. I was more of a technician. There was a big battle at James Monroe High School, and I brought my whole system. I was battling Disco King Mario. Bam was there. Mario saw what I brought and called for help, asking others to pull their systems together to beat me. Then they had another DJ, Deadbolt, playing against me, and he didn't know what he was playing, so once I finished him, I saw Bam and yelled, "Bam, I know what you are doing! I know what you are trying to do! You better stop that shit!" And I think that's when he knew I was for real, fully recognized my technician skills on the tables.

I remember one of Bam's DJs, a young Jazzy Jay coming to Monroe High School, seeing me, at that time doing tricks, as Bam says, "doing acrobatics," on the turntables and saying to me, "I wanna do that." There were rumors afterward that Bam was getting DJs like Jazzy Jay and a young Islam (who both later went on to become well-known DJs) and putting them on and placing them to compete against me. But all Bam was doing was building his empire. He wasn't trying to pit other DJs against me. When you went to a Bambaataa party, that's what it was: an empire. The whole party was full of ex–gang members that he was able to bring together in peace.

On the flyers it used to say, "Come in peace or leave in pieces." The words were a warning to all. If you came to a Bam party, you better act right. None of this would have happened or become what it did had he not been able to bring the people—the gangs, the crews, the street dudes at the time, the Black Spades, the Black Pearls, Savage Skulls, Seven Immortals—together in unison through music. Because if he doesn't pull that off, we never would have had the block parties which were the cornerstone of what eventually grew into being what shaped the culture of hip-hop. What Bam was doing was wonderful.

In the mid-seventies, gang culture was running wild with lots of death and needing permission to go into certain neighborhoods. But Bam (whom I spoke with for this book just before his untimely death) was a person who watched history, he studied it more than most in our age group at the time. He grew up around activism and also became a member of the Black Spades, he followed people who were instrumental in the revolution, the honorable Elijah Muhammad and the Nation of Islam, Huey P. Newton and the Black Panther Party, all of the things going on in Africa with the Mau Maus and the Zulus, he knew that he had to get out in the streets and do something. He was always one who couldn't just sit back and watch his people—our people—struggle. His influence with the gangs he was with made him be able to speak to other group leaders and group members before they became broken down organizations to explain to them how they had to become, as he would say, "warriors for our communities." He would tell them how they had to fight the struggle in our communities that many of the parents were going through in the sixties as members or followers of the Black Panthers and Young Lords of their time. He just tried to put common sense into many of the gangbangers' heads.

"Stop killing your brother. Stop killing your sister. Organize! Organize! Organize! Take care of your community. Fight against police brutality. Stop letting the police walk all over you. Keep your community sharp like the Zulus; keep it organized like the NOI." Bam created an environment.

For some people it worked. For others, they disagreed with

what he was trying to do and they started their own crews. The ones who believed in what Bam was doing, followed him, and that's how he started building an organization, the Zulu Nation. But he maintained a connection with the others who were starting their own organizations, which established a calm situation. He knew what it took to organize our stuff in the streets, organize the projects, organize certain hoods, and that's what started bringing everybody in the Bronx together. "Peace. Unity. Love. And having fun." He'd always say that and always stood by that.

And it trickled down to the music he played and the songs he selected. It was all about calming things down. When he was planning the sets for his parties, he'd be ready for Mom and Pops, people's parents who lived in the neighborhoods, to come to the parties, just to check, to see if it was safe. He would see them and take them back to the old days and play a Temptations song, then bring them up to date by playing "Fly, Robin, Fly" by Silver Convention and the disco songs, then he'd play the funk records, "Flashlight" by Parliament, and from there he'd ease them into the breakbeats. And that's how he would grab people, they would gravitate to the way he played the music. His philosophy was to use music to soothe the savage beast.

He was changing the paradigm; all of us were in some way. I was doing it in my part of the South Bronx; Herc in the West Bronx; DJ Breakout, DJ Baron, and the L Brothers in the North; Bam in East Bronx in Bronx River. (And some would say they were drawing decent crowds at DJ Smokey and the Smoke-a-Trons' on Grand Avenue.) We were like four corporations. Bam would always talk about how, not just the song and its title, "Say It Loud—I'm Black and I'm Proud" by James Brown, impacted him, but hearing James Brown say he's Black and he's proud in the song, talking about dying as opposed to living on our knees, changed everything for him. Same with "Stand!" by Sly and the Family Stone. Those were powerful words that stayed in his mind. Lyrics he lived by. That's what made him get in the streets all over the Bronx to organize.

When it came to records and the knowledge of the history of those records, no one could touch Bam. I can't remember exactly when this was, we were much older then, but Bam invited me to his house one time. It was in the projects. I remember walking in, going into three bedrooms, and seeing crates and crates of nothing but records stacked from floor to the ceiling of each room. Mountains of records. I had never seen anything like this. Seeing this fucked me up the same way it did when I first experienced my father's collection. But my dad had a closet full, and Bam had three whole rooms!

I asked him, "Do you know where every song is?"

And he said to me, "I know where every record is."

Nobody could touch Bam when it came to records. He had records that had different versions of records. The song "Indiscreet" by D.C. LaRue, I had the album versions and on those versions the break is about eight seconds, so I had to keep cuttin' it when I played it. But when Bam played it? I always wondered why the breakdown part was almost five minutes long. And when I went to see what version he was playing, he had it white labeled. Same with "Apache."

It wasn't until much later in life that I found out from Bam that outside of going to record stores all over the city and in the Village; going to the backroom in Downstairs Records where I would go; and being in many record pools and getting promotional records from different radio stations like WBLS, WWRL, WLID and other stations in New Jersey, he'd make his own test plates of songs. Same as a lot of the disco DJs were doing at that time. For battles he would make special plates where the breaks would repeat themselves, to extend the beat. I spent years and years wondering where he found so many different versions of "Apache," it was a mystery to me, only to later find out that he was making his own test plates of it.

I know for a fact, that at this time, nothing we were doing, all the theories I was trying to create with my scientific approach to music would have meant anything without what Bam was able to do as (what I call) a "community organizer." Before the rappers came into what we were doing, we were just playing music, and before we were playing music, Bam was taking people who were wildin' and calmed them down, which gave birth to the block parties. There could never have been block parties if everyone was still wildin'. Gangs going against gangs. Savage Skulls going against the Black Pearls, Seven Immortals against the Intruders. It was messy, but he changed that. People then didn't have a better music to speak on until I did what I did, but I would not have had people to play for out in the streets if Bam didn't do what he did, and Herc doing what he did. It wasn't just me who made this thing what it became.

* * *

It's the early seventies and breaking was bigger than DJing. EZ Mike, Dwayne, Mean Gene, and I would go to various areas and territories in the Bronx to dance and battle. I thought I was a breakdancer and graffiti artist for two seconds, realized I wasn't shit at either.

On the dancing side there were guys like Black Jerry, Bumpy Face Melvin, Avery, Hoik, and then there was the one everyone knew as Trixie—the godfather of breakdancing. Started in the late sixties, became famous in 1970, stopped dancing in 1975. He came up in a problematic household with a father who was an alcoholic. As a kid Trixie would beat up classmates; that's how he dealt with his pain. Dancing, he told me, took away a lot of the anger he had for his father. "Dance took out the 450 years of all of that anger God gave me," is how he puts it. James Brown's "Give It Up or Turnit a Loose," "Skin Tight" by the Ohio Players, "Love Is the Message" by MFSB were his songs. He was that dude, born and raised on the west side of the Bronx, he grew up with and in the same neighborhood as Herc. To the point that I always thought he danced for Herc, which he never did. He'd put on these amazing break dance performances at Herc's parties and parties all over the Bronx and no one would challenge him. Trixie had other dancers scared. He would go to clubs, and they'd ask him *not to* dance because he was *that* good, they knew who he was.

Trixie's first battle, he'll tell you, was against another legend, Wallace Dee. Legend is Trixie burned Wallace Dee twice. Once by jumping straight over his head in their first meetup, then jumping over his head again, came down, did a roll on the ground, did a spin, came up, and, in Wallace Dee's face, shook it off, in their second meetup. His second real battle was against, Dancin' Doug, one of the original, original b-boys. Doug was from Harlem but ended up going to Cardinal Hayes High School in the Bronx. And it was "stumble bum luck," as he calls it, that Doug met Herc and Coke (La Rock) at a mutual friend's house, and they told him to come to a party they were having later that day. No one in the Bronx at the time knew that Doug was a known dancer in Harlem. That he'd been breakdancing in community centers and at the Audubon and the Polo Grounds all over Harlem only. And when he decided to go to the party Herc and Coke told him about, he already knew who the established breakdancer there was: Trixie. And that's when Doug introduced himself as a dancer to the Bronx. Walking up to Trixie and saying, "Let's go."

They became good friends and each other's nemesis. Their battles became big, legendary as well as stories of legends. My favorite one is when during one of their battles Trixie pulled out a dildo, began throwing it on the floor and hitting himself in the head with it. Crowd went crazy. He slayed Doug. To which Doug tells the story about being in Germany and someone asking him, "Are you the guy with the dildo?"

"No," he tells them, "I'm the guy who was dancing against the guy with the dildo."

But the next week Doug and his break dance partner learned the Lindy Hop, a dance from the 1920s and 1930s made famous by dancers like Shorty Snowden and Frankie Manning and the Nicholas Brothers and turned around and did that, along with the dance the Charleston, against Trixie and Wallace Dee with the DJ playing James Brown's "Give It Up or Turnit a Loose." They did splits. Throwing one leg over the other one's shoulders. Jumping over each other's backs. It was crazy. Destroying Trixie and Wallace Dee.

Under them there were other great breakdancers who were probably just as important: Sasa, the Amazing Bo Bo, Rossy, James Bond, who used to do the move we called the "Maxwell Smart," where he'd fall on the floor, slide back, take off his shoe, put it up to his ear, and start talking to it like it was a phone, just like the detective did on the TV show *Get Smart.* Crews like Rock Steady and Dynamic Rockers. Then there were the b-girls: Kimmie, Duesy, Janice Rock (who had this move where she'd dance like a spider), Sista Boo, Mother Earth. There was a place in Harlem called the Chuck Center on "the Hill" in

Harlem where a lot of the dancers would go to hone their skills and come back up to the Bronx to test them out on the weekends. And in the middle of all of this was a guy by the name of Kurtis Blow, who was from Harlem, who started off back then as a dancer, who ended up coming to the Bronx later to hang out with Kool Herc and eventually with me.

It was around 1973 when Kurtis Blow, according to Doug, battled him at Nell's in Harlem. They'd battled before but this particular b-boy battle rose above the norm. Kurt, according to Doug, said, "it was a big beat that turned out to be a 'D' beat," with the D apparently standing for Doug's defeat.

So even though no one knew Doug danced when he came to the Bronx, he had an underground reputation in Harlem as someone who could dance and would battle anyone. But the Bronx was not going to let anyone from outside of the Bronx come on our turf and defeat us, especially in something we believed we created. We had Trixie.

Now, according to Trixie, who again grew up with Herc, the "first" party that Herc had that really started it all was not the one everyone talks about. There was one before that in the little rec room where Herc lived, in the Valley, as they called it, 1520 Sedgwick, in 1970. It was so cold that night, Trixie said he wasn't going to go but Coke convinced him to go. And it was there—at that party—where Herc first played on his sound system. Said the first record Herc played at that party was James Brown, said the sound of the music ran right through him, said that's what changed everything. Because before then all of the parties were either "house" or "like house" parties, 25- to 50-cent parties where everyone was using their record players to play records. Them thinking that Herc was going to have a record player playing records at the time, not knowing that he was going to be playing music on a system. It was then that Trixie said, "they recognized him, and he (Herc) recognized us" because it was Black American music that he'd heard that he ended up playing at that party.

Trixie always said that Doug and Wallace "brought out the Trixie" in him. Anyone else that came in his circle, his presence, was easy. But those two brought out the best in him. Trixie to me was like a gift from God when it came to doing what he did. He never—*never*—practiced any of his moves or routines.

"I would wake up, let God put a move in my head, and go out on Fridays and Saturdays and do what God gave me," is his recall of this time in our lives.

He set a standard of what breakdancing could and eventually did become. He's owed a lot when it comes to what he gave to this culture. Flowers that he'll never get. He was like our Fred Astaire, our Gene Kelly. Our Bill Robinson, the one everyone got it from. But he was never discovered, so at around seventeen or eighteen years old, he stopped. Left home at seventeen and got a job and has been on his own ever since. Found out he was also talented.

Doug, he ended up dancing for Herc for four years. He would always say what set Herc's sets apart was that the b-boys would go to them—they were the ones who set Herc's spot off. Everyone came to see the b-boys. And Doug would tell him: "You were a great DJ, but if it wasn't for b-boys rockin' your spot, and people seeing the dancers there every week, you might not be who you are." According to Doug, Herc gets mad when he says that to him. There were great DJs at one time playing all over the Bronx; b-boys had opportunities to dance and showcase their skills at a lot of places, but a lot of what was being played was deep disco (like in Harlem) and R&B. But Herc was playing that hard sound, as Doug called it, "that hard sound, that real raw shit." Because we were all ghetto kids, our dancing would at times be aggressive. It was real physical. They called it "burning." Where they'd do things like mushing people in the face while they were dancing, taking peoples' caps off their heads, and throwing them across the room and stomping on them. Burnin' was rough. It evolved from "burning" to "breaking."

Doug claims the first "real" break move was b-boys falling down going backward and tripping people. They started tripping people instead of mushing them. Once dancers started going to the ground, it changed things. Anything to get muthafuckers to laugh at who you were battling. It was embarrassing, sometimes humiliating. It was intimidation. Dancers were chased out of parties by other crews. Sometimes thirty deep. Doug tells about one time after a party in Castle Hill where after he "busted" someone in a dance battle, the Black Spades chased him and he was trying to escape. He got halfway to the place he was trying to get to where he'd be safe, but instead he dipped and snuck into another place to hide. Smart. And when Doug and them thought they were safe, some white boys chased them the rest of the way.

Same thing happened in Red Hook. He danced against some crew there, lit the place up, and they chased him out of Red Hook. He got chased out of places all the time. B-boying was a contact sport. And the girls were as ruthless as the guys. Some of the guys were scared to dance with or against some of the girls because there were some bad girls and they would embarrass them. Like (dancer) Kimmie would battle the (Nigga) Twins and give them hell. Then they'd double up on her, but she'd hold her own. She'd dip down on one leg, go over one of their backs, body them up, all of that. It was rough at first.

Then it began to get more "stylish," less physical, and that's when it shifted. That's when the b-boys and b-girls became the show. Which is why I always say: *We, the DJs, played the music, but the breakdancers during the origins of this were the actual stars.* Years and years before the rappers.

* * *

In July of 1971 (July 25, 1971), *The New York Times* did a story claiming Philadelphia the "graffiti capital of the world." This "wall writer," called "Cornbread" in Philly, became famous. The stories going around about him were crazy, that he tagged his name on the Jackson 5's plane once at the airport in Philadelphia when they came to town for a concert and another one about him tagging "Cornbread Lives" on an elephant at the Philadelphia Zoo with spray paint. Apparently he began using buses and trains instead of walls in Philadelphia for his graffiti. Some called him the "Godfather of Graffiti" and say he was the influence for subway graffiti of the seventies in NYC.

"Coco 144"—one of the earliest writers from Upper West Harlem, who began in the late sixties, 1969 to be exact, a year after the whole street-art movement took shape out of Manhattan with "Julio204" and took over Washington Heights—says that there are stories when it comes to "Cornbread's" legend and what built it. He told me, "I've had conversations and contact with many early writers who have not gotten their shine." He told me these writers made it straight that Cornbread is not the legend that some people believe he is.

And in a culture that predates what we were doing—that had its own existence before it became a part of the culture being built by breakdancing, DJing, and rapping—accuracy of who was really who and what was really what is important.

"There's a lot of other brothas who went out there and really fought their way through the system by putting their names up (on walls and public places), risking their lives and freedom for this." But these brothas don't get credit for it. That's how Coco broke it down for me.

He got his name "Coco" (also "Coquito") at three-months old as a term of endearment because his head looked like and was the size of a coconut. His crew coming up were Tan 144 and Ace 137. Guys attached the street number they were from or street they lived on as codes on their signatures (later called tags) to let the world know where they repped. As an artist Coco 144 lived in the era of signatures and hits (simple block lettering). He outlined a few trains but never did what we called "tops-to-bottoms" where artists painted the entire car. It wasn't until later that T-Rex and Top Cat brought what they called the "Broadway elegance" style to the forefront, a flavor they got from Philly. Using small dry markers (before the wide markers even came out) and Red Devil spray paint (before Krylon)—or whatever he could get his hands on from Woolworth's—Coco was part of the original crews doing what was called layups. Layups were where the trains went to sleep, where they'd go after their last run, stabling yards or switching yards or overnight storage or for maintenance. There was a layup between 137th and 145th, and on the weekends that's where and when Coco would make his hits. Writers back then would risk their lives, jumping onto those tracks to tag the cars.

Very much like I was attempting to discover something new with sound and music, they were discovering and creating something new with art. Just like I was taking turntables apart and experimenting with my mom's needles to be able to do what I wanted to do with the records, Coco and them were doing the same thing with markers and spray paint cans. Taking the original nozzles off and replacing them with the Easy-Off oven cleaner nozzles to get a wider spray for their work. They were just young cats out in the streets inventing things. They, like me or me like them because they were before me, had an undying love to get something done that wasn't getting done. Believing the thoughts and ideas they had in their heads should be tangible, should be seen. Saying, "Since the art world ain't going to do it for us, we're going to do it for you." To get their visual representation out, they had to do whatever it was they had to do to let the world know.

The mission for them was for people, especially other writers, all over New York to say, "Yo! Did you see where my man put his name?" That was a big deal. Often you weren't respected in the game until you were either arrested, almost arrested, or threatened. You had to be willing to take the risk of either losing your life or getting locked up. Doing the impossible and the level of danger involved in tagging your name was a part of building your legend. The tags and reputations of Super Kool 223, STAY HIGH 149, Taki 183, SEEN, Blaze, Doze, Ray-B-954—who was the first person to tag his name on a TWA commercial airplane, and no one ever found out how he did it—and especially Phase II were swelling and popping up everywhere. Their work was becoming some of the most seen and known of the graffiti movement in New York. They were heroes, visual movie stars to us. In particular Phase II, who probably had as big if not a bigger following than Herc, Bam, and myself. What separated Phase II from other artists was his style. His exaggerated, super-large bubble letter style—a lot of times with arrows—was distinctive and different. No one had really seen anything like it.

And it was Phase II, when he and Coco met in early 1973,

who said that it was what Coco and his generation of writers did on the Broadway line that opened it up for him to do what he began doing in the Bronx. Just being kids of the '60s and '70s almost made them rebel. They spoke the same language of revolution and militancy. Phase II talking about the Black Panthers, Coco talking about the Young Lords. They're way of rebelling against what was happening and what they were experiencing as kids at the time was to hit up walls and trains and other public spaces. Not that any or all of us were politically educated on exactly what was happening, but we knew things were a mess. So we went into our own worlds. I like to say: "Walking down paths that nobody cared to or nobody dared to." And while for them their art was developing, the artists themselves were elevating with their styles, which kept the art itself constantly moving forward. And it was growing fast, spreading like a forest fire all over New York. No one can specifically say who but someone "lit the match." "In the writing culture generations happen like every ten years, but with us it was like a generation of new writers came every week," is Coco's way of describing how it took off. Comparing his generation to the Olympics: "We were the cats who lit the torch, and everyone else carried it."

It was an era that was ahead of its time. Whenever the press wrote about anything related to graffiti they'd always relate it to "These are just some ghetto kids," or "These are just kids from the ghetto." Which sometimes was true, but not always. Coco was from a working-class neighborhood in Harlem. I know of other famous graffiti artists whose parents were accountants and architects and sent them to private schools. One of my favorite Coco stories comes from the time he got caught by the police, and what they'd often make graffiti artists do was make them clean the tags off of the subway trains, tags they didn't even put on the cars. This one time they made Coco go to Brooklyn to clean a subway station, there he met other writers, they were all there to do the same thing: Clean cars and the station. Later that evening, after being "released" from cleaning duty, they all went back to the same station and graffitied the whole place up.

By 1972, before many of the writers became super famous, Coco had stopped writing publicly on brick. He was sixteen and had become a dad. Coco had to grow up quick, becoming an original member of UGA (United Graffiti Artists), which became the transition of writers from writing on trains to painting on canvas. In March of 1973 they did the backdrop for the *Deuce Coupe* performance for the Joffrey Ballet, at a time when they were considered "vandals and criminals," and in September of that same year they did the first major show at the Razor Gallery in Soho. RIFF 170 was in the group, so was Phase II, Ray-B, Charmin 65, BAMA/AMRL, SNAKE I, all started apparently by a NYC City College student named Hugo Martinez. UGA was the foundation of the aerosol culture before the media named it "graffiti." A term that the group attached "artist" to inventing the term "graffiti artist," which was their way, led by Phase II, of taking graffiti out of the negative context that it was being framed in and not letting anyone call them who they were as young people from the inner city.

Phase II would tell Coco that what they were doing was bigger than they thought it was. They knew there was something there even though they couldn't put their fingers on what exactly it was. Coco likes to say, "there was a certain energy" going on. Something powerful. Many thought it was just a fad; a form of art that would soon die.

Later on in Bed-Stuy, though, there was this kid who was

"writing on walls and shit," as he liked to say, and was a part of a graffiti group called the Fabulous 5. Fred Brathwaite. He and one of his crew members, Lee Quiñones on the Lower East Side, took the original subway concept of Phase II and Coco to a different level. Fred and Lee became known for painting the entire sides of subway cars not just tagging them. Fred had an eye on the downtown scene and a plan bigger than New York.

* * *

When I was doing parties at 75 Park on Hoe Avenue in the South Bronx there was a DJ whose parties I went to because we were kind of both doing our thing around the same time. He went by the name of DJ Smokey. As mentioned earlier, word got around that his parties were decent. That was an understatement. He gave some of the dopest apartment parties. The setup was legendary. Every room in his fifth floor apartment was filled with people anytime he threw a party. Absolutely amazing. If I wasn't DJing somewhere, I'd go there to hear Smokey. And he'd be spinning on *two different stereos*. He's like a folk hero.

We'd go to Downstairs Records—probably the most important record store in the country at the time—spend hours there, getting into that backroom, dealing with the owners, Barry and Nick. Spending eight dollars on an album twice so that we had two copies, just for four to five seconds of one song we were going to use. The block parties he had on Grant Avenue were just as dope as the apartment parties. He drew crowds in. The Nigga Twins (aka the Legendary Twins) started out at Smokey's. The original Clark Kent started out at Smokey's. Smokey just didn't have the sound system. Some people say he was doing what we were doing before Herc. I always had a lot of love for Smokey.

He played a role in paving the way. I thanked him in my speech when I got my Grammy Award.

In other boroughs there were stories of other DJs and other MCs doing many of the same things we were doing in the Bronx. In Queens, in Brooklyn, in uptown Manhattan. Names of DJs like Master D and crews like NuSounds, names of MCs like K.C. the Prince of Soul who was on the mic for Grandmaster Flowers. Stories that go back to the late '60s, 1968 and 1969. In the Bronx, we had DJ John Brown playing at the Plaza Tunnel. The Black Spades would go there. Herc from what I heard went there, and it became his inspiration. The club would end up closing a few months before Herc's famous party in 1973—thrown by him and his sister—which people believe started it all.

So many DJs' stories have been lost in this history. Way too many of them have been forgotten.

* * *

The drum break on Baby Huey's "Listen to Me" was another song kind of like Curtis Mayfield's "Move on Up" where the break came at the back end of the song. The break was about sixteen to eighteen seconds; you had to get in and out quickly or the song would be over. It was a song I never liked but had to play because the people loved it. I always wanted to get to the break, the drums, and work with that part of the record because that's what I did. But I couldn't with this one. Everyone wanted to hear the whole song.

As I got older and began DJing all over New York, that song became the song when all of the stick-up kids would come alive. To the point that later I stopped playing it. The kids, especially during the summers, would have summer youth jobs and wouldn't get paid until the first and the fifteenth, and before they'd get their checks they'd come to the parties and hide in the bathrooms and take other people's sneakers as they'd come to use the bathrooms. And it would always happen at the parties when any of us—Herc, Bambaataa, and Breakout—would play Baby Huey. The song was very haunting. Even the album cover didn't seem right; it didn't look like the rest of the album covers. Black and white with this four-hundred-pound guy on it. Very unprofessionally made. At a Flash party people would start fighting; at the other parties people would get shot. There was just something weird about this song.

Once at a party on Boston Road I played the song, walked away from the turntables, next thing guys came out, guns out, people ran into the bathrooms, jumped behind the bar, everyone threw their hands up, and the guys were like, "Put your muthafuckin' hands down! We ain't announcing no damn stick-up. We lookin' for somebody. Anyone seen him?" Then they just left.

But "Apache" evoked an exact opposite emotion. There were so many rumors all throughout the Bronx about that song. It's like the song itself had built its own mythical legend. The song was originally done in 1960 by a four-piece rock instrumental band in England called the Shadows (written by another English songwriter, Jerry Lordan, and recorded before that by English guitarist Bert Weedon), who gave it a guitar-heavy, almost Spanish/Italian spaghetti western–type of sound. The beat was very faint in the background. You barely noticed the drums. In 1973 the Incredible Bongo Band did a cover of the song, adding bongos, congas, bass drum, horns, and organ, while keeping the guitar riff, with an eight-second drum beat opening and a two-part, two-minute break in the middle of the record that at that time, for what we were creating with music in the Bronx, that drum break just sounded so big. As a teenager, I could say that break was the attention grabber. As a grown person who learned and studied music from the perspective of a DJ, I can say it was the way they put the reverb on the snare, and the kick was like thunder and lightning—which I tried later in life to replicate that sound in two different studios and failed miserably. Whoever engineered that record was a genius. It annoyed me the way Herc played it, but just hearing it on his sound system was like nothing else. The song gave people joy.

I always wondered, because there were rumors, about how many versions of that song existed. Bam, it seemed, had versions that no one else had. Then I found out that Bam was doing his own test presses of certain records, which explained all I needed to know about—and killed—the rumors about different versions existing of "Apache." While Bam and really Herc kept "Apache" in heavy rotation (another rumor I heard and later found out to be true: One of Herc's DJ's, Timmy Tim found the *Bongo Rock* album with "Apache" on it, was the one who gave Herc a copy of "Apache" first, and Herc's other DJ, Clark Kent, gave Herc a second copy later as a birthday gift), I was constantly using Bob James's "Take Me to the Mardi Gras"—a Paul Simon song originally—to break a song down to its very last element. When I played that song it caused such a stir at my parties. I guess from there it became street talk. "Flash is playing this record with these bells in it." That thirty-second drum and clavinet and xylophone/bell-sounding intro for "Mardi Gras" was everything, magical. Now Herc was playing the record with the big drums in it, but I was rocking the bells. The songs were literally 1A and 1B at the time. "Mardi

Gras" was me; it distinguished me from both Bam and Herc. That record became my identity.

The drums on that record were masterfully produced. And they had this one accompaniment of a melodic bell that sat alongside the drum break that was, to me, genius. I wasn't deconstructing the song as much as I was reinterpreting the song. Repurposing it for a new audience. That's one of the things I believed separated—I'll say differentiated—me from Herc and Bam and the other DJs.

It's the kickoff of real turntablism, the beginning of what would later be called/labeled hip-hop, the introduction of my Quik Mix Theory, the birth of the culture, the origins of the technique of scratching, the early invention of sampling, the prelude to the explosion of the recording industry, the innovation of our generation.

PART II

THE PARKS (LEVEL 1: 1971–1975)

1. **"Gotta Get Away"**
   Flaming Ember (1971)
2. **"Kool Is Back"**
   Funk, Inc. (1971)
3. **"Think (About It)"**
   Lyn Collins (1972)
4. **"'T' Plays It Cool"**
   Marvin Gaye (1972)
5. **"The Mexican"**
   Babe Ruth (1972)
6. **"Apache"**
   The Incredible Bongo Band (1973)
7. **"Misdeameanor"**
   Foster Sylvers (1973)
8. **"Impeach the President"**
   The Honey Drippers (1973)

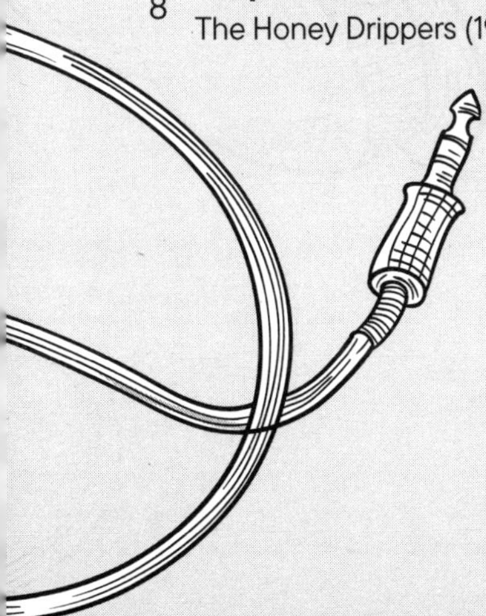

9. **"Take Me to the Mardi Gras"**
   Bob James (1975)
10. **"God Make Me Funky"**
    The Headhunters (1975)
11. **"The Jam"**
    Larry Graham and Graham Central Station (1975)
12. **"Long Red"**
    Mountain (1972)
13. **"Bra"**
    Cymande (1972)
14. **"I'm Gonna Get You"**
    Joe Quarterman and Free Soul (1974)
15. **"It's Just Begun"**
    The Jimmy Castor Bunch (1972)
16. **"The Assembly Line"**
    Commodores (1974)
17. **"Rock Creek Park"**
    The Blackbyrds (1975)
18. **"Give Up the Funk (Tear the Roof off the Sucker)"**
    Parliament (1975)

Chapter 4

There was this 1972 song called "The Mexican" by a band called Babe Ruth—named after the great New York Yankee legend—out of England about the battle at the Alamo in Texas; it became a classic within our circles, if you can believe it. The break in that song came at around the 3:17/3:18 mark, and that became the get down. It lasted less than ten seconds, eight beats. Nothing but bass, drums, and two guitar licks. I'd extend that part when I played it until the needles sunk into the wax of the vinyl.

A song about a Mexican, a guy named Chico, by a white singer in the UK, that was recorded in the same studio where the Beatles did most of their recordings, Abbey Road, that has a Spanish sound from South America, that Blacks and Latinos in the Bronx were groovin' to. That was the essence of what I was trying to do: Bring different elements of life, elements that no one believed should be together, all together through sound.

I wasn't DJing as much as I was *theorizing* what could be done by a DJ. The first place I ended up playing was in the park right across the street from our hangout. 75 Park, Bryant Avenue Park. This was 1971, 1972. When we were rolling our equipment down the streets in shopping carts, and we'd hook up the system into the streetlight post to provide electricity. I remember when I first started playing the block parties I would beg people, either at grocery stores or who had homes close to the parks, "Could I plug my extension cord into your socket so that I can do this block party?" The grocery store owners would say, "No." The people who lived near the parks would say, "No." So when I saw the light post, my mind went to: "Remember your teachings at Gompers. Remember the laws of electricity and how it works."

The lights in the parks came on every night automatically, and I knew someone from the city didn't come out every night to every neighborhood in New York, so I got my screwdriver, opened the faceplate door at the bottom of the light post, and noticed a switching device. To me that meant the switching device had to be connected with something that had an eye to sense darkness and light. During the daytime it would automatically shut off, during the night it would turn on. In order for this to do this by itself, there must be a constant flow of electricity. But it also had to have some form of an electronic arm to break the circuit so the light would shut off as programmed. So I grabbed the wires and traced the circuit and found where the electricity in the light post was flowing constantly and where it was connected to the device controlling the light. I cut it, stripped the wires, ran the wires to the park, put black electrical tape over the open wires, and had electricity. With electricity I had sound, and I could play the parks anytime I wanted to.

My first battle: St. Mary's Park. Against DJ Grandmaster Flowers. A damn good blendologist, could transition from one record to another flawlessly. The first "Grandmaster." But at this point I was deep into my theory. I had a little teenage following.

I didn't know too much about a lot of other DJs at that time. I hadn't even heard Herc yet. I was doing little block parties on Hewitt Place and Fox Street and doing the little parties at our clubhouse.

And that's when I met Mean Gene. Again, a breakdancer at the time who became very important in the history of what we were creating and ended up being my other DJ partner. We both had sound systems, but we both needed things from the other's sound system to make our systems better. So I took my sound system from 927 Fox Street to 1199 Boston Road, where Mean Gene lived, and now we could combine our systems together. But the theory of mixing I was inventing wasn't finished yet. And it was Mean Gene's mother, Ms. Mary Livingston, who was the reason I finished it. As I was finishing up the Theory, my ideas would come 2 p.m., 2 a.m., at any time. While in her house, she could have very well said to me, "Joseph, shut that off!" "It's too loud!" "You can't do this here like that!" Instead, she would walk up to me while I was on the turntables trying to figure this whole thing out and say, in a calm voice, "Boy, just turn it down because I have to go to work tomorrow." Or she'd be in the kitchen cooking and she'd say, "Okay, I just don't want to hear it too loud." She allowed me in her house, as I was trying to complete the last technical aspects of the Theory, at any time, any hour of the night, to turn on the system and work on the ideas I had in my head.

And 63 Park, which was not even a block away from Gene's house, was where I was able to have the block parties and begin to really put on display what I was working on.

EZ Mike was the first person I'd ever really shared with what I was doing and the first I showed the unfinished theory to. But because I was in his mom's house, I was trying to show Gene what I was doing too. Now again, Gene was a great dancer, Mike was a great dancer, Dwayne was an okay dancer, I was kinda wack, so I tried to instruct Gene on how to do exactly what I was doing. It was time to teach Gene what I'd shown Mike—how to make a record go backward and forward, how to make it go counterclockwise. Gene just could not get it. Kind of like Mike, but Mike got it on a very basic form. He could do it in the privacy of him and me, but once he was in front of a block party crowd his nerves took over. Now Gene's younger brother, Cordio, kinda got it, but he couldn't master it as I showed him.

The theory I was developing was based on many things. Time and space. The time I had to continue the same beat on duplicate copies of the same vinyl record, the space I had between revolutions on each disc. Timing and precision. Hands on the record, marks on the record. Follow the pattern, follow the rhythm. Never lose the beat. Speed and accuracy. The formula I developed only worked within those elements if you could master the quickness necessary to extend a beat of a song that was usually somewhere between 90 beats-per-minute and 130 beats-per-minute. Something no one had ever done before.

I called it the Quik Mix Theory because to do it you didn't necessarily have to move fast but because the breaks in the records I was using (of the same record) were so short that you had to really know what you were doing and how to keep that break going. The taking two of the exact same songs, using the breaks of those two compositions and repeating the same break, extending the same part, the same section of the song or interchanging one part of one song with another specific part of another composition, regardless of the genre of music, in a span of minutes, sometimes seconds, without losing the beat—"Quik" might have been an understatement, but that was the only word I could think of to describe what was needed to execute. Your hands and movement had to be quick, but your mind had to be quicker. Again, this is science even though no one saw it the way I did.

It's equivalent to a scientist putting different color liquids into a beaker and shaking it up a little bit. I called it the mechanics. But my formula was the felt, the wax paper, the coins, and the crayons. The final part was the instrument, the turntable. And on it either you are rubbing or juggling beats or a combination of both.

People later on called it an invention when it, the Theory, really should have been called "an extension." Because you can't reinvent the wheel. You just make better treads, you make advancements in rubber. So when people call what I was doing an invention, they take away the three years it took me to violate the turntable, to violate the needle, to violate the vinyl, and to violate the way a mixer is supposed to be used.

This is what the Quik Mix Theory was. The *operating system*. The operating system that now almost every technique done on planet earth, when it comes to DJing, uses. I had notes and index cards with all types of math computations on them as a formula for how the Theory worked. Hypothesis and variables and analysis all written down. I was "misappropriating" technology. I was "disrespecting" music. I was hated for it. But if I were someone else, I'd be considered "innovative." I didn't want to change the way music was made; I wanted to rewire what people thought they wanted when listening to music. Which to me made the Quik Mix Theory the beginning. Maybe that's why it was so hard for my guys to catch on once I showed them what the Theory was. The Theory itself in execution was too quick.

* * *

The journey to get here is a story within itself. Most geeks will understand it. Cartridges. Needles. Styluses.

The first cartridge that I used, that I was really cool with, and this was 1971 to 1973, the one that stayed in the groove, with a conical needle was the Audio-Technica ATXN1. It was the first magnetic cartridge I used. Prior to this, I was trying to use the ceramic cartridge, and the fidelity wasn't great. Technology was advancing and companies were introducing newer cartridge models. Then I went from that to the Pickering XV-15. Then I went to the Stanton cartridge. And all of the Stanton cartridges were pretty good. Eventually, after going through several cartridges, I got comfortable with the Shure M44 needle stylus.

The search for turntables was different. I would judge a turntable, even if it was one that I'd removed from an old stereo, on its torque factors. Meaning: While the turntable was in the state of inertia, how long would it take to go up to full speed? The worst turntable would take a long, long, *long* time. A better turntable would get up to full speed in half the time, and a great one would go up almost immediately. In my search for that turntable that could go up to speed immediately, whether it was inside of a stereo I removed or in the junkyards, like a Magnavox, Zenith, Fisher-Price, Garrard, the problem with all of them was the "reject gear." The reject gear was a gear that you'd see when you lifted the platter off the base and looked inside. You'd see this gear that allowed the tonearm to return to the post, the arm rest, once it got to the end of any record. It would pick up, go back, and seat itself on the lever.

I had to remove this gear. But it had a cotter pin that would lock the gear down, the reject out of it's normal position so the turntable in any location would no longer send the tonearm back to the lever. Because if the drum break was at the end of an album and I'm DJing, the tonearm would know it's at the end of the album, it would lift up, go to the right, and go to the lever. But that might be the song that the crowd is rocking to. The tonearm with the gear installed would fuck up all my block parties whenever I would play songs that had breaks at the end of the record. Example: "Funky Drummer" by James Brown. I needed a dead tonearm. For me, the turntables I was dealing with played a major role in their torque and how quick they picked up speed in their state of inertia because most of them failed. I had to find a turntable that could pick up to speed in at least half a turn or a quarter of a turn. And I remember one day coming home from school, walking by an electronic store and there was this turntable in the window. Battleship gray. The platter had these ugly bumps on the side.

The name of the store where I saw the turntable in the window was Vic Marr. On Southern Boulevard in the Hunts Point of the Bronx. I walked in. I'm about fifteen or sixteen years old at the time. I saw this salesman and I ask, "Would it be okay, because I'm doing this study on turntables, to take that turntable out of the window and plug it up so that I can check it?"

He looks down at me, says "Excuse me for a second." He proceeds to the back of the store.

Then he comes back with these goons. I'm looking at them, they're looking at me and I'm saying to the salesperson, "Sir, I just came from school, and I'm doing some research on turntables."

Then this slim white guy comes out from the back, his name was Victor, and he was the owner. He said, "Oh, let the kid look at it. Take the turntable out of the window. Let him do what he needs to do."

They get the turntable from the window, plug it in, power it up; it goes up to speed in a little less than a quarter of a turn. I take my fingers and gently put them on the platter to see what the variance is of the platter slowing down and speeding up with a little bit of hand pressure. This turntable was pretty damn good.

I look at the model because I want to make sure I know what it is. It says, this company I never heard before, Technics by Panasonic. Model number SL-23. I ask Victor, "How much do the turntables cost?"

He says, "Turntables?"

I say, "Yes."

He asks, "How many do you need?"

I reply, "I need two."

He said, "They're gonna cost you $75 each."

So, the conversation with Victor and I goes back and forth. As I'm studying the turntable, thinking of the price, I wonder, *What are those bumps looking like mumps on the side?* I also noticed that the rubber mat was on there. I had to make that $150.

So I started my hustle at the supermarket. To get those tables I had to work from early in the morning so that I could be there as long as possible. And this was only on the weekends because I was still in school. My job: To help the elderly take their food, with my shopping cart, to their residences. Eventually I found another job as a delivery boy for Crantex Fabrics in Midtown Manhattan. They were in the swatch business, dealing with materials before they entered the fashion world. So I'd work at Crantex Fabrics on weekdays and help the elderly with their groceries on the weekend. I worked while I went to school and did my chores. It took me around three to four months to earn $150.

I remember getting the turntables home. It was so exciting. The first thing I wanted to look at was the torque. It was crucial that I was able to put the wax paper on the metal platter, the felt on top of the wax paper, and the album on top of both. I needed to turn the turntable on, go in a backward-and-forward motion, and then go counterclockwise. When I turned this turntable on there was a little orange light to the left. And those little things that looked like the mumps, they were like lines moving. In that moment I said, "Oh those must have something to do with the slowing down and speeding up the pitch of the turntable."

Once I discovered that I needed to set the speeds on both turntables to where the dots—I'm sorry, "bumps"—would not move, then I'd go back and put the wax paper on the platter and the felt on top of that and the album on top of that. I could watch the dots and they were steady, so the problem was solved.

The next problem after that: the DJ mixer. At this time, I tried everything from a battery-operated mixer that ran on nine-volt batteries to mic mixers. The battery mixers had knobs that were the enemy for all DJs that you could plug audio items into them, which really didn't work out well. The mic mixers you could hook three to four microphones up to didn't work out well either. After trying multiple different types of mixers, I tried this mixer out by Sony, the model was MX-8. This mixer didn't have a crossfader, it went up and down. It also didn't have a way for me to pre-hear the song that I wanted to play for the crowd. So I had to come up with a way to hear the next song in my ear, so I could line it up with the song presently playing to the crowd. In my searches, I found out about a company that made DJ gear. Speakers, mics, amps, mixers. I took the train and found the Gemini Sound Products factory in Brooklyn, and I met the owner, Ike Cabasso. When I walked in it felt like the clouds parted and I saw the pearly gates. Everything that I'd had to hand build this company had it already built-in.

I was walking around the factory, seeing all of this DJ gear, then I turned and saw this DJ mixer. It had everything I could ever imagine being on a mixer. What I saw was the Gemini DAC X-2000 Silver Face mixer. It had the cue on the top left, it had up and down faders, but it also had a crossfader. All the things I had to hand-make for years, this mixer had it all. I asked Ike, "How much?"

He said, "Sixty dollars."

So I had to raise money for this mixer. Which I did.

Now I have the SL-23 turntables, the Gemini Silver Face mixer, slip mats, wax paper, and the proper needles. With all the things going on in my head, I can now physically try. If there was a break in a pop record I could switch it, go to another. Then another. "I've got something here."

I gathered a pile of records of different genres. All records with drum breakdowns. Funk, pop, rock, blues. I began feeling more confident and decisive as I was playing all of my breaks and playing all of these records. In my excitement I was grabbing different songs throwing them on the SL-23s to see what I could do. "I really have something here," I said it to myself again. All the years of developing the Theory and all of the items that I had to gather, everything came into fruition. Everything is possible.

I can remember when I brought that system out, my mixer and my turntables, lots of DJs weren't only watching what I was doing but what kind of equipment I was using. The Technics SL-23, I finally retired them, and eventually the SL-220s became the industry standards for us hip-hop DJs in the '70s. Some would use the Pioneers; they were popular but those Technics were the most. And they were all belt-driven turntables.

As technology improved Technics came up with this turntable called a direct-drive turntable. And even with my schooling, I was puzzled by what direct-drive meant. I did some research and discovered the part that spun on the motor was the integral part of the platter, and the torque factor on these direct-drive turntables were ten-fold compared to the belt-drives—which was the reason belt-drives eventually were discontinued. And that's when Technics came up with the SL-220 and the SL-1100s. The 1100A, which I never saw but heard a lot about, were what Herc spun on.

And then the 1200s came.

* * *

One day when I walked into Gene's mother's living room, there was this little kid. And what I could do circularly and seamlessly with the Quik Mix Theory, he was able to pick up and drop the tonearm of the turntable in almost the exact same place every time. If he did it ten times, seven or eight outta those ten it would be on time. He was doing it on Gene's mom's stereo. Picking up the needle and dropping it. On beat. The song he was doing it to, Herman Kelly and Life's "Dance to the Drummer's Beat."

I asked Gene, "G, who is that?"

He said, "Oh that's just my little brother."

I said, "Well, do you mind if I teach him the Theory?"

Now, not only was Mean Gene a really good breakdancer, not the greatest DJ, but when it came to fighting—that muthafucka—if there were two people in a crowd in a fight, Gene would be one of those two people.

When I asked him could I teach his little brother my Theory, he said, "If I catch my little brother on the set, you and me are gonna have problems."

I couldn't outwardly show his little brother, so I had to be creative. When Gene would go out, I'd say, "Theodore, come on." And I'd grab a milk crate, go to Mean Gene's room, and instruct him on the Theory completed; he caught on quickly.

Theodore was about nine or ten years old. He had a knack for being able to mirror me when I showed him something. For a period of time, again whenever Gene wasn't around, I would show Theodore my new style of DJing.

I couldn't understand why other people in my age group couldn't catch on, saying to me, "What do you mean you are putting your hands on the record? Why aren't you just using the tonearm? What do you mean you're keeping one area of this composition and continuing it seamlessly? How are you doing that? Why are you doing that?" So for me, it became very frustrating because there weren't many people close to me interested in learning what I was doing or who could comprehend how to do what I was doing. But a kid could.

For those who came to our side of the Bronx, especially DJs, they had to retool doing the old-fashioned style of DJing. They looked at me, Flash, and they couldn't get it, and they looked at Theodore and were embarrassed that they couldn't get it. If this little kid could get it then they had to.

Later this became a gift and a curse when I DJed at 63 Park. I thought playing the drum breakdowns of a pop record, a funk record, a jazz record, of records people knew, I'm going to have the crowd losing it! They're going to be jamming with me. Dancin', groovin', party'n'. But the opposite happened. Instead people were pushing behind the ropes to see what I was doing to the records. They were quiet, they weren't partying. They thought I was doing some type of magic trick or something. I was heartbroken. They weren't dancing. It almost broke me. I spent years doing this, inventing this new style, and this is what I get?

* * *

By 1973 to 1975, we were deep in the parks. Mott Haven Park. Arthur Park. 23 Park. 63 Park. Bryant Avenue Park. Testing out my style and theory in front of any crowd that would come to any park to hear me play. Trying to do whatever the other DJs weren't doing.

DJ Kool Herc had a crew of DJs. They'd come on during

his sets to relieve Herc when he wanted to take a break from being on the tables. Later, they became known for being on the microphone, some of them actually called themselves rappers which I never understood because I knew them—*and only knew them*—as Herc's DJs. Coke La Rock, Timmy Tim, the (Nigga) Twins, and the original Clark Kent. Whenever one would walk off the turntables, the other would walk on. By that time he had assembled them into what I liked to call his "second-in-command DJs," Herc was getting deeper into building his American music collection of records. James Brown, Jimmy Castor, and Rufus Thomas. But his system was still built from the foundation of his Jamaican heritage, many say by his father, from the sound systems made famous for reggae and dub in Kingston.

Before the Herculords became the Herculords, Herc had a partner, called El Marco. Now Coke La Rock and Herc did the parties, but El Marco was the one who hooked up the sound system. Herc's father from what I was told had a band, and he supplied Herc with what we called the Brain, which was actually an amplifier that had outposts to hook microphones to it. El Marco apparently showed Herc how to hook two turntables up to it with preamps. From my understanding that's how it all started. From there, Herc was able to build his system. And the more money Herc made from parties, the more he invested in his sound. One day Herc, with Clark Kent who told me he was with him on this day, went to Harvey Electronics in Queens and purchased a McIntosh MC2300 amplifier—I called it the Blue Face—and the guys who worked there apparently told Herc, for what he was trying to do, "You're going to need more than this." They continued, "To make this sound what you want it to be you need a crossover." That was the piece of equipment Herc had that no one else had. That's what made his sound unique and different and bigger than everyone else's.

Their system included a five-band JVC equalizer, preamp, and the crossover—which basically was a dual subwoofer filter. And what the crossover did was make the fidelity on all frequencies of what they were doing sound crystal, crystal clear.

And it was Clark Kent who, being a low-key nerd like me, would watch El Marco string up Herc's system. So when El Marco left (I never found out why), Clark was the one who told Herc how to really string up the system because according to him Herc had three or four amps he wasn't even using. Kent showed Herc how to hook up the other amps to use both sides to make the system sound more powerful. The rest is history and the story goes that the only time they brought out the whole system, full sound, was at a party at the PAL (Police Athletic League) on 183rd and Webster Avenue. They had the best mobile sound system in the Bronx. Period.

There was one time that I remember being able to get on one of Herc's crew's systems. It was a party Clark Kent had at the 3rd Avenue Ballroom on 166th. I think it was the first time Clark did a solo party, he invited me to come. I went, and he let me play. Which I'm almost sure didn't make Herc happy because he was about protecting his people and his brand. He had rules. But we were kids, we didn't care. Clark told me the separation of crews didn't sink in until he started spinning for Herc. The whole Herc telling them don't go to certain parks and parties and places, and for them not to take pictures with certain people, other DJs, and other crews.

"If you wanna be down with us, this is how we get down," Clark told me was how Herc got down when it came to them.

But, again, as kids we really didn't care about all of that. Like, Clark Kent and Melle Mel, who ended up being a rapper in my group, were friends. Them and Scorpio ("Ness" as we called him), who like Mel would also end up being a rapper in the group. To show how small our world was then, Scorpio stayed in the building right next to Clark's. Scorpio lived at 1420 Washington Avenue, Clark lived at 1385 Washington Avenue. When Mel would come to see Scorpio and they'd see Clark Kent, they'd always stop and chop it up with him. They'd all be on Washington Avenue together. Clark told me once, "Flash you know at your parties you would stop the music a lot and people would get annoyed because once the music stopped people couldn't dance until the music came back on."

Now I would stop the music at the parties to get the rappers—or MCs (Masters of Ceremonies)—time to do their routines. Anyway, Clark was like, "One day I told Mel, 'You know what you gotta do? When the music stops and you all are getting ready to set up the next routine, you gotta do something until the music comes back on. So, speed up your raps. Make the people have to listen to what you are saying in order to *hear* what you're saying.'"

Little things like that happened on the side, unbeknownst to me and probably everyone. Because back then, for them, it wasn't about competition, it was just three young teenagers seeing one another in the neighborhood and chillin' with each other while they were on the cusp of making history.

* * *

The jams were always a different experience for different people. An experience that I personally never experienced. I never "experienced" a Flash party, I was too busy doin' 'em, working them. As a friend says: I would "climb inside of a record." I'd go to other jams just to hear other DJs to see what they were doing, to be normal, but I kept hearing how my jams were different.

With Gene on 168th Street and Boston Road, again right down the block from 63 Park, we would also have parties at his place, and people would just show up. People were hearing about my sound, about how I was DJing differently. One of the first people I remember coming there consistently was this girl we called Little Terri (Terri Martin). *Little* because of her height and at the time she was around fourteen years old. She would come with her sister Debbie. They would play hooky from school just to come to the parties at Gene's apartment.

We took those parties from Gene's spot to Clark Park on 145th Street. There we had the Casanova Crew—Tiny, Dicey, Peanut, Little Jay, Crazy Eddie, Lance, etc.—who were my security. They made sure while I was DJing at the jams, nothing happened to me or anybody. Then we'd be at Behagen (Playground) on Tinton Avenue, and I'd look up and it's Little Terri and Debbie again. Then I was DJing at "Over the Dover," which was a theater in the Bronx on 174th Street, where upstairs above a theatre we used to have jams and who was there? Terri and Debbie. They were true, they followed and stayed with me from the beginning.

Terri would always tell me how much trouble she and Debbie would get in for coming to my parties. How her mom would give them a curfew to be home, usually around midnight, and they wouldn't get home until the sun was coming up. Another friend of mine who always came to the jams would say, "We gonna get the same beating for coming home at 1 a.m. that you're going to get at 6 a.m., so you might as well stay." And all of them would tell me that it was worth it.

One time when we were at 63 Park, Terri screams out, "Somebody say, Ho!" The people would scream back at her to, "Shut the fuck up!" They'd call her names, but she didn't stop. And once she started, Debbie joined in. "Somebody say, Ho!"

One day Keef Cowboy, another future member of our group, picked up on the Terri-and-Debbie chant and screamed out, "Somebody say, Ho!" But when Cowboy said it, everybody picked it up. No one told him to shut the hell up. They all screamed back, "Ho!" And Terri was like, "Alright, that's what I'm talking about." It made her happy.

When I formed the group with the Furious Five and we were recording the song "Freedom," Ray Chandler, who was managing us at the time, had sent four of the guys to Terri's mom's house on Tinton Avenue to pick up Terri and Debbie to be a part of the song. The plan was to have them in the background saying, "Everybody say, Ho! Scream it out and say, Ho!" They came to the studio and according to Terri never got in to record. Apparently, we'd gone through so many takes and cuts, that we ran out of time to add them in the recording. Ray went out and told them, "It's too late now, you all won't be able to get in there." I think that crushed them. I know for sure that Terri was pissed off. She told me she felt betrayed because of how hard she was out there just telling the world about me. She felt that I was moving up and leaving her behind.

She was the one who came up with the "Somebody say, Ho!" phrase so this was like her chance to be recognized. "Flash, I was so ticked off because that moment was high hopes for us," she's told me. They were about to be on a song. But it didn't happen. When I speak with Terri now, she laughs about it. Says, "That was one of our downfalls with you." But they still would come to the parties.

And not only come to the parties, she did security at parties for me, helped carry crates, got angry if I missed a beat on a mix, she and her friends did work promoting the parties—on their own, without me ever asking! Going to schools, local businesses, on foot, on the train, in the winter when they'd put plastic bags over their sneakers, they'd pass out flyers, tell people, "Yo, you gotta come to Flash's party." All over the

Bronx and into other boroughs. They'd push me, encourage me. They wanted the best for me. And they weren't the only ones. It was like one big family get-together every weekend.

Terri came from a family with a musical background. In fact, her parents were in a group called the Willows, whose hit song "Church Bells May Ring" I used to play, not even knowing at the time that her parents were in the group. And one of the things that Terri would tell me when it came to coming to my jams was directly related to the variety of music I played. It wasn't just about me breaking down breaks, it wasn't just me finding and extending drumbeats. It was just a part of it. That I'd spin for hours even as people would come to see me do the one thing I was becoming famous for—breaking down drum breaks and manipulating parts of records, but they stayed for the music I was playing because I was doing it differently.

"[Herc, Bam, and Breakout] just stuck to one brand of music," she'd tell me. "Yours wasn't that. You played a lot of music. You played 'old school,' you played 'doo-wop,' you played 'break-beats,' you played 'hustlin' music, you had a variety, a style about the music you played. And a style about yourself. The other parties, it was like one brand of music, at a Flash party, there'd be a variety of music. If someone didn't like what you were playing they'd go sit down, take a break somewhere, eventually you were going to play something to get them back on the dance floor."

For them, they'd always tell me, "Flash you are our life." They lived vicariously through me, as I grew, as this thing I was doing grew, and so did they. "What you are doing Flash is bigger than what you think," is what Terri kept saying. She started with me, following what we were doing at fourteen years old, and it stopped when she was twenty-one years old. Seven years. Terri's last Flash party was a big DJ battle at the Armory in Harlem. A big brawl broke out, it was really bad, thousands of people inside, and at the time Terri was pregnant. She was like, "I can't hang out like this anymore." The risk was too much, and that was her last party.

* * *

Then there's the story of Keith Williams. A b-boy from Manhattan, raised in Georgia, moved to Harlem, living in the Bronx. You would see his tag T163 on buses. He would always be at Bam parties, and he'd sneak out of school to go to Herc parties at the Executive Playhouse on Jerome Avenue where Herc would have what they called "hooky parties" because the kids would play hooky from school and go to his parties in the middle of the afternoon. Keith came to my parties before he built his own set. He'd be at Downstairs Records too, trying to buy all of the b-boy records. He was able to get into the backroom. Just like Disco Bee, Keith after a while stopped breakdancing and turned into a DJ. His name was Breakout. Even though he was a few years younger and came into it a little after us, Breakout was like the fourth cornerstone to what we were doing at the time. I called him, because he stayed so far uptown in the Bronx, the King of the North.

Bam was kind of the reason Breakout became DJ Breakout. Bam at his parties would give Keith records to take home to practice with. I think they were for him to practice breakdancing too, but Breakout used them to practice DJing. Like me, he was fascinated with sound. One of his friend's (Baron) brother had a system and when Keith saw it, he said, "Let's get something together."

Breakout took apart his mother's Zenith stereo, made a big speaker (I think) out of garbage cans he got off the streets, and he had another stereo system which was a console record player with the radio in the front, rolled them down the block to a school yard in a shopping cart, broke in the school, got power from one of the outlets, and . . . he didn't have a mixer. Didn't even know he needed one. All the times he watched Bam play, he never got close enough during Bam's sets, never got behind the ropes, to see how Bam was actually doing what he was doing. He just took the wires from both components with the record players on them and connected the wires from both of them into one speaker, put the needle on one record, and every time that record phased out, he'd drop the needle on the other record. And that was the beginning of DJ Breakout.

Once he got a mixer, Breakout went to Murphy Projects off Babylon Avenue, DJing there and then to Edenwald, where he played at the same spot every weekend and started to make a name for himself. He had uptown on lock. Boston Secor Houses, all the high schools, all the parks. His sound system was a magnet for me because my sound system was shit. I was technical—I was always, always tweaking what I was doing, so I didn't really take too much time to go hear other DJs. I'd go to hear Bam, I'd go to check out what Herc was doing every now and then, but when I heard about this system called the Sasquatch I was like, "What the F is this?"

I jumped in a taxi to go to where I heard this system was. I remember the taxi pulling up, me getting out, me walking toward the Center to get in, and hearing Breakout playing "The Big Beat" by Billy Squier. "Whoa! Oh my God!" is all I said.

They were those garbage can speakers he had with twenty-inch woofers in each of them. That's why he called them the Sasquatch. And every party he'd blow out those speakers, take the money he and Baron got from the party, buy speakers to replace the blown ones, and put them back in the garbage cans for the next party. He and Baron didn't get a real set of speakers until they had to go up against Bam. After that, they went and bought a new, bigger system. They kept reinvesting in themselves.

I admired Breakout. I would never have any reason to go that far uptown, 226th Street—except to hear him. Back then I didn't even think there was anything that far uptown in the Bronx. Going up there was like a discovery: "Oh shit, there's people and land up here." But Breakout had it rockin' up there. Pretty much like we had it rockin' in the other three corners of the Bronx.

* * *

I met these girls: Cookie (Francine Gutierrez), Anna (Monroe) and Dee Dee (Denise Hairston) around 1970. At maybe a basement "club" that EZ Mike and I played. I think I met Anna and Dee Dee first. Anna and Dee Dee were in junior high school and convinced their school to let me DJ at their school's ten-cent party during lunch time. Let Cookie tell it, as she's older than them, I then went from there to being the first DJ, replacing the live bands, to do the world famous—from (Grace H.) Dodge Vocational High School to (Parkland Park) Rye Playland—boat ride sets.

Anna, Cookie, and Dee Dee were a part of a crew called the Invaders. They'd come to all our jams, at the parks and clubs. They even followed me on Tuesday nights when I spun at the Disco Fever. Over time, Cookie, Anna, Dee Dee, and I became more like family. There were other b-girl crews—Charlie's Angels, the Intruders—but the Invaders stood out. Lee jackets with bleached names of the crew across the backs. Plus Anna was a rapper, but she never got the chance to rap. She really was one of the original ghost writers; she was gifted. Anna would have these rhymes that she'd just drop off the top of her head. "Dip, dip, dab. So, socialize . . ." That was her. "The roof, the roof, is on fire. We don't need no water . . ." That was her too.

What I found out later was that some of the things the guys were saying at the jams while I was DJing came from Anna and

Cookie. Anna, mostly I was told, and Cookie would be writing down rhymes on sheets of paper from a five-cent composition notebook and passing them to the guys to say. Anna tells me these stories of how she'd come up with sayings and lines.

"Grandmaster/Cuts faster," that was her; "Gotta rock it, don't stop it," that lyric came from her. The whole "willing and able" line, her. She says she was the one who told the guys that they needed to go back and forth, passing the mic to each other when they were rhyming.

Cookie and Anna also were the ones who came up with the names for the guys in the group. Anna would say, "We gave Cowboy his name because he was bowlegged." Cookie started calling Scorpio Mr. Ness because he always thought he was fly before he changed his name to Scorpio. Rahiem's real name was Todd. They started calling Danny Kid Creole because he had that "New Orleans, creole color to his skin."

When Anna tells people these stories no one believes her. She'll say, "What do I look like? Do I look like I'm capable of [creating] things like that?" But she knows how important she, Dee Dee, and Cookie were in helping build this art form. To this day Anna will tell you: "I gotta lotta haters because I do a lotta stuff that people make money off of." I know there's some truth there because when we started doing the jams, she was always around. She was there when Ray Chandler and I were hustling around trying to book the parties.

I'd tell her, "Stay here until we get back. Don't go nowhere, don't open the door!" And she'd be there, using her imagination to come up with rhymes. She studied everything I did on the tables. She learned my DJ patterns. When I'd hit one of those grooves, I'd do this dance while I was spinning she used to call "The Goose Neck." I'd hit that perfect part of the record of a mix and my neck would start moving back and forth. That's when I knew I'd found that pocket. I had a long neck and used to wear turtlenecks a lot, and at times when I'd dance to what I was spinning my neck would stick out from the turtleneck. Anna used to say I looked like a goose, so she was the one who put a name to my dance.

Cookie always told me: "You saw us." That I played to the crowd. That I looked out at the crowds when I was DJing, and I knew exactly what I *needed* to play. And that's why they never went anywhere or followed any other DJ.

I played music for women, at times. Hustle music to slow jams. At times. But I was still trying to invent something with the music I was playing that didn't exist. I don't want to call them groupies, but I had a crew of women from the Bronx that came to the parties in the park that I'd call the Original Fly Girls. All from the South Bronx. Little Jackie (Jacquenette Casey), Kya (Farrow), Cheryl (Bordies), Dee Dee (Deidre Bordies), and Big Jackie (Jacquline Tucker). They lived for Fridays because on Fridays, they'd tell me I always "stepped it up a little bit." And they wanted to see what I was going to do. They'd call them Flash Jams, not parties. And for them it was a whole production: outfits, matching clothes, sweatshirts, farmer jeans because that was the style. They would pay to get in the parties when they could have gotten in for free. That's the type of support they gave. They did the footwork, getting the word out every week about the next jam. It could have been considered cultish, but, we were kids, high school, it felt more like a family.

We were a village. I met some of their parents, and I became responsible for them while they were at my parties. A lot of times this meant putting them in taxis to make sure they got home. The girls had a policy that one of their mother's enforced: "Five of you all leave together, five of you all come back." No exceptions. And they always did. They were out at fifteen and sixteen years old until 2 or 3 a.m., and some of that flexibility came from their mothers having trust in me.

The Fly Girls would always be up front, close to the stage, and they waited for me to bring out the beatbox. They'd make the most noise when I'd work the beatbox and count the number of times I'd switch from one song to the next when I was quick mixing. They would count the cuts out loud like a hype crew. "Ten! Eleven! Twelve!" And even though Little Terri and Debbie didn't make it into the studio when we recorded "Freedom," the girls, Kya, Cheryl, Dee Dee, both Jackies, were there, in the studio, in the background, when we recorded the first record "Superrappin'." They knew we were making history.

* * *

From my understanding the only real props the guys in the group, the rappers, ever gave Anna and Cookie was when they'd call out the name of their crew during the jams, "The Invaders are in the house!" Now the other girls and crews would get shouted out for always being there, for being like our family, for being loyal to us, so at the parties they'd get recognized. But Anna and Cookie were never singled out for what they were contributing and according to them that only began to happen after they approached the guys about giving them and their crew credit. Also Anna, Cookie, and Dee Dee wanted acknowledgment at the parties because when the dance floors were empty because all of the people were watching me DJ, the three of them would "invade" the dance floor and light the place up. They'd start hollering, "Go Flash! Go Flash! Go!" And the people would go into a frenzy. The rappers would use that energy when they'd get on the mic.

Anna would say (to the guys): "You all are up there [on stage], but you all ain't in there." From her point of view, without her crew's help the guys were just mouthpieces. Not rockin' the parties like they could have. The b-boys and b-girls crews were the ones who kick-started the parties, they took the energy from what I was doing and transferred it to the dance floor by hyping the crowd up and breakdancing, and that became the energy the MCs used when they got on the mic to say their rhymes. We all had a part to play.

Here's where this gets deep. Sometime around 1976, Anna told me her brother was going into the military, to the Kokomo Armory in Indiana, where some of the Tuskegee Airmen came from. Her exact words to me were: "Flash, he's about to go to the service, because he's going to 'Hip-hop-hip-hop,'" saying it like she was a drill sergeant.

Now, Anna had five brothers who were in the military, and they would come home and teach her and her sisters cadence. So when her other brother was going to Kokomo, they were chanting, like they did with me at the jams, "Go Kokomo! Go Kokomo! Go!" Then Cookie started teasing their brother in cadence, "Your left, your left, your left, right, left!" And as she was doing that the other girls, including Anna, were saying, "Hip-hop-hip-hop, it don't stop," in the same military-type cadence, but with a rhythm like we were at a jam. She said they were doing that because that's the way the soldiers walked. "One-two-one-two, pivot, turn, one-two-one-two."

"Hip-hop-hip-hop-hip-hop it don't stop. Make your body rock. My back is aching, my bra's too tight, shake my (ass) from left to right."

And if you ask her or Cookie—and I was there at that time and had not heard the term used before—that's where the theme of hip-hop started. That hip-hop was not a thing until they started teasing their brother about going to the military, going to Kokomo. And the very next day I was DJing at the Boston Road Ballroom in the Bronx, they told Keef (Cowboy) to say, "Hip-hop, hip-hop, hip-hop, it don't stop. And don't stop that body rock" when he got on the mic that night. Even though Lovebug Starski along with Keef are the ones credited with using, or as they say "coining," the phrase hip-hop first. The rest is history versus her story.

Later in life, I found out that Anna got really sick and her kidneys shut down. This was years later, in 2019. Cookie found me and told me Anna was going into surgery (a kidney transplant), and she wanted to talk because there was a good chance she might not make it. So, I called. I called after the transplant. I called every day. She told me I was one of the reasons she got through, that I was one of the reasons she held on. "I held on like I did back in the day to get to one of your parties."

It means a lot to me to know that I played such a role in people's lives. Them saying, "Flash you laid the groundwork for this music, we did the footwork. We were in the streets, with the flyers, in the schools, promoting. We had a connect on every block. You guys made it for what it became. If it wasn't for you, there would be nobody else." Cookie was one of the people who followed me from nothing and will tell me to this day: "This movement started with your birth. They keep saying 'birth of the *nation*,' no. The birth was you. You are a genius, a mathematician. You built your system, and we watched you get a response from the crowd through music. You earned your name, 'Grandmaster Flash,' and fought to keep it, and none of your trials changed that great personality. I'm proud of you like a mother to a son. We loved you first but had to give you to the world. To let them see how great you were." I knew I was making people happy, doing something that gave people a good time, but I didn't know I was *moving* people. Making them experience something that they'd carry with them for the rest of their lives.

When I heard someone call one of our jams "like being in *Alice in Wonderland*," I knew for people who were living like us this was different. Their reaction was just as important as me supplying the music. I know I wasn't alone—it was Herc, it was Bam, it was Breakout all at the same time pretty much. But it's nothing like having the people who were there say, "I was on the listening side of it and *you* made me—you made us—feel this way," that it was "magical," and our jams were the most magical times of their lives. A lot of times, the other DJs had bigger crowds, but I always felt the crowd we drew was the best. Just something about it.

Cookie: "When you had the block parties there was peace in the Bronx. Wasn't nobody fighting, wasn't nobody shooting, wasn't nobody killing, wasn't nobody bothering anything. When Flash was outside the police knew where everybody was. They were all in the park. So they never bothered you. 'Oh, that's Flash. We can sit in our patrol cars and not listen to our radios.' Radio silence. Because they knew nothing was going to jump-off because of your music."

Truth told, I had a good relationship with the police departments in the parks I played in. We would see rows of cars out there parked, but people would just be out there drinking sodas or just sitting in their cars, listening to the music, not causing any problems. And I'm talking about some of the most notorious stick-up kids, some of the biggest named gangsters. They'd be like, "Flash, you okay?" We're talking children, grandmothers, all out in the park, just jammin'. It was very peaceful. It was like a village. In the ghetto. As the girls like to remind me, "Flash's parties did something for people who lived in poverty." I had no idea at the time what this was or what this was going to be, but I know if I looked to the left, my fans were there; when I'd look to the right, my fans were with me. Wherever I went, they were with me. What I was doing could have missed, but it didn't.

The E-mu SP-12 sampling drum machine. One of hip-hop's first sampling drum machines. It became one of the most important pieces of equipment in the entire music industry.

The SL-23 by Technics. Herc had the 110A, I had the SL-23. In my opinion, more DJs were using the SL-23 turntable. This was hip-hop's first official "economical" turntable.

CHAPTER 5

I never understood why Herc never liked me. I often use the word hate, but I don't think he hated me, but I *know* he always seemed to treat me like there was no love. I'd go to parties in other territories in the Bronx to hear the other guys play, Bam's territory, Breakout's territory, somebody else's territory, I'd always get mad respect. They knew who I was, people would say hello, they'd let me in for free, all of that. But whenever I'd show up at a Kool Herc party, I'd always ask: Why in the fuck am I getting disrespected so much?

I'd walk into a Herc set—now I'm not sure if he saw me or someone told him I'd walked in—and he'd put on "The Mexican" from the very beginning. At the top of the song were the guitars—*bling, bling, bling, bling*—and, as always at a Herc party, I marveled at the sound of the system. Then he'd get on the mic. "In order to be a great DJ, you gotta have highs." *Bling, bling, bling, bling.* The guitars would come in. It would sound like birds fighting. "In order to be a great DJ, you gotta have horns." His midrange frequency sounded crystal clear. Then the tambourines in the intro of the song come in. *Ding, ding, ding, ding. Ding, ding, ding, ding.* And then when it'd get to the end of the intro, he'd say, "And most importantly, in order to be a great DJ you gotta have bass." Then "The Mexican" beat would start. And that shit would shake the floor, it would hit, *Boom, boom, boom, ba-boom, boom!* By this time everyone there is looking directly at me. They know he's directing this at me; everyone knew I had a shitty sound system. But I'd just stand there and really wonder, *Why is this guy fucking with me? What did I ever do to him?* He has the biggest crowd, great records, the best system, he's it. His sound system could easily crush mine. He's the bomb dude, had the upper hand on almost all fronts. Other DJs were trying to make names for ourselves, but he was the King. *So, why are you doing this? Why are you fucking with me?*

EZ Mike was with me once when I asked Herc if we could do a party with him and Herc straight said, "No! Don't nobody come see you."

The words broke my heart, and it continued for years. If he'd see me at one of his parties, which I was rarely able to get to because I didn't have many off nights, unlike other DJs who had me escorted to the DJ booth or have me come up on stage to get me away from the crowd, Herc would never do anything like that. Never allow me to go up on stage or to get close, like, "Stay the fuck away from my system! Stay the fuck way from me!" Just bitter for no fucking reason.

I never figured out why.

There's even this thing about the Merry-Go-Round. To me the Merry-Go-Round was three DJs standing behind each other on one song with each individual taking turns cutting up a break. Then one standing to the side, while the second DJ cuts the break to the right, cuts the break to the left, then he'd step off and the next DJ would step up. The "record boys" and I we had a routine: We had to run around up to the turntables and catch the records and spin it back for the next person to catch. I would start it. I would take a record with a good break, and I'd start it. Leave it be for maybe four to eight, sometimes depending on the break, sixteen beats. Then I'd step back from the tables, and Disco Bee would step in. He'd do something with the break, then he'd step back, and EZ Mike would step in. And he'd do the same thing. Then he'd step back, and I'd come back in. I remember us doing that and back then calling it the "Merry-Go-Round." Herc has said, and it's something he argues with me about, that he came up with the Merry-Go-Round. Saying his DJ "style" was a merry-go-round. That always confused me. We had a whole routine going on: *It was a literal merry-go-round.* Us taking turns going around the turntables, one after another, extending the same break or playing different records in a very short period of time. If Herc wants to take credit for it, I'm not necessarily cool with that because what we did was literally a merry-go-round and what Herc did wasn't the same as our Merry-Go-Round. I'm not taking anything away from Herc. But this DJ thing and the mechanics of it, it took years for me to come up with, and that concept of using different DJs.

I had a great conversation with Clark Kent about this. He told me, "Herc never said, 'I can't stand Flash.'" He used the word *never* twice. But I knew for many years on the few occasions when we were in the same room, I'd always try to be cool with him. Herc? He'd direct his ire at me. Putting me down. EZ Mike would always ask, "We don't even know this dude, so why is he like that with us?" To me it went back to "the what," we were both DJs and "the how," in how our styles of DJing were drastically different. I was the exact opposite when it came to DJs of what was the norm at the time. Maybe that was it.

I looked at Herc as a selector. He had no consideration for

BPMs or the law of transitions. Which is in the family of DJing, but the technical aspect of DJing wasn't there. My approach and purpose, for lack of a better word, was totally different from his. He cared about the selection of the songs he would play, not necessarily so much about how the songs were played. And what wound up happening was his crowd started to come see me with my wack-ass sound system and they pretty much ended up staying. I for the most part was making new songs out of songs; Herc was playing songs. What Herc was doing and what I was doing was really, really different, which led to this misunderstanding on the "styles" of DJing.

But Clark Kent informed me that Herc just had a way about not letting people get close to him or inside his circle, that it wasn't just me. He was a very private person. Very protective, as I knew, about his brand. Clark told me stories about how he and Herc would get into it. He would tell Herc he's going somewhere and Herc would apparently tell him, "You ain't going over there." But at the same time he told me of one time when he made Herc come to the Dixie Club to hear me play. I never thought Herc ever came to see me play. He told Herc when they had this one night off, "Man, we ain't got anything going on tonight, and I'm not sitting here all night on this bench, let's go to the Dixie Club." Herc said he wasn't going because that was Flash's thing. To which Clark said, "Okay you stay here, I'm going." And Herc came with him.

But I know Clark used to get on Herc's nerves a lot when they'd have private conversations because he told me. About times he'd tell Herc, "You know, [Ray] Chandler got that DJ AJ and Flash show going on, if we get down with that and put our system with them in front of those kids, we'll blow up so big!" He said Herc wouldn't, couldn't see it. Like he couldn't understand that concept. That concept of collaboration. I idolized Herc's sound system so much that if he wanted I would have possibly joined him or at the least taught him the Theory. But he didn't. As Clark likes to say, "Rome was not built by one man," and we at the time were the heavy hitters. And neither I nor Herc were building this movement by ourselves. He was the Pied Piper, I was the scientist. But with my hands on his sound system, with our record collections combined, history and hip-hop probably would have been totally different.

Herc was getting into and playing in clubs at this time that Bam and I couldn't because he was a couple of years older than us and started a few years before we did. Like the club he made famous, the Hevelow, was a gentleman's club, Herc had an "in," he had his own thing. And as Clark says, "When people are making a lot of money they don't see collaboration as making more money." To most people it's all about them. Clark kept trying to make Herc understand that for them bringing a few more people along with them . . . man. I could imagine: Clark as chief engineer, Herc as the leader, me moving those turntables on *that* system. It's scary to think about. It could have been phenomenal.

* * *

"I'm not a pioneer, Flash. I'm late to arrive but I was already up on all the G.O.A.T.'s games, like, I already saw how they were doing it, where they were doing it. I approached it early on like, 'I'm gonna do the recon of the New York subway system.'"

Futura came on to the scene wanting to write every line, a fanatic by his own admittance. An only child with freedom to roam and chase his interests, the shit he was into. He chose graffiti. The whole lore and mythology of the Writer's Bench on 149 Grand Concourse Station in the South Bronx, where the writers went, talking shop, mingling, engaging with one another, Futura never went into those cyphers. Instead, he was about fifty yards away, on the other side of the platform, scoping. Staking people out. On the edges. He was the observer.

He arrived somewhere between 1970 and 1971. What some might call the second generation or second wave of the graffiti culture. Stanley Kubrick's movie *2001: A Space Odyssey* from 1968 registered with him. Not just the film, but the numbers in the title. No writer of graffiti in NY was using four digits in their tags. Everyone had three, two, or one number attached to their names. So, well aware of that, Futura added "2000" to his public domain. It was a fantasy projection. He was fifteen years old at the time, in New York, forty-five years old was never something he foresaw reaching.

That's why he was surfing trains like LA kids were surfing waves. Leaving his mark and art and name on welded sheet steel that would last years. Doing shit kids were dying doing. "Graffiti and hip-hop culture spun out of gang violence that we mighta had, and even if you are breaking minor laws by painting (they called it vandalizing) you aren't really gang banging. Graffiti was a different lifestyle. And I was grateful for that," is how Futura looked at it.

By 1974, Futura 2000 was no longer on the streets of New York. He'd joined, like so many others, the armed services and went into the navy. He went from subway tunnels on 180th Street to flight decks for aircraft carriers. In 1978 he returned, back to the block and sadly to exactly what he left—the same people doing the exact same thing.

"Four years later everyone is still on that stoop. Nobody moved. The graffiti hierarchy of who was who, the same.

Older cats still on top, little wannabes still on the bottom. They hadn't moved an inch in their lives," is all he could think. A feeling in life I would later relate to and live with unfortunately. His life experience of getting away broadened how he saw life and his art.

Graffiti on transit between 1976 and 1979 was wild. Lee Quiñones, the legend of legends, was becoming a star but also shaping the larger acceptance of graffiti art in New York. Futura and Phase II became close friends, as did Futura and Rammellzee, and Futura and Dondi basically, according to Futura, became the best of friends. They'd do things outside of art, like fly pigeons from the roof of Dondi's crib, which helped Futura in his visualization of the art he'd create. "When I was on a block or on a particular street, ground level, I didn't visualize it from where I was standing, I saw things from above," is how Futura explained it.

Dondi, being one of the most influential graffiti artists of that generation, was the one who was raising the bar. Some of the work Futura did after 1978 was a result of his connection with Dondi. Getting out of the New York City grid mindset where POVs can be trapped and limited. Him being able to train his mind to rise above to see "the canvas" of NY—then the world—with a much larger scope. In the shadow of Dondi, Futura 2000 was also becoming a legend.

Even though Futura didn't consider himself a pioneer, he and I remained on a parallel path of the same timeline. We were both the quiet ones. Never coming into the room talking about all the shit we'd done, neither of us the showy ones, taking in our surroundings knowing how lucky we were. Getting love and admiration for who we were and for our contributions. Him a tunnel kid, me a parks kid. It was in 1980 that Futura, along with another legendary graffiti artist Zephyr, held down a two-month project called the Graffiti 1980 Studio (or Esses Studio named after Merryl Esses's father who championed the art work of graffiti artists), where they gave space for the subway legends of the culture to do the same thing on canvas they'd been doing for years on trains and walls. His contributions and vision becoming larger than his actual art.

Case in point: In 1982 Futura was also a part of a five twelve-inch record release compilation where he had his own record titled, "The Escapades of Futura 2000." The other four records were by Grand Mixer D. St. (who later became Grand Mixer D.X.T.), Tribe 2, Phase II, and Fab 5 Freddy with a French female MC named Beside. They did it for this independent record label out of Paris called Celluloid Records. They became somewhat of a collector's item. Not just for the records and the artists but for the artwork Futura did on the backs of all five of the record sleeves—if you put them all together next to one another they formed one singular piece of art.

Unknown to me that same year Futura did a piece entitled "Future Look for Flash," which was very similar in concept with what he did for the five twelve-inch record set. A four-foot each, three-piece aerosol painting on metal of me as a DJ representing my contributions to the culture. I heard about it. "I was inspired by you Flash because I thought at that moment if there's elements of hip-hop and there's someone on the turntables, you are that person." He never commercialized the piece. From his book he reads me the words he wrote for the piece after the painting's title: "Flash as in the Grandmaster. I imagine him as a prisoner of the influence. The governmental force who controlled the populous being subjected to mixing classical music with industrial noise. Playing weeks without sleep. The timescale is 186 hours-a-day. The climate for a revolution is ripe. GM Flash on the 1s, 2s and 3s." Me being a *Star Trek* fanatic and him being a *Star Wars* fanatic, it made perfect sense. I never saw the piece until 2025 when Futura told me it was in an art exhibit in Paris. How fucking futuristic is that?

* * *

My personal life by 1974, 1975 was all over the place. Father at eighteen years old. Opening sets for Pete DJ Jones at ballrooms and disco clubs in Manhattan and Midtown just to get money and my name out and my rep up. Working as a messenger boy just to get steady money to help Paulette (ex-girlfriend and mother of my first child) with the baby and buy more records. Still waiting on the Quik Mix Theory to really catch on and make sense to everyone, not just a few. The parks were still my haven and heaven.

"This thing that you're doing on the turntables is quite amazing." I heard the words before I saw the man saying them, even though I noticed him staring at me through the fence. I remember him approaching me. Tall dude. Like *tall.* Light-skinned. He said, as he came into view, "We can make money with this." We? I look up at him and say basically, "Whatever." After that he left me alone. Then he shows up again at 63 Park. Same thing. He approaches me, "C'mon man, we can make money with this." I didn't at that time say "Fuck off" or "Get the fuck outta here," but that's how I came off.

I had no idea who this guy was. I thought he was just some poor guy in the neighborhood just messing with me. Then the word got back to me from someone from Boston Road, "Yo, Flash do you have any idea of who you talkin' to like that?"

I'm like, "No." Really didn't care. They told me he was Ray

Chandler, one of the Chandler Brothers. Still, meant nothing to me. "So. Who's that? Who is he?" The answer made it simple for me: He controls everything in this area." Everything that happens in the streets. *Everything.*

Now I'm shitting bricks because I shut this muthafucka down religiously a few times. Six, seven, maybe ten times. So the next time he approached me I looked at him with fear but at the same time with much respect. I said, "You can probably pull this off." In a calm voice Raymond Chandler, a former police officer mind you, said to me, "You need to give me a chance to do this. I'll find a place, and we'll charge at the door."

That door was black. The place was on Boston Road. Literally right up the street from 63 Park next to where the jazz spot Goodson's once was. We called it, what else, "The Black Door." He said he'd make these paper things called flyers to promote the parties. I'm looking at him and am like, to myself of course, "Who's going to pay for all of this?" After successfully bringing people into the park whenever I wanted to for free, for no money, who's gonna now all of a sudden pay for the same thing?

This was a Business 101 lesson, supply and demand. Ray Chandler knew what he was doing. Marketing-wise, business-wise. The Black Door from the minute it opened stayed jam packed. And with that newfound popularity of now being inside came a new order of necessary protection. EZ Mike while still running the streets, doing street shit, being a fly guy, he was still very protective of me. If anyone got out of pocket and he was there, he made sure nothing would ever happen to me. Best friend shit. The money that we had the chance to make at the Black Door meant nothing to Mike because he had his own money from the streets coming in. But as more people came and as our street cred grew, the more real security became needed.

All the other crews giving parties during this period, whether it was Bam or Breakout or Herc, they all had protection, I didn't have any. I *had to* have protection. Even though we moved things inside from the parks, wildin' was still going on in the Bronx. Ray Chandler would hire guys off "The Infamous Nine" from the Boston Road Crew, Lance, Joe Kidd, etc. to make sure no one brought guns in, that no one brought knives in, anything besides fists and feet that could hurt people. Now the people Ray hired to make sure no one came in with guns, them muthafuckas themselves always came in with guns. And I'd have to ask them, "Hey Joe, hey Lance, please go back there and take your guns and put them behind the crate of records. I don't want you all walking around the parties with a pistol on your sides." I would beg them to do this.

The crowds became too large at the Black Door so Ray Chandler moved our parties to a place called the Dixie Club on Freeman Street. The Dixie became our home. Eventually the Dixie couldn't hold the amount of people we were bringing in so we moved to Broadway International on 146th and Broadway in Harlem. It was much bigger than the Dixie, but we always went back to the Dixie. And as our rep got bigger as we moved to different areas in the Bronx, so did the need for protection. So there were people who were a part of the Black Spades, which later became the Casanovas, who became our security. The two things the Boston Road Crew and the Casanovas did when it came to being our protection crews: They didn't allow anyone attending any of the Flash parties to get hurt and, equally as important, if anyone was caught with any type of recording device it went straight into the bathroom of the clubs. Ass beat until you blacked out. Calling for your mother. The crew leaders, including Tiny of the Casanovas, made sure no tapes or recordings of our shows leaked out in the streets from behind our doors. Tiny and I had history.

Tiny's godmother, a lady by the name of Marion Rose, who was the first Black district leader of the South Bronx—and was very instrumental in connecting me with Pete DJ Jones and getting me permits to do block parties in the Mitchel Houses/ Patterson Projects—always kept Tiny involved in politics even though he was in gangs. He'd just come home from doing a one-and-a-half- to three-year bid in jail when Ms. Rose rolled up on her godson and said, "I need you to do me a favor." That favor? "I need you to put this boy under your wings and make sure nothing happens to him. His name is Grandmaster Flash." (The "Grandmaster" name given to me by Joe Kidd while I was breaking the equipment down on New Year's Day the night of my birthday at the Black Door and he claimed, "Damn Flash you played those turntables like a Grandmaster.") Tiny's response to his godmother, "And?"

Ms. Rose knew in the South Bronx once DJs brought their equipment out brothas were just running up and snatchin'. In the park, while you were spinning, snatch, grab, gone. All of your shit. It was like a wind came by, swept everything up and stole everything. You almost didn't notice it when it happened, that's how fast they were. She was looking out for me. So Tiny heeded his godmother's request, well, demand. We bonded. Both teenagers at the time. And that started our journey together and my reputation as Tiny would always say, "the most hated DJ in the Bronx, not because he wasn't good but because he couldn't be touched. The most well-protected DJ of his era."

To the point that I played almost every high school and damn-near every park in the Bronx without getting got. Between the Black Spades and Casanovas, they ran those neighborhoods. Nothing happened without either one of those factions being involved. And I had Tiny behind me. Ray put Tiny in charge. And it wasn't just me, the girls who came to our parties never feared coming and felt well-protected too because nothing would jump off. For as long as I played, they never had to close down one of our parties. That, along with other things that he was doing, gave Ray Chandler a name for having the biggest party platform in the Bronx. He was becoming the biggest promoter. No one could touch him. For parties where he'd charge five dollars to get in, he'd clear five thousand dollars.

The killers of the killers who would come to the parties would be told by Tiny, "Put your guns over here." They'd always give them their guns back out of respect because they were very aware of who these dudes were, but Tiny wouldn't allow anyone to come in strapped. I had one of the most powerful crews in the Bronx on my side. The other crews were powerful—Zulus, Gestapos—and would go against one another, but they'd all come to my parties and even hang out with the Casanovas.

Ray Chandler, he instinctively saw what was being done at the disco clubs with the disco DJs all over New York, especially with Blacks and Latinos, and believed in the energy generated by what we were creating, and asked himself why couldn't the same thing exist? I think he saw me as a catalyst who could make that same kind of thing happen. I was very much a scientist, and every scientist needs a businessperson to help bring their inventions to the masses. Edison had Grosvenor Lowery and Menlo Park, I had Ray Chandler and the Black Door.

Part III
The Explosion (Level 2: 1976–1979)

1 **“Johnny the Fox”**
Thin Lizzy (1976)

2 **“Seven Minutes of Funk”**
The Whole Darn Family (1976)

3 **“Frisco Disco”**
Eastside Connection (1979)

4 **“Sing Sing”**
Gaz (1978)

5 **“I Like Funky Music”**
Uncle Louie (1979)

6 **“Groove to Get Down”**
T-Connection (1977)

7 **“Was Dog a Doughnut?”**
Cat Stevens (1977)

8 **“Let’s Start the Dance”**
Bohannon (1978)

9 **“Dance to the Drummer’s Beat”**
Herman Kelly and Life (1978)

10 **“Good Times”**
Chic (1979)

11 **“Rapper’s Delight”**
The Sugarhill Gang (1979)

12 **“Daisy Lady”**
7th Wonder (1979)

13 **“Bustin’ Loose”**
Chuck Brown and the Soul Searchers (1979)

CHAPTER 6

Club 371 to many people was their coming-of-age spot. The Fever, Ipanema, Nell's, the Roxy, none of them was like it. For me, 371 was the place where I had to put on hard bottoms (dress shoes) and a blazer and a white button-up shirt and take my hat off. It pissed me the fuck off. But that's where I wanted to see what the hard-bottom crowd was doing because we were just *come as you are* in the parks. To see what was happening at 371, I was like, "Okay, this is different." I remember meeting DJ Reggie Wells there. And I asked him, "Reggie, do you think I could get on the turntables for a little while because I want to just play this style of DJing?" He said, "I heard about what you are doing (in the Bronx)." He let me get on for fifteen minutes of his set. I wanted to see if what I was doing could work with a hard-bottom crowd. It ended up working extremely well. And at that point I started looking for jobs at different clubs.

There was a distinct difference between clubs that myself, Breakout, and Herc were playing than the hard-bottom/disco-type places that were popular in the Bronx and in Harlem. We couldn't get into a lot of the clubs with sneakers on or because of the way we were dressed. Which further made us keep doing our own thing. But DJ Hollywood, in my opinion, did have an impact on the game. His influence came from not just the records he was playing but also the way he was playing them and what he was saying on the mic while he was playing; which was considered a form of rapping, but it was Hollywood's concept of doing one-hour sets instead of the seven-hour sets—which we learned and conditioned ourselves to do while spinning and throwing all-day parties in the parks—that changed the ways we were playing. He gave an "Oh, I see how this is done" moment. We could do an hour, hour-and-a-half set, be done, get off the stage, go out the back door, jump in the Cadillac with the engine already running, and be off to the next set to DJ somewhere else to make some more money.

While we would be setting up our systems, bringing in our systems to gymnasiums at like 6 p.m. to spin until 3 or 4 a.m., Hollywood would have three-to-four flyers out in the streets for sets he would play all in the same night! We'd be, "How the fuck is he playing in Harlem, in the Bronx, then going to Brooklyn, *then* going out to Queens all in one night?" I did some research on how he was doing this, and then I watched him. He had a driver, driving that Cadillac, and all Hollywood had to do was jump out of the car with his records and all the places he would go had turntables already set up. Once I saw that, I told Ray Chandler.

The problem with Hollywood was he played in the Bronx, but he lived, I believe, in Harlem. And when disco was poppin' off crazy he was the muthafuckin' man!

I've heard Hollywood feels like he's a part of hip-hop, and I've been told he's disappointed that he's not included with the pioneers the way that some of us are. Yet, I still have the highest respect for Hollywood and what he did. We have, I think, the highest respect for each other. He doesn't have a problem with me, but I heard he's upset about not being considered one of the main faces of this culture.

I read somewhere, I can't recall exactly where, but someone wrote that Herc was "the man who wrote the genetic code for what we call hip-hop today." Personally, I believe from the DJ standpoint there are three architects of this culture. There's Herc, Bam, and myself, with Breakout maybe being the fourth since he came later. We did the *sacrificing*. I totally disagree with anyone who has the power to promote and tell this story to say that one person created this. There was no one, singular mind or event that did this. This shit never would have worked had I not done the technical things I did to and with the turntable. This shit would not have worked if it weren't for Bam taking gang violence and gang members and turning them into Zulu Nation members and musicians and artists and bringing the community together though music. This thing probably doesn't happen if Herc doesn't do what he did, followed by Breakout. These are the pillars as I see it. I think it's somewhat of an injustice for it to be in the history books claiming that one person—or anyone besides us four—put this together and made this multibillion-dollar empire happen. If any one of those four DJ elements, in my opinion, had not been in this from the inception, meaning Bam, Breakout, Herc, and myself, hip-hop would not have had the legs nor the foundational strength to transcend fifty-plus years as a culture.

* * *

By now, the rapper, or MC, is becoming prominent. No longer just guys and girls saying a few words and shouting out names on the mic during DJ sets, jams, and parties, but rhythmically putting full rhymes and poems together, telling short stories. Which is why it always confused me—the, I'll call it, misinformation of Coke La Rock being credited as the first or original rapper. He wasn't! At least not in the sense of what a rapper actually is and/or does. And Clark Kent backed me up on this when I spoke with him about it. His exact words to me were, "I think like everybody else people pick up these narratives and they run with it. They act like we all forgot what really happened. I don't know when they ran with that, but we know Coke did talk on the mic, he would give us our nicknames and things like that, but he wasn't an MC. I wouldn't classify him as an MC. Because I did the same thing Coke did on the mic. And I am *not* an MC. So I too am confused. But if Coke was here or on this Zoom call right now, he couldn't tell *me* that he's the first MC of hip-hop. I would challenge him on that. Because I was *there*." That's all I needed to hear.

The first rapper attached to what I was doing was Cowboy. He was with me when Ray opened the Black Door. I needed someone to "vocalize inside the spaces of my groove." I remember asking him, "Keith, can you be my talker?" So the two of us kind of intersected. He allowed me to go into my bag, to give the Quik Mix Theory another dimension. When he would talk on the mic and ask people to do things in the crowd it would set me up perfectly because prior to him whenever I DJed people would annoyingly do things like look under the DJ table or they would try to get up on the stage to look at my hands just to see if I was doing magic tricks. Cowboy eliminated all of that.

This allowed the situation to be less of a classroom and more like what it was meant to be, a jam where I rocked the crowd. Cowboy's signature thing was he could get a crowd motivated with his hands, movements, and the whole thing. "Say what!

Say wee-ohh! Throw your hands up!" He had a way of taking the attention off me and getting the crowd rocking. Which I loved him for. Plus, he had that voice. That nice, deep, P.T. Barnum and James Bailey's ringmaster voice.

Once Cowboy knew how to speak in line with this new style of DJing I was doing, it was that gentleman Nathaniel Glover, the one who ended up with the name Kidd Creole, let's just say he "tried out." If you wanted him to say a rhyme on one day and ask him to say another rhyme on another day, he would not use the same word twice. That's how deep his vocabulary was. And he was very long-winded. They were my MCs for a period of time. Then Creole said, "I gotta little brother who is a really good breakdancer and he knows how to rhyme too. Can I bring him to you?" "Sure," I said. The kid passed with flying colors. He understood; he got it. His name: Melle Mel. After a while Mel came up to me, same thing: "Flash, I have a best friend, he's not so much a prophetic writer, but I think he could work really well in the group. He asked could he be invited to join?" He ended up not being a great rapper, but he had great stage presence. The best friend was Eddie Morris. He went by the name Mr. Ness. He ended up with the name Scorpio.

We used to battle against Breakout and his group the Funky 4 MCs. Their lead MC was incredible. His name was Rahiem. But their secret weapon was this female rapper named MC SHA-ROCK. Once their group broke up there was a meeting held with my MCs. They came to me and said of Rahiem, "Flash, we need to get him." They didn't want him to go to another crew or anyplace else because whenever we battled, he was always able to hang with them verse for verse. So it went in like a two-to-three-year period from Grandmaster Flash and the 3 MCs in and around 1974 to Grandmaster Flash and the

Furious Four in 1975 to finalizing as Grandmaster Flash and the Furious Five sometime around 1976 once we finally added Rahiem.

Lovebug Starski wanted to be a part of our crew because he lived in the Forest Houses where I used to play the block parties on Tinton Avenue and 163rd. But I could never fit him in and that's when I introduced him to Pete DJ Jones, and he became the direct influence on Pete's hip-hop style of DJing. And this was before Starski became one of the in-house DJs for Sal Abbatiello's famous Disco Fever. Someone brought Sal to one of my parties at another club, and afterward he asked his father, who owned the Disco Fever (Sal ran the club), if he could do these types of shows one night a week? It was at the Disco Fever where I did the first ever hip-hop DJ set that became their Tuesday night showcase. I called it "Terrible Tuesday." In two, three months time it blew up, rivaling his Saturday disco nights. After the success, Sal started inquiring about rappers because he wanted to bring more hip-hop to the club. From that point on, the disco nights went out the window. Not too long after that the Disco Fever went from doing Terrible Tuesday nights to doing rap shows and playing rap music *every night*. It was like us having our own version of Studio 54 on 167th and Jerome Avenue.

I guess without realizing it, pairing Cowboy and Creole together—two different styles, with Creole being able to rhyme from now and twenty-four hours from now, never saying the same rhyme twice, who also had a magic way of taking my inventions with the echo chamber and knowing how to flip the switch at the exact time in his rhymes—was magical. And to me it was what made me know that I had the best MC crew. Their styles were not just different than everybody else's, but individually their styles were totally different from one another. From that point, we didn't want to acquire any other pieces to the group. It was me, Disco Bee, EZ Mike, and the Furious Five.

But building voices around what I was doing was essential to everything at this point. And one day at a party we were doing at Club 125 in Harlem, I saw a gentleman come in. He was so noticeable that I said to myself, "Who's that?" He was respectful, looked around sixty years old, he went to the bar, had a drink—I watched him all night. I was like, "either he's the police or he's looking for somebody or he's somebody's parent." To the point that I said something to Tiny: "Keep an eye on him. If he does one thing wrong, you know what you gotta do." *The guy won't do anything wrong.*

Then as we were taking the sound system down, he approached me, saying, "Hello, Mr. Flash . . ."

I cut him off. The club was empty, everyone was gone, and he'd been there the whole time. "Who are you, and who are you looking for?" is what I asked him. The party's over, no one's there, so did I do something? I'm thinking he's po-po.

He says, "My name is Bobby Robinson, and I own a record label not far from here in Harlem. I was just wondering would you and your group be interested being on my label to make a record doing exactly the same thing you all did tonight?"

Now I wasn't sure what the fuck he was talking about, but I kept in touch with him. I wasn't going to make the same mistake that I initially made with Ray Chandler. I knew there was something about what I was doing, but I also knew there was something about what the rappers were doing that was serious.

If you ever needed a history lesson on rap and rapping, Bam, even then, would give you one: "People have to look at the history of our people as a nation within a nation or as a people within a world community. And they have to look at the fact: We got soul. We are a soul-power people. There are others that came before us who were rapping, who were using rhymes. Before Grandmaster Flash, before Kool Herc, before Afrika Bambaataa and the other pioneers put that name and label on it as 'hip-hop' we had Mother Goose rhymes, we had Rudy Ray Moore with his nasty types of rapping, we had Moms Mabley, we had Pigmeat Markham, who really gave us that beat and break-beat and put the rapping on it, we had the poetry of the Watts Prophets and the Last Poets, Sonia Sanchez, Nikki Giovanni who was doing all of that with Gary Byrd and others. So our people always had it in us. And the Europeans had it too because when they were selling our black asses in auctions they would speak in their version of a fast rhythmic pattern to get others interested and to buy."

And although it was only one element, it was a major one, and it was slowly becoming the most important one.

* * *

MC SHA-ROCK is kind of a mystery. As the one many people consider to be the first b-girl of the culture, how she entered the game and when has always been an all-over-the-place discussion. One she never had a problem straightening out.

"I was born in Wilmington, North Carolina, and I was introduced to music by going back home, back down South, every year as a kid when my mom would send my sister and brothers and me down there." Growing up in New York she knew the music was different than what she'd heard down South. The music played in New York had a different feel, blaxploitation soundtracks and songs were everywhere, *Cleopatra Jones* movie-type sounds. So going back to North Carolina for her was like a breath of fresh air. Her mom and stepdad gave her a varied foundation when it came to music: the Stax label sounds, the Isaac Hayes, the James Brown, the Beatles, the Jackson 5, Nikki Giovanni, Tom Jones, Betty Wright, Elvis Presley. Her mom was a music connoisseur. She was given the best of two worlds of music with the time she spent between the South and the North.

A young Sharon Greene—Sharon = SHA-ROCK, get it?—was still a product of the Bronx through and through. She represented when she started as a b-girl in 1976, when she started on the mic in late 1977, and when the Funky 4 made her the plus-one in the group in 1978. Which not only made her a pioneer (she'd probably call herself more of a "revolutionary" than a "pioneer") but made DJ Breakout and them geniuses for adding her voice to their sound and crew.

For me, MC SHA-ROCK was eliminated from too many conversations. Her name never came up enough. People claiming that they came before her or that they were better than her, this and that. She believes that happened (and believes to some degree it happened to me as well) because we "figured everyone just knew the deal" with what we were doing at the time and there was no reason to promote or defend our contributions. The information was out there, whether it was word of mouth or flyers or parties or performances she didn't feel like she—or I—had to solidify who we were.

"When they talk about me being the first female MC, the first thing they look at is me being a part of the Funky 4 +1. They think about the music era in 1979, when we all made records. But unless they were out there, they don't know the hustle and the work I was putting in or the things I was doing before then," she told me when we got into this discussion about her place in the culture. "But when you have different people spreading the untrue gospel, you have to go back and solidify exactly who you are and what it is you did. So when other females talk about, 'I was there with SHA-ROCK doing this and that.' *No they were not there!* I was the only one there. I can name a hundred things that SHA-ROCK did before any other woman. For every ten things someone says that I didn't do, I can show them ten things that *they* didn't do and another ten things that *I did do*! I'm coming with proof. They learned from me!" As the saying goes: She gave birth to most of them MCs.

Starting out as a member of the Sisters Disco crew, MC SHA-ROCK's Mom, also a "radical who was into the whole Black Power movement," wrote SHA's first rhymes for her. She came through the game hardly ever battling against other female rappers, "I had to contend with not only the Funky 4 but all of the other MCs out at that time, the Melle Mels, the Cowboys, the Scorpios, the Creoles. There were no other females out there doing that; there were no other females on my level" is how she puts it. At a birthday party for Bam and Herc (their birthdays are one day apart) in 1979, she was the only female MC on the flyer. She wound up through it all being on more than five hundred flyers.

She learned how to MC and how to become a bonafide MC from the Quik Mix Theory. The continuous beat, the continuous breakbeats that were the foundation of the Quik Mix Theory, allowed the MC to rhyme for longer than eight or sixteen bars. For MC SHA-ROCK it was how she learned and developed breath control, so that she could do her thirty-two, sixty-four, ninety-six bars which she became known for. Rhyming back-to-back for ten to fifteen minutes. Things some of the male MCs couldn't do. She did things that a lot of other MCs stole from her too.

She would often find her flow through a song by Edwin Starr called "I Just Wanna Do My Thing." I would play it. MC SHA-ROCK's DJ Baron, who was Rahiem's DJ before he became part of the Furious Five, knew she loved to rhyme to that particular song. Now, to me, "I Just Wanna Do My Thing" has always been what I call "a man's" beat. It's monstrous. Some rappers—and I'm talking male rappers, who I won't name—were scared to fuck with that beat! It was just so killer. And MC SHA-ROCK, in her own words, would say, "I used to ride that muthafucka!"

Baron would use the Quik Mix Theory on that song for MC SHA-ROCK because in the break of the song there wasn't a lot of noise so the MC wasn't fighting against too many instruments and sounds to be heard. You could hear very clearly using that break what the person on the mic was saying. As MC SHA-ROCK says, "My DJs began to start playing that song because of Flash, because if you were *that* MC you wanted every fuckin' body in the party to hear what you had to say—*clearly.* And the continuous way Baron played that song, after Flash introduced how to play it, was the catalyst for every MC out there who wanted people to hear what the fuck it was they had to say. It let the MC shine."

This was exactly why I'd tell people that I come from and helped create an era where I had to support the rapper, the MC, the breaker. The beat had to be steady with minimal scratching or interrupting because it was critical to the rappers flow and what he or she was saying, and it was important to the dancer's moves and what he or she was doing.

* * *

Downstairs Records was in the subway station on West 43rd Street—the godfather of all record shops. Nick, Barry, and Elroy ran it. If you knew one of them or all of them and were in good with them, they'd allow you access to the backroom where the rare records were. The ones all of us DJs were searching to find. For me, the more obscure and unheard before the break the better. We'd spend hours in Downstairs. It was probably considered the first real element of crate digging. We made record searching, buying, and collecting an art form. Because there is an art to it. Some were actual masters of it. Smokey and I would be in Downstairs all of the time. Disco Bee and I would be there all of the time. Bam was a legend there, even though he was getting his records from many other sources. And the key was to never let another DJ, if they weren't in your crew, see or know what records you had. Your crates and what you had in them were sacred.

Which eventually led to another cultural phenomenon of the time: the mixtape.

One of the reasons the Casanovas and Tiny were so dead set on not allowing anyone to record our parties was because of the value they knew our parties had on the streets. "Grandmaster Flash tapes were worth a hundred dollars," he'd always say. In 1975, 1976, a hundred dollars was good money. That was the rate. Now as our parties didn't allow anyone recording any of our sets, and the beatdowns if security found out you did or were trying to were serious, tapes were made for certain people. We did them at home, at least I did, mostly. It was like a separate income. For me, I would use the tapes to barter. Example: our limousine services, our OJ car services, our Godfather car services, if you came to one of our parties using one of those, you had arrived. You were the shit! If you rolled up in either a Cadillac or an Impala or a Lincoln, you were the bomb. I'd make tapes for drivers because for them, if they had Flash tapes and people could hear them during their rides, they'd call on those drivers more. And they would ride longer just to hear more of the tape. For me, my primary driver for the car services was Joe, same name as mine, I called him 1-double-0. I'd have the car service request 1-double-0 saying, "Flash is looking for you." That was the code for him to pick me up. Now I would tell Joe, "I'm going to give you this one-and-one-copy-only of this 'Flash tape,' and you'll be the only one with it but you're not going to charge me anything for the pick and ride. I want to go on hold."

Going "on hold" meant being in the car for a couple of hours, and for that time he was my personal driver. So I'd go to the west side of the Bronx or I'd go to the east side of the Bronx or I'd go to Bronx River, wherever I wanted to go in this car. Sometimes it would be with my crew, sometimes I would be with my girlfriend, sometimes it was just me. And I'd get them to do it for tapes. This is where the actual thing that was called the "mixtape" was born. After a while people were calling me saying, "We want a tape without rapping on it. We want a tape with just you doing the Theory." And the people who were asking me for this were straight-up, stone-cold gangsters; they had feared reputations. They had amazing cars, dope-ass sound systems, lots of money. They would come to me, and I'd say to them, "Give me two songs you love and give me a couple of days. Just tell me how long you want the tape to be." It was mostly ninety minutes. But then they'd say, "But you gotta say my name every few minutes through the tape." I'd say, "Okay, this is how this is going to go. I'ma put this tape together, but it's gonna cost you a dollar a minute." So 90-minute tape, $90.00. 120-minute tape, $120.00. No problem. And some of them wanted them for their cribs, not just the rides. They wanted them for their reel-to-reels at home. Those were 120 minutes each side. So $240 to $250 a tape. Again, for them, no problem. It was the beginning of the mixtape business and what caused the Theory to begin to really spread around the Bronx and Harlem.

But the tapes of us in the parks became a thing of legend. They were being passed all around New York. Someone recorded on cassette everything we did the night, the only night, we went to Bronx River and played the same set with Bam. And even though we weren't making any money from those tapes, they were helping us become famous. And those tapes years later would have an impact that I never could have dreamed of.

What we were building—even if we didn't know it—was a whole muthafucking forest. Not just the DJing. Other elements of this new culture existed—graffiti, breakdancing, rapping, the style, the energy, the people—what I was able to do was give the culture a soundtrack and its own sound.

"The Box." The JVC R500. If you had a boom box like this . . . you were official! This was the One! This boom box, if you had one, all of the chicks wanted to be around you and you could start your own street party on the corner with this box right here.

CHAPTER 7

Two things happened within the span of a year that changed everything for me and so many others who were a part of this journey we were on in New York.

One day Ray picked me up and told me he wanted to show me something. Show me a room. He said, verbatim, "Flash, you done played all types of rooms, we've played every club, every school has called us to do their graduation party, and we've knocked it out, we did the Ritz, we've done all of it. I wanna take you to a place I want you to play. Something we haven't done." He's doing this while he's driving us to the place. At the time, we were a little corporation without us knowing that we were a corporation, and with my arrogance, being cocky I was like, "Yeah, let's do it!" without even thinking about the place he was talking about. He's prepping me.

After a while, on 165th Street, he parks the car and says, "We're here." And I say, "We're where?" He says, "At the place." Now, I'm not paying attention to the building we're walking along the side of as much as I'm concerning myself with what I know. And that's *usually* on a block—blocks I'm used to seeing and blocks I'm used to doing parties on or clubs I'm used to playing—you'd have apartment buildings, grocery stores, liquor stores, etc. But the one building we're walking along the side of is just one long building, and I'm asking Ray, "Where is it?" We got to the corner, we make a left, we go into this entrance, and I see four flights of stairs. And at the top there was this little guy, looked like one of the Mario Bros. before they came out. He was the superintendent of this place. Just like Truman's father was in the place where we had our clubhouse on Faile Street. So we walked up the stairs.

At the top I saw the fire-capacity size of the building on a notice on the wall. It read, "3,000." Right then, I turned around, looked at Ray Chandler, and said, "No!" He immediately grabbed me and said, "We could." Our average max at the Dixie or any party was seven hundred to a thousand people. Average. A thousand people at the Audubon Ballroom, where we were standing, was a failure. Too much space. Ray said, "Just give me a couple of months." He said, "We can pull this off." Again, we?

I had never been so nervous in my fucking life. But Ray said, "I'm going to promote this harder than I've done anything in my life." Which didn't mean much to me in the moment, but he said, "Flash just gimme the 'go' sign." To which I literally said to him, "I don't think so." But he kept persisting, kept pressing me. And then he said, again, "Just give me two months."

Ray Chandler, throughout that whole summer, because the party was on September 2nd, kept promoting and promoting it in the streets. And all I kept thinking about was with all the success that me and this man have had, this was going to be our first failure. That this place right here was going to be our end.

So the day comes up. September 2, 1976. We're bringing in the sound system, we called it the Gladiator. Halfway through the sound check there's a loud *pop*! Sounds like a gunshot. It was the main transformer of the amplifier. This is the amplifier that is connected to the base bottom of the Gladiator. It blows. Doors open in five hours. Now we have this homemade vacuum-tube amplifier that these Jamaicans made for us, and we had to pick this thing up and somehow get it back to them—*and beg them*—to fix it. The Audubon is in Washington Heights, the Jamaican where we got the Gladiator was on Gun Hill Road in the Bronx. When we got there, the guy stopped everything he was doing and fixed it for us.

We hauled ass back to the Audubon. At around 5:30 or 6 p.m., once the amp situation was straight, I left. I got in a taxi and went home. Went home with the weight on me that with all the success that I'd been having, this one was going to be my fail. That we—with my name up-front—might not be able to pull this one off.

Little did I know Ray Chandler had called the girls, the crew. Told them to meet him at the Audubon Ballroom. He said to all of them, "Listen, your boy is moving up, you see these flyers? I need you all to get out there and get all these damn flyers out there about this party tonight." Ray put them to work. They did, skipping school and everything. Some of them even went back to school, gave out flyers, and left, never going to class.

Terri: "You packed that place so deep. You were nervous. You didn't think the room would be filled. And we went out to look. Virginia. Georgia. North Carolina. License plates. Cars from all over the place. They came to the Audubon that night. There were even people scaling the walls coming through the windows to get in. I don't know if there was a balcony or anything but they were coming through the windows! It was amazing. People were coming from all over the States to this one party. It was a huge sea of people, and all they wanted to do was dance to your—not anyone else's—music. And you said to me before that party, 'I don't think anyone is going to come.' And I told you, 'Naw Flash, they're gonna come.'"

Terri would tell me later that she (they all) felt weird. They felt guilty about coming there for a party knowing what happened to Malcolm X and that being the place where he was killed. Then they heard that "*boom, boom, boom*" from the system, that sound, she said, "God, forgive me."

I left home to come back at around 7 p.m. The taxi had to drop me off on 164th Street because of the traffic, so I had to walk a block. And while I was walking all I saw were license plates from DC, Florida, Louisiana. And all I was thinking was, *Somebody must be doing something around here*. And when I got to 165th, to the building, the line to get in was wrapped around the corner. People saw me, they started screaming. Oh. My. God. I say, "So, this is goin' down." Tiny grabs me, pulls me into the Audubon; I go upstairs.

About 9 p.m. there were maybe fifteen hundred people in there—it still looked empty. About an hour, hour and a half later, even after seeing that line and all those cars from outta state, I don't know where these people came from, but the room was packed. Kool DJ AJ was our warm-up act. By the time me and the MCs got on the floor, it was shaking. And we didn't help matters because at the height of our show—when I was playing "Mardi Gras," "Apache," and the records are flying back and forth, and the beatbox is on point I can see the tonearm vibrating because the floor is literally shaking! It's shaking to the point that, even as Cowboy and the rappers are still doing their routines, all any of us on the stage were thinking was: *We're going to die. This building is going to collapse.* But it didn't.

That three-thousand capacity was closer to, if not over, four thousand. The fire marshal came and had to shut the party down due to the size and overflow of the crowd. It was that night at the Audubon where me, Bee, and EZ Mike really perfected the Merry-Go-Round and maybe intro'd it to the world. We'd done the Merry-Go-Round at smaller clubs and parties—like at the Savoy—but at this party, at the Audubon, this made us kings of hip-hop at that point. It was the biggest room at the time. It was *the* event. It was at the Audubon where I really put the QMT (Quik Mix Theory) to a test. As I'd said before: "A new way to cut without cueing." I just watched the intersector as it went forward and counterclockwise. It was at the Audubon that we became the most successful in the streets of New York. The night was record-breaking for us to pull off a space that size.

For the rappers it gave them more freedom and cachet to get more girls, get more booty. For me, I was under protective custody for the rest of my career. I could no longer go to another area unprotected. From that night on, I never went anywhere without Mike or one of the Casanovas or someone from the Boston Road Crew as protection. I was well protected, well loved, but dammit I couldn't run around the way I wanted to. I hardly did anything by myself anymore. I could no longer go to a block party or anything by myself. I went from the apartment into a car either with people or a girlfriend, to the movies or to a club where I was playing, then back. That was it. I became famous. That night my life closed in. But the style, what I was doing on the turntables, after that night, that's when it exploded.

* * *

Then there was the blackout. The only time I can remember being able to be by myself after the Audubon was almost a year later when the blackout hit New York on July 13 and 14 in 1977. I was nineteen years old at the time, sitting by myself in the crib when the lights went straight out. It was too dark to stay in the house, so I sat on the stoop. Even at night there's usually light from the stars, so I'm thinking, *Okay, maybe a transformer went out somewhere in the Bronx. It won't be that long.* That shit lasted two days.

When it happened, and the whole city went dark, I saw people walking with mattresses on their heads, carrying dressers, stereos. This was when the thieves came out, both my fans and my friends, hustlers, who were also good friends of mine. People came by wanting to sell things, knocking on my door, bringing me equipment that I could not afford. At the time all I had was the Plush amp I'd had forever. Them telling me, "Flash, you can use this." Them asking me, "Flash, do you need this?" I'd look down to see what they had. One time it was the Bozak mixer, which was the most expensive and best disco mixer in the world. I said, "I'll take it, but I don't, I mean, can't use it because it won't work with the system I have." Then one person brought me an amplifier, another brought me a speaker. They'd stole them from a club called the Hunts Point Palace on Southern Boulevard. The Bozak was a knob mixer. I didn't even know how to use it, but I took it and learned. And that speaker with that amp with that Bozak gave my sound system a whole new twist.

The blackout was wild and impacted the city for decades. MC Serch likes to call the blackout "The plight that gave us the light that gave us the mic." It was because of the blackout where the direct and indirect weight of it on the culture would emerge. In people, places, and ways no one would ever expect.

* * *

There was a kid from Texas who visited New York all the time because it was where his grandfather lived. His grandfather, Grandfather Bill, was a jazz musician. Every year their annual family trip drove from Prairie View, Texas, to South Carolina, stay a few days, then North Carolina, stay a couple of days, drive to Baltimore, stay a couple of days, and the finale of their summer trips would be New York to visit Grandfather Bill. And every year Grandfather Bill would take his grandson to Yankee games and afterward to Playland in Times Square, where the kid would beat everyone in the place at pinball. The kid's introduction to real New York was once he stepped out of Playland to see the breakdancers with boom boxes doing their thing.

The kid, all of eleven years old, happened to be in New York during the blackout. And what he witnessed he wouldn't forget, saying, "I was around and seeing the most craziest stuff in New York during the blackout. We were driving to Yankee Stadium and people are stealing the front tires off of bicycles that were already chained up. As a kid I'm like, 'They're stealing in broad daylight. I wanna live here!'"

Not long after that, in Long Island in August of 1978, a student enrolled in Adelphi University. Set to change everything. He was one of hip-hop's first babies and someone who would carry the torch. He started in radio. Resembling the vocal tone of Hank Spann of WWRL and the rhyme style of K.C. the Prince of Soul, from the early '70s, both looked at as originators in the history of this thing we were starting to call hip-hop.

Somewhere in-between the group War released an album titled *Galaxy*. The first song from that album shared the same name. To the kid at Adelphi, the song was like an alien. To the kid from Texas, it was 1972's "It's Just Begun" by the Jimmy

Castor Bunch that had a similar effect. Both in "space-age" ways. To the kid from Texas, seeing the b-boys and the boom boxes doing their thing off that song made the kid curious as to "What made them choose this record?" Doing things that hadn't reached down South yet. He saw it all in real time, in the streets, when he came to New York. It became a gravitational pull.

He vowed to become a part of it. He'd go back to Texas and tell his friends what he saw. "Man, they take two records and repeat the beat on top of one another." And his friends would ask: "Why would they buy two of the same records?" It was equivalent to telling them he'd seen a UFO. "Flash," he'd tell me, "you were a UFO."

At a party, the kid from Adelphi heard "Galaxy" for the first time not on the radio. As the DJ played the song, bass line loud, amplified, rolling, young fella waited for the words to come in. They didn't. He looks at the DJ because there's a light on the DJ and he's moving side to side. "Now I'm asking myself," he recalls, "*Why aren't the words coming in on this song?* And then I'm looking at the DJ and saying to myself, *Why is he going over here? To his left, then to his right?* Then the words finally came in, *minutes* later." Mesmerized. The DJ had extended the intro of the song, something unknown to the young man. He stood there at that party and watched as people did the hustle to the mix. He wanted to dance because he'd never heard anything like this before, but he didn't know how to do the hustle. So he just stared at the DJ, trying to figure it all out. "I'ma tell you how countryfied I was," he said, even though he was from Long Island, opening his arms out wide, "I thought, *Damn, size of that record most be* this *big.*"

About a year later there was a show. A DJ performing with an MC. "It was the first MC I'd ever heard who was clear. There were other MCs, but they all sounded like kids to me. Until I heard Grandmaster Flash and Melle Mel at this spot." Until that moment, what he'd conceived after watching the DJ did what he did to "Galaxy" this was all a math and science thing. Then he heard Mel. In the corner of the stage, spotlight on him, darkness all around. "*One-two, one-two. From the top of the world to the depths of hell/I rock so well/I am Melle Mell/And on turntable Number One and turntable Number Two . . .*" And then I came in with "Mardi Gras."

The atmospheric composition of the room changed. "Shit," he said in that moment. "Now this thing is not just a science or electrical science anymore. This thing is theater."

Chapter 8

I'd heard about the stabbing but had no idea how bad it was.

I asked Clark Kent about the place where it seemed the culture was without really considering the circumstances surrounding the full scope of my question. Because then, with everything going on with me, the group, everything that Bam had going on, everything with Breakout and Baron and their people, it was just beginning to feel like a change was happening.

Me to Clark: "When you saw the change, when things started to change, there were some things that Herc could have done to change his career too, but I've heard he didn't want to. When you saw the change I'm sure you were the first one to say, 'Herc, we need to make some changes.' And I'm sure he didn't want to listen to you. What did you do when he didn't want to listen? Did you say it was over? Because, this was like your child. You helped birth this thing. And when it was changing, I saw the baby dying."

His response set a whole different understanding of the history of how this culture unfolded.

"Let me give it to you exactly how I lived it. Herc was the

pied piper of hip-hop; there's no question about that. Anyone, anybody who tries to say different, we know better than that. But then Herc got stabbed at the Executive Playhouse. Damn near fatally stabbed."

Now I'd heard that Herc had only been stabbed in the hand. Not true.

"He got helluva lot more than just stabbed in the hand," Clark told me. "I was on the turntables, playing the music when it happened. That dude stabbed Herc about eight times."

He continued. "You know how the Exec [Club] was, there was a narrow hallway and you had a curtain but once you come past that curtain you had full view to the stage. It was a straight line. Herc and I were on the stage and someone came to Herc and said to him, 'Yo, something is going on at the door.' Something had transpired; there was some sort of beef. Now Coke [La Rock] was supposed to be at the door but left. Herc looked at me and said, 'Keep the music playing.' Because one of our main rules was if something happened at the party never stop the music. If somebody got shot: Keep the music playing. Never stop the music because if you do, you are putting all the focus on the negative situation. So I watched Herc leave the stage and go through the curtain. No sooner than he walked through the curtain he came back through the curtain backpedaling. And the guy was trying to kill Herc with that knife. He stabbed Herc all the way back to the stage. And by the time he got back to the front of the stage a couple of the guys doing security started stomping the dude with the knife. They were able to get the knife from him. They beat him back out of the door.

"Herc was sitting on the floor, leaking from many places. I looked at him, called his name, and he said, 'Pack up the set. I gotta go to the hospital.' Believe it or not, but he got up and walked up the hill to Bronx-Lebanon Hospital. He was strong enough to take those stabbings and walk to the hospital. When he got there, that's when he fell out."

According to Coke La Rock, he wasn't on the door at the time of the stabbing because he'd gone home, which was only three blocks away, to go to the bathroom because he didn't like going to the restroom at the club. And when he came back the police were already there, and he was told what happened. While at the hospital Herc told Coke not to go looking for the guy who did this, to wait for him to get better, and they can go look for them together. But apparently Coke didn't, and he and Mike (who was at the door at the Executive Playhouse at the time of the stabbing) went looking for the dude the next day. Coke believes the guy slipped by them in one of the places they went to find him and some of the guy's people "sent him down South" so that he couldn't be found.

Clark admits, "It took Herc two and a half years before he got himself back to what he felt was presentable to go out into the world." And according to Clark, all the club owners they were playing for—who Herc showed "this is how you make money"—because Herc was out of commission, it opened the door for DJs like Bam, Breakout, and myself to get to places like the PAL, Sparkle, the Playhouse, etc. It opened the door for everyone to be everywhere. Clark believed that the club owners were "fiending for that money Herc was bringing, that he was no longer bringing because he disappeared." As he said: "The game didn't stop because Herc got hurt."

* * *

A guy from South Carolina who moved to New York started Enjoy Records and opened a record shop in Harlem in 1946.

Bobby Robinson, that guy who came to Club 125 who I thought was the police, launched Enjoy in 1962. His idea that he said to me at Club 125—of capturing on wax what we were doing in the parks and in the clubs—stuck. The sound, the voices, the energy. Reducing thirty-minute routines into fourteen- to fifteen-minute twelve-inch records. Sometimes eight minutes. Sometimes five minutes.

For us the result became "Superrappin'." A song the six of us went into the studio and recorded as "Grandmaster Flash and the Furious Five." Our first record.

After us, Bobby Robinson began to build a small roster. He had a nephew named Spoonie Gee who was already on the scene, who he brought in to make a record, and he signed on a group called the Treacherous Three, who was known for turning out block parties in Harlem. And they had an MC named Mohandas Dewese in the group, who went by the name Kool Moe Dee.

When we started going into Harlem and listening to the groups, and their group Treacherous Three, with Moe Dee—very, very dangerous. And that's dangerous in a good way. Speed rappin'? If Melle was 1A, Moe Dee was 1B. Talent-wise? Totally incredible. He had a split-Harlem style. The way he melodically spoke on a record against the way he spoke in battle mode displayed how dangerous he was. He was a fuckin' force to fuck with.

Fast forward a bit, about eight years. The aftermath of the breakup of the Treacherous Three and Moe Dee leaving their record label, Sugar Hill Records, was massive. Sugar Hill would never be the same; they shut the label down in 1986, the same year Moe Dee released his first solo album on Jive Records, and Moe Dee would become a star. The minute his first song hit the streets and the radio, you knew his life was going to be different from that point on. Him going solo was like Lionel Richie when he left the Commodores or when Michael left the Jacksons. But what made "Go See the Doctor" work besides Moe Dee's stories in the song was the production of an eighteen-year-old kid named Teddy Riley. Who at seventeen-years old, along with Dennis Bell and Ollie Cotton and Doug E. Fresh, helped produce "The Show." A year after that first album, Moe Dee and Riley changed the game with "How Ya Like Me Now." Putting Riley, not Moe Dee, at the forefront of a new music genre they called "new jack swing" all based on the sound the teenager Riley had invented.

Anyway, back to the here and now, before any of the rap records on Enjoy were released, Cowboy and I were chilling in the VIP upstairs at the Disco Fever where I was the resident DJ, and we heard a friend of ours, Grandmaster Caz of the Cold Crush Brothers' rhymes over Chic's new song "Good Times," but it wasn't Caz's voice. We ran downstairs to see who was on the mic, only to find out it wasn't someone impersonating Caz on the mic—someone was actually doing it on a record. That was our introduction to "Rapper's Delight."

* * *

Going back, by the end of 1976 two groups had pulled off tagging full trains, top to bottom, all ten cars. Caine 1, known as the "King of the 7 Line," pulled off the "Freedom Train," on July 4, the bicentennial, doing full-scale patriotic work across a whole train and a group called the Fab 5 did a whole Christmas-themed train that ran during the Christmas season of that same year. Those trains became inspirations.

From that a true artist—in every sense of the definition of an artist—emerged. Left a mark, then left. I've watched it happen, especially in this culture, especially when it came to women. The b-girls go unrecognized; the female rappers go unrecognized. In the culture of graffiti there's Sandra Fabara. To the world she's Lady Pink. Queens born and bred. Third generation graffiti artist. Came on the scene in 1979 at fifteen years old and turned professional as an artist at sixteen.

Graffiti—because it began long before the culture became a culture and it was indoctrinated into what we were creating even as it had its own thing going on—has always had levels and tiers when it came to its artists and timeline. Their first generation predated ours in this culture. What made Lady Pink so unique is that she understood that from the beginning. She found graffiti, graffiti didn't find her. She was already a budding artist, whose work was being exhibited in "aboveground" galleries at sixteen years old, and a student majoring in architecture at the High School of Art and Design in Manhattan when her stubbornness got the best of her, hearing guys who were graffiti artists tell her that because she was a girl she couldn't do what they did. Her response: "Well, watch me."

Starting out in Brooklyn, her first tags were Brooklyn-style even though she was from Queens. All the cool cats at her high school were from the Bronx. She came up under the inspiration of Lee Quiñones and Dondi and Futura and Zephyr and Doze and Crash. Legends. She met all the guys who were using subways as their canvas. It to her was artistic, fun, and outlaw-ish. She wouldn't have it any other way. She was there for the excitement, the thrills, the "kicks and giggles," as she put it, things that at the time were important to all teenagers illegally using public platforms as places for their art.

Fame came along with her name, she being one of the first

and only females out there at the time. Her tag stood out; there weren't too many other Lady surnames spread across New York, even though she hung tight with another female artist named Lady Heart, who was only in the game for a couple of years. Then there was Spanky. But for Lady Pink being a female came at a cost with people thinking she was not doing her own work.

"Being the only female was a novelty, so I already had fame," she told me. "I didn't even have to do anything. But what came with that was I had to prove it to everyone that I could paint my own trains. The repercussions of that—sneaking out in the middle of the night, being around nothing but a bunch of guys—was that people were going to talk. They were saying, 'She ain't really painting her own trains, she's just doin' the guys to get her name up on that train.' Therefore I *had to* paint with groups from all over New York City, and they all had to watch me paint my own trains. Proving that I ain't doing nothing else but painting my own train."

She'd sometimes dress up like a boy when she tagged trains and subway tunnels with her teenage friends. But at the same time, the fame that came with her name got her into parties and nightclubs where she'd be the exact opposite, dressing like a princess. Her name showing up on nightclub guest lists, drugs and liquor surrounding her, hanging with Andy Warhol, and contributing (footprints) to future legendary artist's paintings at seventeen years old, parties at rich people's and art collectors' houses.

She learned the protocols of graffiti as respect came with her work. Learning how the train yards and layups process worked, a system set up by the first and second generation of artists. How to get to the trains without getting caught was a military-style operation. A member of a crew would send a scout out, someone who knew and studied the train schedule, the ins-and-outs of the times the trains would retire for the night. You had to be a member of the crew who was painting the trains in the yards that night to get in. If another artist tried to join without being invited while another crew was there, they would not get in and get "dealt with, taught, and schooled" or sometimes "robbed" because they were making the place hot, a target for the police. You couldn't just go loitering in train yards like that, when another crew was there that yard belonged to that crew. You had to be down with the right people to join them.

All the laws of graffiti had been laid down for decades before Lady Pink entered the game. There was hierarchy and ethics. Very much like the unwritten rules we had to operate by as DJs when it came to territory and neighborhoods, graffiti itself was its own entity. Even as a third-generation artist, she still represented what the graffiti culture stood for before it became aboveground and they lumped all of the four elements together and put a name on it.

Lady Pink stayed true to the style importance in graffiti and how it was the epitome of graffiti. The fonts, the letters, you had to know, you had to learn and be taught. She was—endless hours of practice until she got it right before anything went up on a wall or a train. Learning, like all early and real graffiti writers, how to get the lines straight in the dark without sometimes even seeing what you are doing because there is no light in those tunnels, in those train yards, in those layups. Styles were done so precisely that they could tell if a tag or someone's work is from the Bronx or from Queens, or from France or Australia. Strictly by the way they did their letters.

Style also often dictated era. When talking, Lady Pink broke it down to me that style (in graffiti) was like fashion. "Like when you look at clothes and can tell something is from the sixties and you know that clothing is from the nineties. It changes over the decades. So fonts, letters, style, you have to study it hard, and you have to be taught by a master. You couldn't just make shit up."

The shelf life of most graffiti writers was somewhere between two to five years. It was too dangerous. Most began as kids, and they grew up and had to get a life. A "real" one. Because, similar to breakdancing, after a while the underground graffiti—staying in it as a writer with all the risks they took—didn't make sense. Out every weekend grubbing with other writers in dark, dirty, cold subway tunnels; climbing walls, waiting in swamps, dodging rats, hiding under trains for hours, basically risking injury, life, and freedom just so they can bomb trains. Which she did nonstop from 1980 to 1985. This after being told since she was sixteen: "The art market is very fickle. It's like a fad; it will change its mind in a year when something else is hot, when something else is interesting. So ride the wave while it's here because this might not last."

Lady Pink's view of it helped shape mine. "We had to put aside the vandalistic stuff, find and hold a job, get an apartment, get a wife, get a husband. . . . We couldn't just be out there risking all that stuff just for the sake of getting famous. After that you're just doing it for the thrills, the excitement. That's an important part early on when painting. Sure it's nice to see your paintings in a gallery, but it's not the same thrill as in 'Ohh, I got away with something naughty. No one thought I could do it.' And you did it. To see a train rolling by with your work on it, it's a different kind of excitement. You don't want money for your work, you don't want an exhibit, you don't want any of that glory shit, you just want to go out in the middle of the night to paint. It's the adrenaline rush that you crave."

A trap that she later avoided. When she took her talents inside, aboveground. Her knowing there was more.

Meanwhile, that brotha with the Bajan roots like mine, who's godfather was jazz legend Max Roach, who was wallpapering subway cars, had begun to invade the downtown Manhattan scene. Fred's vision was different than most of the other graffiti artists in the city. To him it was visual art. Something that should be looked at and appreciated as "fine art." He wanted people to accept what was going on all over New York—something that outside of those of us who were in it was hated across the board—to look at as an elevated art form. Art he believed the world should see.

So Fred immersed himself and made connections with the punk rock/new wave people downtown. He thought because they seemed so wild and sorta open, he could connect better there with people who would listen to what he was talking about in terms of some graffiti being looked at as visual art. Part of his idea was to put a positive light on graffiti artists and other black youth who were creating in hopes that it would destigmatize the negative depiction in the press. If he could put a light on what they were all doing as visual artists and the innovative new music being developed and created in the Bronx and uptown by DJs, he could present it as this whole new culture, and he could get a film done that could showcase all of us in a better light than the racist and negative ways we were always shown.

In his downtown journey, Fred, who was becoming known as Fab 5 Freddy to stay connected to his original graffiti group, Fab 5, befriended many people. Chris Stein and Deborah Harry of the new wave group Blondie; Charlie Ahearn, an underground filmmaker who was on the scene doing a martial arts film about kids in the projects on the Lower East Side, and, most important, a young visual artist who was a member of a two-man crew who went by the tag SAMO—short for Same Ol' Shit. He saw what was going on with us in the Bronx: rebellious energy and coming from the streets, just a different rhythm. The people he was connecting with agreed. They listened to everything he was telling them. And after bringing Chris and Debbie to a few spots uptown to see what we were doing, they eventually went into the studio to make a song about what they'd experienced seeing rappers rap and DJs spin the way I was spinning. Freddy thought it was a joke when they first played what they recorded for him; he had no idea it was a legit record they were making. Literally what they played him was Debbie's, as he called it, "goofy version of everything I'd told her." He told her that "there's fly guys and fly girls," and that "Flash is fast," he was in their ears. Telling them repeatedly that there was something going on in a whole 'nother part of New York that no one knew about and that he felt it was just as hardcore as their punk rock thing.

Rock and roll had lost its edge. Now there were the Sex Pistols and the Clash, cutting-edge groups that were wild, rebellious, on some revolutionary shit. Freddy was deep into their scene. He knew to them the "rock-and-roll motherfuckers had gotten corny" and were on "some rock star shit." Punk rock wanted rock and roll to be back on some raw, rebellious, "out of the garage" type of vibe. And it no longer was. But to Freddy, he believed that hip-hop, what we were doing was in a similar place to punk rock. Both had the same sensibilities. We were both doing things the way we wanted. The cultures were different, but the attitudes and energies were close to the same. That is exactly how he presented it to Chris and Debbie, which was reflected in the song they recorded. When it was done, they not only name-checked Fab 5 Freddy in Debbie's lyrics but also me. And at the time, this is before the actual song was released, Sugar Hill Records had not released their first record.

Two very significant things happened almost simultaneously that would play a role in reshaping how graffiti would be seen and how what was happening in the Bronx would be introduced to the world. And Fred was at the center of both. First, in SoHo, Freddy, almost strictly going by Fab 5 Freddy now, and his guru graffiti partner Lee Quiñones partnered with some people they'd made connections with in a big loft in SoHo and threw a party. Lee and Freddy, to outfit the party, had done a couple of huge paintings on plastic sheets for the backdrop. All the artsy types are there and both members of SAMO show up. Unknown to anyone, because while they were still somewhat anonymous, their tag wasn't. Until at that party one of them tags SAMO on one of the visuals in the room, and everyone is like, "Oh shit, you're SAMO!" Black kid with a wild mohawk. Took everyone by surprise. From that point on Freddy and that one member of SAMO linked up, were tight, and became friends. That SAMO member's government name: Jean-Michel Basquiat. The same artist whose work Lady Pink would later put her footprints on.

The second would be the relationship Freddy was able to build with Charlie Ahearn and the film that would come from it.

Jean-Michel and Freddy were like the outsiders in the outside world of hip-hop. They were the ones running in a different crowd yet still being themselves in those crowds. Extensions of the culture expressing themselves in the same way I was, Trixie and Dancin' Doug were, Anna and Tina were, Coke La Rock and Clark Kent were, Mel and Moe Dee were, Phase II was. They simply wanted their work to be looked at the same way, in the same arenas the world was looking at Andy Warhol's and Keith Haring's works were. Even before those types of street artists—not really known or considered in circles as graffiti artists or writers—became big and famous, Freddy would say there's a "certain type of space, certain type of gallery you want to see yourself in in the beginning" just like they were. Two young black art nerds who went to art museums as kids, learning about Picasso and Rembrandt, finding each other as artists who "were trying to hit it on a historical art level to be right up in those museums" with all the other greats they saw. As Freddy said: "Everything with Jean was executed according to plan even though that wasn't 'the plan.'"

CHAPTER 9

Bill Curtis, a founding member of the legendary New York group the Fatback Band was in the studio working on the band's twelfth album and had an instrumental song "Catch the Beat" included as a track. Kind of based on what I was doing with records "catching the beats" and breaks on songs. "Catch the Beat" was missing something in Curtis's mind. It needed some type of voice. One of the roadies for the band had a friend, Timothy Washington, in the projects who could rap. The group brought him in. He recorded his rap in two takes. It was something between what Cowboy and Mel were doing and what DJ Hollywood was doing, like he was part rapper, part on-air radio disc jockey. They gave the friend from the projects the name "King Tim III." And changed the name of the song "Catch the Beat" to the same.

When Sylvia and Joe Robinson released "Rapper's Delight" on Sugar Hill Records, "King Tim III" had already been out a few months as a B-side song to Fatback's "You're My Candy Sweet." But there's belief that because the song wasn't registered as a lead single the official copyright registration date of the song is August 29, 1979, even though it was officially released on March 25, 1979, while "Rapper's Delight" has a copyright registration date of August 25, 1979, four days ahead of "King Tim III." But Bill Curtis and Timothy Washington technically did have the first recorded rap record on record, which I consider the first record for postmodern hip-hop. Then everything around us seemed to explode all at once.

All in the same year, 1979, "Superrappin'" was released; Chic released "Good Times;" "Rapper's Delight" was released; "King Tim III" released; "Christmas Rappin'" by Kurtis Blow on Mercury Records was released, the first by a rap artist signed to a major record label; a song with Cowboy, Rahiem, Mel, Creole, and Ness recorded under the name the Young Generation called "We Rap More Mellow" was recorded in October of 1979 and released before the year's end; the song that Debbie Harry and Chris Stein and their group Blondie called "Rapture" was being conceptualized and was recorded, and was released the next year; an MC/radio host on WHAT 1340 AM out of Philadelphia named Lady B (Wendy Clark) released a song called "To the Beat Y'all," and it became an under-the-radar hit, to the point that it was picked up by Sugar Hill Records a year after its release; two rappers from Brooklyn, Master Jay and Michael Dee, released a song called "TSOB" (The Sound of Brooklyn) early the next year. *And* on the B-side of Spoonie Gee's first record for Enjoy Records called "Love Rap" was "The New Rap Language" by the Treacherous Three with Kool Moe Dee, that would be released the following year as well. This was the beginning of what we'd been doing for all these years being commercialized. And you could feel it; you could feel the change.

Sylvia Robinson could technically be called and considered the first hip-hop record producer even though she didn't produce the first rap record. She created the Sugarhill Band—the instrumentalists performing the songs the label sampled—possibly to avoid legal action based on copyright infringement. Later the label still faced a legal threat for re-creating the bassline from Chic's "Good Times" in the hit "Rapper's Delight" and eventually settled with the song's owners. I thought Sylvia was also trying to re-create what Herc, Bam, Breakout, and I had created. She would bring in in-house producer Jiggs Chase to produce and arrange songs with her. And although there was another Sugar Hill Records label out of North Carolina that dealt in bluegrass music, Sylvia had an entire record label only dedicated to producing and recording what people began calling rap music.

It was less than two months after "Good Times" by Chic was released that Sylvia was in the studio reproducing the bass line and drums for "Rapper's Delight." Atlantic Records released "Good Times" to the world as the first single off Chic's third album, "Risqué," on June 4, 1979. Sylvia went in to record what would become "Rapper's Delight" with the bass player and drummer playing the chords of the song uninterrupted for fifteen straight minutes on August 2, 1979. "Good Times" was still #2 on the *Billboard* charts, three weeks before it went #1. She didn't waste any time. She'd approached a few other rappers about her "idea" of doing the song that would end up being "Rapper's Delight" before she found the three in New Jersey who would become the Sugarhill Gang; before Big Bank Hank imitated Caz's personal style and even borrowed a few of his rhymes on the song, very similarly doing the same thing to Caz that the Sugarhill Band did to Chic.

* * *

By now the graffiti artists were doing all the flyers for parties at the clubs. Phase II was our guy. We had the baddest artist in the game making flyers for our Flash and the Furious Five parties. We had raggedy flyers, but once we met Phase our flyers were proper. There was no photoshopping, he would do them on Letraset sheets, rubbing the letters in, drawing the lines. He put detailed work into it.

Flyers would become the main marketing tool for everyone's crew and every DJ to let people know where to come. The doper the flyer, the more people.

One night at the Armory in Harlem that year in 1979 some of the best DJs and MCs of that time got together for a jam. It was huge. But it was shut down due to a shoot-out that occurred during the event. The very same one that ended up being Little Terri's last party. A kid, all of eleven years old, named James Todd Smith was at the show. So young his mother had to drive him and come in with him. She sat in the stands. They'd gotten to the show early so James could stand in front of the stage. So closely he saw the Crash Crew walk in. He saw Sequence perform. When they started shooting (an urban myth)—he enjoyed it. He jumped over the stand and under the stage and was like, "This is great!" He needed to be a part of it. The same kind of feeling as the kid from Texas had experiencing the blackout.

"This gave me an opportunity to get closer to this shit," is how the then eleven-year-old told it to me later. "I had to leap to get over the barricade to get under the stage. I was already in that zone. I was all in it. I didn't know this at the time, but there's this concept called *mimetic desire*, and that concept is about people desiring things only because other people want them. Like, 'He got that shirt, I want that shirt. He got the car, I want the car. Somebody has this, I want this.' Even as I was exposed to what became known as hip-hop early, it spoke to something on the inside. In other words I didn't need anyone around me to tell me that I wanted to do this. There were, of course, outside stimuli, but this was different because as a kid it was an organic desire. Internal and intentional."

He was part of the first generation who literally grew up on the culture. Eight years old hearing and listening to tapes. Nine, ten, eleven, twelve, thirteen years old, deeply immersed in it. Back and forth between Long Island and Queens. He'd be all around Queens, often ending up in Harlem. By the time he's fourteen or fifteen years old, he's going uptown, Grant Projects with Silver Fox and the Fantasy 3. Memorizing the rhymes of Fearless Four. Their freestyles, "F-4000," "Problems of the World (Today)," their cadences stood out, stood different. The way they put their words together. There was a sea change from lyrics to lyricism.

Every element touched young James. From the graffiti to the breakdancing, which he never did, to the DJing and rhyme saying, which spoke to his spirit. He gravitated to it because of the musical choices made by DJs—big beats, strong beats. The voices of the MCs; the "Yes, yes y'alls," the echo chamber. All of it sounded powerful to him. Sounded stronger than he felt. He'd ask his grandfather for some equipment. So that he could "do what Flash was doing," he used the microphone to do what every member of the Fearless Four was doing. All of it helped him escape the pain.

He literally told me, "Flash when I wrote, 'Write my name up on a cloud. Make the world turn twice . . .'" that was his destination, that's where his mind went to get away from it all. "That's what we wanted to do," he'd say. "What we *didn't want to do* was deal with the bullshit we had to deal with around here. With the friend getting killed up the block, with someone's father getting shot, all of the problems we were stuck with to deal with." The rhymes he wrote helped him get away from the pain that was life.

Young James may have been the culture's first true prodigy. Down the line the prodigy would become a target.

* * *

Of all the DJs, Herc, Bambaataa, Breakout, Baron, Smokey who'd left the scene, AJ, Theodore who was my first student, Islam, Mario, it was Jazzy Jay from Bam's crew who fell deeply in love with the Theory. He studied it, he was at all the high school events I did, he was at all of the different venues I'd play, and he'd be there studying me. But I never felt threatened or intimidated by anyone who may have tried to perfect what I'd started. I was very cocky. There was no one in my category as far as I was concerned. The Theory was new and not everyone incorporated it, but it wasn't just the QMT, it was the beatbox, the Five, the echo chamber, Ray Chandler, these were all my war tools. Even though I was public enemy number one and all the DJs in New York seemed to be gunning for me, I didn't have any problems, feel threatened by, or fear anyone.

I also had a secret weapon. The Five had dance routines while they were rapping. Of all the MC crews out there, they were the most dynamic. There were certain records we'd use to rehearse our routines. Like "Celebrate the Good Things" by Pleasure. They would do these moves as they went into their rap thing. And on the tables EZ Mike and I had our routine. Then one time when I was in the Jackson Projects on 149th Street I heard this sound, and I kept going back there to see if I could hear it again. Finally I met the guy who was producing the sound, his name was Stanley. The sound was coming from a machine. Stanley and I became friends. I told him, "Man, if you ever want to sell this box, I'm going to be the first one to buy it." With my electronic knowledge, once I got to see it and examine it, I knew what I had to do, I knew what connectors I needed to have. Once he decided to sell it to me, that went on the flyer. "Grandmaster Flash and the Beatbox."

I learned how to play this manually operated drum box with these little, teeny-ass buttons, and the Five came up with this song we'd perform called "Flash to the Beat." (Sugar Hill Records ended up releasing a studio version of that song called "Flash to the Beat. (Part 1)." It was wack. People hated it. Asking me, "Why did you make that record?" The studio version didn't have the rawness and the dopeness that my manually operated drum box/beatbox had.) So we had all this talent intermingled into this thing that was based around me, and me with that machine made us as a group the best in the business. And no one could mimic the beatbox because they couldn't find one. If they could, they would have gotten one. It was our secret weapon. I put black tape over it so no one would know the brand name. Same thing we did with covering up record labels in our crates. I kept it in covers. I did everything I could to protect it because I didn't want anyone else to buy it and try to emulate us. Now once we got into the record business and I put the beatbox away, I started seeing people do the same thing that the beatbox did with their mouths. And even though I couldn't copyright the beatbox because I didn't create it, I was the only one using it the way that I was using it. While I didn't birth it, I gave it life.

I was paying attention to everything around me that seemed to be growing at the same pace as DJing happened to be growing. There're so many moving parts, so many of us doing different things in different places all at around the same time creating the same kind of energy around what we were doing and all circling and interacting with one another while exiting in the same circles. I keep calling it a solar system without a sun.

Dancin' Doug, I believe, put it best years later: "Everybody had an element that played a part in how this thing grew. I worked organized crime as an adult because my brother got killed and my life changed. I got sent away to school; my life turned all the way around. I became a Fed. And like Cosa Nostra, this, hip-hop, is our thing. Everybody had a hand in making this thing what it is. No one person can claim it. When I hear people try to claim it and say, 'This is mine,' or 'I started this,' I say, 'This belongs to all of us!' No one person did this!" Then he tells this story, always tells this story, which to me places everything in perspective: "I was in Paris, France, in 2012. I went to a club out there, and I saw this fat white kid doing my move. I used to call it the 'Curly,' they call it the 'Shuffle' now. I'm standing right next to him and he's doing this dance and I say to him, 'You have no idea you are doing my dance that I was doing in 1973 and 1974.' And I'm in a whole 'nother country, forty years from when I was doing it. That's how beautiful it is this thing we got."

Part IV

The Culture (Level 3: 1980–1989)

1. **"Square Biz"**
Teena Marie (1980)
2. **"Bounce, Rock, Skate, Roll"**
Vaughn Mason and Crew (1980)
3. **"The Breaks"**
Kurtis Blow (1980)
4. **"Never Too Much"**
Luther Vandross (1981)
5. **"Before I Let Go"**
Frankie Beverly and Maze (1981)
6. **"The Adventures of Grandmaster Flash on the Wheels of Steel"**
Grandmaster Flash (1982)
7. **"Risin' to the Top"**
Keni Burke (1982)
8. **"Genius of Love"**
Tom Tom Club (1981)
9. **"Sexual Healing"**
Marvin Gaye (1982)
10. **"Candy Girl"**
New Edition (1983)
11. **"Walk This Way"**
Run-DMC featuring Aerosmith (1986)
12. **"I Know You Got Soul"**
Eric B. and Rakim (1987)
13. **"Straight Outta Compton"**
N.W.A. (1989)
14. **"6 in the Mornin'"**
Ice-T (1987)
15. **"Roxanne Roxanne"**
UTFO (1984)
16. **"The Show"/"La Di Da Di"**
Doug E. Fresh & Slick Rick (1985)
17. **"Rapture"**
Blondie (1981)

Chapter 10

In the summer of 1980, when Kurtis Blow followed up "Christmas Rappin'" with "The Breaks," the shift in the culture seemed to shift even more. It felt bigger than most of the other "rap" records out at that time. Maybe because KB was on a major record label and the rest of us weren't. I didn't know. But "The Breaks" was huge. Ended up being the first rap record to be certified gold by the Recording Industry Association of America (RIAA). Second-ever certified-gold twelve-inch record after Barbra Streisand and Donna Summer's "No More Tears (Enough Is Enough)" just a year before.

Some, if not a lot of that, had to do with the radio play "The Breaks" got once it was released. Stations that didn't even play rap music (outside of "Rapper's Delight," of course) seemed to have "The Breaks" in their rotation. Which really cracked the doors for other rap records afterward at radio stations in New York that begin to play on a still less-than-regular basis. The Frankie Crockers and Gary Byrds followed by Mr. Magic later played major roles by taking the hinges off the doors that led the way for rap blowin' up all across New York.

On both "Christmas Rappin'" and "The Breaks" there was a

bass player by the name Larry Smith. A session musician from Queens, who became as important to Blow's music as Marcus Miller would be to Luther Vandross's beginning the following year. A young entrepreneur by the name of Russell Simmons was KB's manager at the time. He started a management company, Rush Artist Management. While he was getting and booking shows, he was also all over New York, in every borough, promoting parties. Getting to know and build relationships with everyone who was anyone. And Russell had a little brother who was madd eager to get in the game. By then, Joey, Russell's little brother, had already told his friend Darryl while they were both in eighth grade two years earlier: "When my brother Russell ever lets me make a record, I'm putting you in my group."

Russell put his little brother Joey under Kurt's wing.

"The Breaks" put KB on the top. He became the MC all the other rappers began to look up to because he now had stature. Real stature, major-record-label, major-record-sales stature, not just that "you the shit in New York" stature. He kept setting the table. It seemed every year, another classic. "8 Million Stories," "Basketball," "AJ Scratch," "Tough," "If I Ruled the World." Earning Kurtis the first MC to have the title "King of Rap."

While Russell was introducing the world to artists, Smith was literally introducing the world to sounds. "The Bubble Bunch" (Jimmy Spicer) sound, the "You've Gotta Believe" (Lovebug Starski) sound, the "Fast Life" sound (Dr. Jeckell and Mr. Hyde), the "Action" (Orange Krush) sound, the "Jail House Rap" (The Fat Boys) sound, the original Run-DMC and Whodini sounds, the "U Know What Time It Is" sound by me. He may have been, more likely was, more integral in giving rap music a sound in the '80s than any single individual. He and

Russell's early business and musical partnerships with Kurtis Blow helped make KB one of the first solo rap artists to have real commercial success but also were the innovators in showing us how professionalism in rap could look and sound in the music business.

The one other thing that Russell provided, especially in around 1983, '84, '85, and especially '86 that not many in the business were providing was real, official management. Someone who made club and concert promoters and club and venue owners take rap music artists, at least somewhat, seriously and help change the perception to a lot of them of what rap artists, rap music, and hip-hop as a whole really was.

* * *

When Debbie and Chris and their band Blondie released "Rapture," the song they were working on that Freddy didn't believe was a real song that Debbie name-checked us both in, everything blew up. Even Johnny "Guitar" Watson got into the fray, adding the song "Telephone Bill" to his *Love Jones* album in 1980, which by all standards was a rap song. The *Houston Press* wrote in 2008, "'Telephone Bill' sounds like what would have happened if Kurtis Blow had come from Third Ward instead of the Bronx. Watson's rhyme scheme, humorously woe-is-me subject matter, and musical flow shows a clear influence on Devin the Dude and was years ahead of its time, as was the live musical backing." This was not the blues; it was either blues-adjacent music entering the rap game or something different.

On the roster at Sugar Hill by then was Disco Dave and the Force of the Five MCs, otherwise known as the Crash Crew; the Sequence, the female group formed in South Carolina;

the Treacherous Three; Spoonie Gee; of course, the Sugarhill Gang; the Mean Machine, a bilingual black and Puerto Rican rap group; and our group, Grandmaster Flash and the Furious Five had now signed with them and released the song "Freedom." Our follow-up to "Superrappin'" but also our for real entrance into a whole new ball game because Sugar Hill was a big deal thanks to "Rapper's Delight" blowing up all over the world.

Meanwhile at Electric Lady Studios in Greenwich Village, the punk rock band from London, the Clash, who a year ago were in America doing concerts with both Blondie and Chic, were back in America recording the punk-rap song "The Magnificent Seven." Basically, a merging of the two cultures Fab 5 was saying resembled each other in energy and attitude years before.

While Sylvia and Joe and their investors were trying to "Motown" Sugar Hill, Tom Silverman, who was the publisher of *Dance Music Report*, a dance music magazine, was in his New York City apartment starting a record label he'd name after himself, Tommy Boy Records. Apparently after watching "Rapper's Delight" blow up, Silverman believed he too should dip into the record-producing business, especially since he was running a music magazine for years that specifically targeted DJs. The story goes: On a visit to Downstairs Records he noticed the store was full of people searching for obscure breakbeat records from "the breakbeat" section that we'd made famous by buying our records from there. When he asked what was going on, he was told, "We buy what Afrika Bambaataa plays." Which, of course, led him to one of Bam's sets. From there he built a relationship with Bam to cut a record to launch his label.

The first record they did in 1981 was a song called "Jazzy Sensation" in which Bam and the Jazzy Five crew basically dubbed and rapped over Gwen McCrae's classic "Funky Sensation." Not only was that Tommy Boy's first record as a (rap) label, it was also Bam's first as an artist.

A year later, Bam along with a DJ from Boston who'd come to New York to further his career as a record producer and was a music writer for Silverman's *Dance Music Report*, Arthur Baker—who worked with Bam on "Jazzy Sensation," "interpolated," "Trans-Europe Express," and "Numbers" by German electronic dance band Kraftwerk—created a song they called "Planet Rock." That would be the world's second introduction to the Roland 808 drum machine, which eventually would become the first piece of technology more important to rap music and in rap music production than the turntable.

The song was looked at as the guinea pig when it came to sampling and copyright laws because Bambaataa, Baker, and John Robie never sampled the two Kraftwerk songs for the record. Instead they re-created the synthesizer, drum patterns, and melodies. But their re-creation was so accurate, Kraftwerk said it was copyright infringement. It was equivalent to being sued for sampling without sampling. (The label eventually paid a legal settlement to Kraftwerk.)

Still, Sugar Hill was consistently releasing records. Consistently reinterpreting the bass lines, melodies, bridges, or breaks of songs that we'd play in the parks and in clubs and having rappers put vocals on top of those already familiar sounds. The Funk Four Plus One's "That's the Joint" using A Taste of Honey's "Rescue Me," West Street Mob's "Let's Dance (Make Your Body Move)" from Pleasure's "Let's Dance," the Crash Crew's "Braking Bells (Take Me to the Mardi Gras)" using the Bob James song that was my signature song, Sugarhill Gang's "Apache" using the other same-named classic and on "8th Wonder" using Johnnie Taylor's "Ever Ready," us with "It's Nasty (Genius of Love)" using Tom Tom Club's "Genius of Love."

I felt like nothing I was doing or did to get to this point was heard, at least not on any of the records that were being released. I convinced Sylvia to do a record that really got to the core of what the whole culture and movement was about. So we recorded, edited, and put the concept of the Quik Mix Theory out in a seven minute and eighteen second record called "The Adventures of Grandmaster Flash on the Wheels of Steel."

The boys and I were on tour with Rick James and when you are touring sometimes you get large breaks. I had been telling Sugar Hill that I wanted to make this DJ record. They did not understand what I was talking about at first. After about a year of saying this to them, I get a call out of the blue: "Remember that DJ record you were telling us about that you wanted to make? Would you like to fly in and make the record during the temporary break from the tour?" I wasn't able to take all of the Five with me, so it was just Mel and me. I had about two weeks to strategize the record. The toughest part was picking the right songs to put together for the project.

And Sylvia said, "Well whatever records you pick, you do need to put a couple of Sugar Hill Records in there."

I told her, "I'm already doing that anyway."

I needed some breaks, some pop songs, some R&B, and some funk. Planning the record was the most difficult part. I heard how I wanted to put the record together in my mind, but when I physically tried to do it with two turntables, I discovered what I called the IFs: the Impossible Factors, where it was impossible for me to switch the records quick enough to get to the next record. So, I incorporated a third turntable. After that it was just a matter of me practicing in the Bronx until we were ready to record.

Now, me and my ego figured, well, I'm pretty good on the turntables—scientist, geek—so when I took the turntables and my DJ setup out to Jersey to record, I was ready. I went into the studio and said, "Roll tape." It was a tape recorder called a two-inch, twenty-four track master machine. Just imagine the size of a washing machine with two reels of tape on it with the actual width of each tape being somewhere between six and seven inches wide. And in all the songs that we'd record prior to this, I'd watch the engineers do this thing called the punch. That was what they did when they didn't want to go back to the beginning of a recording to re-record. Basically they were fixing the part of the recording during the recording that was not good. During my first attempt, when I came out of "Rapture" the first time I missed bringing in "Good Times." So the engineers were like, "Fine. Don't worry about it. Let's just rewind the tape back, and we'll do a punch and begin right where you left off." I'm like, "No!" I wanted to do the whole thing clean because I knew that I could. So we went back to the beginning.

On the second one I get as far as "Apache," which is less than a minute into the record, and I missed the cut.

Again I said, "Stop the machine."

They're like, "Flash, we can just punch in this section."

Me: "No, we can't!"

To me, I had to be able to humanly do this if ever the time comes for me to do this live. So the story of "The Adventures," it took only three tries to do the whole thing. No punches. A single take.

When I first heard it, finished it, listened back to it, I was pleased with it and I thought it was cool. But I still didn't know how they were going to press the record up, or whether or not they were going to release it. Mostly because afterward, we had to fly back and return to the tour with Rick James. I remember thinking on the plane: *Damn, is that record ever going to come out?* Because, to me, they really didn't understand the art of the Theory being done on a record. Then the day came when Sylvia said to me, "Flash, we gave the record to Frankie Crocker at WBLS." I was astonished! She said, "Yeah, and he's going to debut it on his opening shift."

Now normally Frankie Cocker, Radio God, does his spiel when he comes on. But this time he said, "Ladies and gentlemen, I'm going to play something for you that's not put together like a normal record. This record was done like a masterpiece using other people's records. I'm going to play this record for you guys, and we're going to talk a little more about it." Then he played it, and five minutes after he played it everything blew up. For Frankie Crocker to say what he said, put a stamp not just on the record but on what I'd been believing for a long time, was a level up. It kind of put me in a position that I'd wanted to be in so people were aware that I was the creator of the group Grandmaster Flash and the Furious Five, and I was also the leader and the DJ. From there the record spread to radio stations across the United States and overseas.

Of all the records we'd put out on Sugar Hill, this one for me, personally and professionally, probably ended up having the greatest, most wide-ranging impact. It introduced the world and brought the culture back to the DJ and the importance of what a DJ does; to what Herc, Bam, Breakout, and Smokey and all the others and I did. The soundtrack, the foundation of it all. The fuckin' reminder. Packaged into a seven minute, eighteen second twelve-inch vinyl disc. Now the world could know what turntablism was.

* * *

A major tipping point for me with Sugar Hill Records came when I found out one of the things Sylvia and the label did behind my back. The young lady at the label's front desk answered a call from someone looking for me, and she forwarded the call to a department that handled talent. The message was: "Someone from Chrysalis Records wants Grandmaster Flash."

Later when the group and I were in a meeting with Sylvia about some unrelated business, I asked her, "Hey, did you get a call from a record label concerning me being in a video?"

She was like, "Yeah, we heard something about that. We turned that down."

This was the "Rapture" video. I was so fucking mad. But here's the shit that I had to understand: They knew, as big as Blondie was, if I'd gotten in that muthafuckin' video, the DJ culture would have blown the fuck up! And that wasn't part of Sylvia's plans.

At the time, I was scared of Sylvia. She held too much power over my career. And what wound up happening in the video, since I never showed up because of what Sylvia did, Fab 5 Freddy, who was on set for the video shoot told them: "Listen Jean-Michel is here and I can show him how to play (act) the DJ thing."

No one had really seen it yet. What I was doing was still kind of unknown to the masses, this was before "Adventures." So Freddy says to Jean-Michel, "Lemme show you, now all you gotta do is do this"—he moves his hands on the record on the turntable—"and all you gotta do is do that"—he moves the record back and forth with his fingertips on the vinyl—"you know, do some hand shit." But what Freddy didn't realize is that Jean-Michel had never seen me spin before, so he had no clue what Freddy was trying to explain to him. It was new shit to him and damn near everyone on the set. When the camera starts rolling Jean-Michel is just standing there smiling, doing nothing. Supposed to be me.

Which spoke to how I was beginning to feel about the whole business. That change I felt was real. It seemed more and more that people who were not a part of what was happening even five years ago were now at the forefront, making decisions, dictating the direction of what we were doing.

* * *

By the time Herc returned, the train had left. Sadly, he was too far behind. Probably due to the stabbing and the time it took him to recover. I'd introduced a whole new style, the Quik Mix Theory had caught on, the excess which was now the "MC" had become the forefront, we, the Furious Five and I, had innovated something that became a hard act to follow or replicate. Hip-hop as a term was used more frequently to label what we were doing and what we'd created. Lovebug, who was a part of what I like to call the Ray Chandler family, and Cowboy probably more than anyone were making the term hip-hop popular. Even though what we were doing was still being called DJing and MCing. I could feel that change, *and* I could feel it slipping away at the same time.

For me: More money, more drugs, more problems. More kids, more backstabbing and betrayal, more fame. More drama, more ego. More b-boy and b-girl crews emerged. In Manhattan, the New York City Breakers came to be. The Floor Breakers came from the Bronx. In Mitchel Houses in the South Bronx a young b-boy "Sidewinder Rob" (Robert Taylor) was about to be the next break dance phenomenon. The world would soon know him as "Lee."

Our story, whether we were a part of it or not, was being sold.

* * *

In 1978, the day Joey told Darryl, "When my brother Russell ever lets me make a record, I'm putting you in my group," Darryl didn't believe him. It's June 1982, right after Darryl had graduated from Rice High School in Harlem he'd gotten an acceptance letter from St. John's University. In August 1982, his phone rings, and it's Joey.

"D, wassup? Remember four years ago when I told you if my brother ever let me make a record? Grab your rhyme book, we're going in the studio to make a record!"

To say the rest is history would be an understatement of all understatements. Because on the day they got into the studio Joey and Darryl would make "It's Like That" and "Sucker M.C.'s." They'd call themselves Run-DMC.

"I'll never forget, the day I got that letter I ran to my basement and wrote a rhyme about it: 'I'm DMC/In the place to be/I'm going to St. John's University . . .'" Darryl McDaniels is telling me. "So when we get to the studio months later Joey is like, 'Just go in the booth and say your newest rhymes.' And my newest rhyme was the one I had about being accepted to St. John's University. And that's my debut to the MC world."

It began for them long before that day. Even before their friendship in eighth grade where Run (Joey) would prophesize they'd one day be a group. For Run, it was almost as if he was chosen by a higher power to be who he became. Rapping at fifteen, known in NY as DJ Run, Son of Kurtis Blow—as he was not only one of Blow's DJs but also Blow's mentee—

Russell's little brother stayed ready so he wouldn't have to be ready when that moment that he knew would come did.

His friend Darryl (DMC) was the exact opposite. A comic book–loving, superhero-identifying, geeky, nerdy kid who went to Catholic school and was deep into rock music along with all the other music he was hearing around his middle-class home in Hollis. "I never wanted to be in show business, the entertainment business, none of this, all I cared about was comic books," DMC explains, "Marvel comics to be exact. I learned about New York—Hell's Kitchen, the Lower East Side, 42nd Street—from Stan Lee. I did not have to leave my room to learn about New York City."

He didn't relate to his surroundings; he only related to Peter Parker, Tony Stark, Dr. Bruce Banner because the superheroes were the only people he saw who were geeky, nerdy, awkward, struggling, traumatized people who were also badass. And while he was becoming aware of the block parties in and around Queens and was there for the death of disco, it wasn't the beats and the rhymes of the new sound that captured him, it was the universality of the music that the DJs were playing.

"When the block parties started, the DJs who were playing the music live in the parks were playing all the music I heard on the radio. The music they played on WABC-FM in New York. They were phenomenal because they played the Black and white music together. Along with all of the funk and soul of James Brown and Sly and the Family Stone. I'd hear Crosby, Stills, Nash and Young, the Allman Brothers Band, Procol Harum, "Black Water" by the Doobie Brothers, "Nights in White Satin" by the Moody Blues, the Steve Miller Band, along with Boz Scaggs's "Lowdown," Jim Croce's "Bad, Bad Leroy Brown," Joni Mitchell, Harry Chapin. The Stones and Led Zeppelin. Creedence Clearwater Revival. Hard rock to folk rock. Music people didn't even know white people were creating."

All of this is inside of him. The reason I've always said rock music and music by white artists played a critical role in shaping what we were doing building this culture. *It was not all a Black thing!* Darryl McDaniels is the embodiment of that. Smart kid, full of comic books, superheroes, and music. As he told me: "Why do you think I called myself the King of Rock when I came into hip-hop?"

But it was the four years when he went into what he likes to call the Shaolin Temple: his ninth- through twelfth-grade years at Rice High School. There he'd encounter "the tapes."

"I was hearing Flash and Mel and Theodore, but not on records. All the kids at Rice coming to school with tapes, 'Yo, this was Flash last week in the Bronx, this was Spoonie Gee, this was Kool Moe Dee and the Treacherous Three!' I had T-Connection tapes, the Audubon Ball Room tapes as my guidelines. It blew my mind. It became a part of my life."

To the degree that his pretending to be a superhero as a kid turned into his preparation to become an MC. "All of the stuff I was experiencing prepared me," he'd emphasize. "I was *pre*tending to be Flash because I had the turntables in my basement and I was a 'pause tape' kid, I was *pre*tending to be the whole Furious Five in my little rhyme book. 'Pre' means 'before.' I didn't know me studying and listening to everything the same way I studied a comic book was an education, *pre*paring me, that it was my training."

D and Joey—and their DJ, Jason Mizell, aka: Jam Master Jay, who they'd crown "JMJ" to match the three letters in both "Run" and "DMC," their producer Larry Smith (whose Cadillac Run was put inside on "Sucker M.C.'s") and producer/

manager/Run's older brother Russell—with the release of their first album, *RUN-D.M.C.*, gave the culture a second birth. Musically, lyrically, stylistically, visually, sonically. It was their rock-infused and -inspired sound on many of their records over the years. "Rock Box" being the first that made them more acceptable and accessible to white teenagers and white audiences as a whole, who up until then—most, not all—looked at what we were doing as jungle music.

And with the drop of *Raising Hell* in 1986, the next golden age of hip-hop officially began. Bill Adler, longtime publicist for Rush Artist Management and Def Jam Records, called them "The Beatles of Rap," Chuck D. called them "The Beatles of Hip-Hop." For a while many—millions—called them "the definition of hip-hop." And they by almost all accounts were. Breaking barriers and stereotypes, especially within radio and MTV, that none of us before them were able to. As DMC said on "My Adidas": Hollywood knew we were good. (And I won't even get into JMJ's use of "Take Me to the Mardi Gras" in "Peter Piper.")

When asked what void in the music of the culture he and Run and JMJ were trying to fill with their revolutionary contribution, what could they add that was missing, D keeps it simple. "The rock [music]. Loud rock beats, that sound. Rock drums reminded me of superheroes. And I knew if we took "The Big Beat" by Billy Squier, "Rocket in My Pocket" by Little Feat, the fourth song on Aerosmith's *Toys in the Attic* album, which ended up being "Walk This Way," and I write my raps like a superhero—Wolverine, Captain America—I had to live up to it." But then he adds, "We also knew that as a group we would never let hip-hop be defined without the DJ. That's why it was Run-DMC *and* Jam Master Jay."

He said later groups including Naughty by Nature *and* Kay-

Gee, A Tribe Called Quest *and* Ali Shaheed, EPMD *and* DJ Scratch, Public Enemy *and* Terminator X to further his point. "Because that's what the pioneers—I'm not talking about people who just made records, I'm talking about the people who *invented* this shit—did. Me, J, and Run always felt that we had a responsibility to keep that alive. Because everything else in the music business can die. But what we are will *never* die."

There it is.

* * *

Fab 5 Freddy approached me when his vision of documenting and turning everything we were doing into a film was possibly happening. The martial arts filmmaker he'd befriended did the same thing that Debbie and Chris did: *Believed in what Freddy was telling them about all the happenings*. In this case, the happenings became an interest that Charles "Charlie" Ahearn believed he and Freddy could turn into a movie. Upon Freddy's suggestion.

Charles Ahearn was fascinated with murals and what he liked to call street culture. Freddy's pitch to him was at an abandoned massage parlor in Times Square. He said to Charlie, "We should do some kinda movie that connected what was going on in the subways and what was going on in the hip-hop world."

Charlie knew enough that Fred was doing stuff with Lee Quiñones so he responded, "If you can bring Lee here tomorrow morning at 11 a.m., we'll start making this movie."

Charlie had been trying to work with Lee for more than two years. And Lee, like most graffiti artists, was not attachable. I call it stealthy. "Bring him here, and you guys can do a piece out in front" is what he said to Fred. Which Fred and Lee did—for fifty dollars.

They did a huge "Fab5" on the wall. In Times Square. Unsanctioned. In Charlie's mind no one saw it, "Now we're getting started to make this movie." And from that moment on, every week, Charlie and Freddy would start "meeting at Charlie's place" to plan the film. They went to the Valley in the Bronx to scout locations to shoot, but it was also a place where a lot of the rappers kind of hung out because they'd have jams there.

A guy was standing next to Charlie that he said "Wassup, man?" to.

That guy just happened to be Busy Bee. Busy was the rapper for Disco King Mario. Mel, Cowboy, and Creole were his inspirations. Charlie took Busy's picture. Charlie took pictures of everything and everyone. He was building a storyboard. Charlie told Busy, "I'm here because I want to make a movie about the hip-hop scene." Busy puts his arm around Charlie and leads him to the microphone at the center of the stage in the Valley and says on the mic: "This here is Charlie Ahearn. He's a film producer. And *we're* making a movie about the hip-hop scene." He literally said, "we're."

That led to everyone there giving Charlie flyers to parties where they were performing. Including members of the Funky 4 + 1. Charlie and Freddy went to almost all the parties on those flyers. Even though I wasn't there that day, Freddy knew me and Charlie knew who I was. They were very aware of what I was doing and knew that I was, as Charlie put it, "key to understanding the hip-hop scene that existed." And that was the beginning of how the movie *Wild Style* got made.

Charlie wasn't writing a script, he was living something. Something that was real to Freddy, that was becoming real for Charlie. He's thinking like a filmmaker, but he's not sitting in a room crafting narratives and plotlines. The movie was going to be told by his actions and interactions with the people he encountered, with the scene Freddy told him existed. The Cold Crush Brothers' story. The Fantastic's story. Their rivalry. My story. Lee's story. Whatever was going on he wanted to be on it. So when I met Charlie the first time, my initial thought was, *Why does this white guy want to come to the Bronx?* I looked at him suspiciously, with a lotta "Ummm." But once he explained himself, and I was able to see the realness in his eyes, that's when I said "Okay." Because the culture wasn't explosive yet and most people outside of the Bronx were terrified to come to the Bronx because of what they'd heard.

"You go to the Bronx, and you die." That's what was being said. For him to want to carry cameras, with a staff, and want to film what we were doing in the midst of the reputation that the Bronx had was questionable but wonderful at the same time.

Both Charlie and Freddy knew that there was a lot of fear, stupidity, and misunderstanding that people on the outside had when it came to the Bronx. And when it came to hip-hop. They told me their movie was going to be a narrative, but they were going to let the music express the graffiti and the art the movie was going to be about.

When it came to the music for the movie, Charlie wanted to have his own original music, and Freddy wanted to use music and beats from actual songs that already existed for the soundtrack. What wound up happening was Freddy as the musical director of the film re-created the breakbeats. He had some breakbeat ideas he lifted from the breakbeat part of the World's Famous Supreme Team's radio show on WHBI out of New York. (Who later would come into mainstream prominence once the manager of punk groups the Sex Pistols, Adam Ant, the New York Dolls, Malcolm McLaren, from London, England, came to New York.)

Releasing together the song "Buffalo Gals" and then later

without McLaren, "Hey! D.J.," Freddy told Chris, "I want the beats for the soundtrack to sound like these" as he played Chris the beats from the radio show. Chris played guitar, added sound effects with some of the gadgets he had lying around and from sound effect records they had in the recording studio; they had a drummer, a bass player, and Freddy producing, in the studio literally re-creating the beats. They made about twelve one-minute tracks for the DJs in the movie to extend. So while the party scenes were being shot for the movie, the DJs were scratching the beats that Freddy produced, the crew was recording it as they shot, and it became the movie soundtrack.

I said to Charlie, "You know nobody really gave a damn about the Bronx until you came along. You had no budget, you had to rent cameras, but you had a vision. Why did you want to do this film?"

He responded by saying, "I could begin by saying that I've been involved in street culture since the seventies, I made a kung fu movie in Lee's housing projects on the Lower East Side called *The Deadly Art of Survival.* I shot it on Super 8. I was deep into kung fu films as an expression of the street culture because there was nothing else out there. I was fascinated by that. But what I became really fascinated with was Lee's murals that were in the neighborhood. These giant, handball court murals."

His first investors came from outside of America. ZDF in Germany and Channel 4 in London. He sent both a cassette tape of an Ecstasy Garage party and a colored Xerox image of a graffitied subway train, with the name of the film and a description that read: "It's going to be a teenage romance of the new culture. It's going to be about hip hop." And at the center of that romance, a love story. A real one. Between Lee and Lady Pink.

Who in the film and in real life were a couple. But Lee wanted nothing to do with acting in the film, remember stealthy, until Charlie tipped the scales. Telling Lee, according to Lady Pink, "If you don't do the film, if you don't take the part as the lead actor and we cast somebody else, that somebody else is going to be kissing your girlfriend."

But this wasn't *Love Story*, and Lady Pink and Lee weren't Ali MacGraw and Ryan O'Neal. And this wasn't Harvard and Dartmouth and Ivy League schools and settings as the backdrop; this was the Bronx. Charlie had a hard time getting anyone outside of the culture to believe. "When I tried to approach anyone [to invest] to get a thousand dollars, to get something from anybody in America," he reflected, "they all said, 'No! Why would we want to give money to people who are going around vandalizing property? Why would we want to give money to something that's obviously not of any interest to anyone except the small group of people in New York City?' They never imagined that this was going to be everyone's culture."

My role was simple in the movie: Be me. No character name, no costume change, no method acting. Just be Grandmaster Flash on the ones and twos. But I had to make it special, so there was a three. The scene was shot in my actual kitchen, where I kept my three turntables.

"We already shot you at the amphitheater," Charlie reminds me. "But I felt it was important to have a very intimate view of Grandmaster Flash. I knew you had three turntables in your kitchen. I just thought it was important to express that part of you. Originally the scene was going to be this hype scene in which Fred is talking to you about you bringing your group to the amphitheater, as if he went to your house to get you to come to the jam. But we didn't use any of Fred's dialog, we just used him sitting there watch you do your thing. It ended up being an incredible scene in the movie."

They were supposed to shoot me earlier that day at another location, basically a whole different scene. They ran out of shoot time with the cameras and had to return them. They took me home first. At the time I was staying at my girlfriend's apartment. And when we get there, the crew said, "Why can't we just shoot the scene right here?" I'm like, "Uh? What?"

Can you imagine coming home from a long shoot where your scene didn't get shot, and they take you home and come upstairs, and they point to an area in your girlfriend's place and say, "Let's do it there"?

I couldn't understand how this was going to work. I'm scratching my head. And since Freddy was supposed to be in the scene with me at the bandshell that didn't work out, they said "Put Freddy right by the couch, and we'll have him looking at Flash while he's on the turntables." I'm still scratching my head. "Okay." So they set up the cameras.

Freddy: "The scene we were lucky we got was the scene in the kitchen. One, we had to reshoot all the party scenes—all the scenes at the Dixie Club and the amphitheater—and the second problem was Flash and them had blown up so big at that time, they were on the road with this one, that one, and a third. They were opening for Rick James and Cameo, so we couldn't get them when we reached out. But I'd been to Flash's crib before, I'd visited him at the crib, so I knew he had the shit set up so perfect in his kitchen, so I told Charlie. So we were able to set the whole scene up with Flash, we called, and arranged it. That scene where he was just cutting in the crib on the counter in the kitchen. History."

And here's the funny part: The character Freddy ends up playing in the movie was originally supposed to be played by Phase II, but Freddy and Charlie couldn't talk him into being on-camera. That's why the character's name is Phade. It was a play on Phase's real graffiti name.

Charlie's biggest fear with *Wild Style* was that no one would see it as a movie and because of the way it was shot that people would feel like the film was a bunch of "stuff." It ended up being far from that. Freddy's whole mission with the film was to, in his words, "connect the dots of the different cultural elements" that represented hip-hop. The film put all the elements together in one ball. One of my friends, Rip, who is a hip-hop historian and member of the brand management agency the Spin Firm, asked Freddy once if he believed graffiti was the first element of the culture? Freddy didn't really have an answer. But he did say, *Wild Style* establishes, maybe for the first time, all of the elements on a table together. Saying that graf, breakin', DJing, rappin' all came from the same nucleus. All at the same time.

Fab was the one who connected us—all of us—to the Caucasians. That's what he did; that's why his role in this is so huge. He was the one who told them our story. He was the one who got us mainstream, which is where we wanted to be because we'd done everything else. We'd done the gymnasiums and the parks and the small clubs and the spots. The only place left for us to go was *out*. And Fred was the one for the culture to make that happen. On *SNL*, in Hollywood with *Wild Style*, later on with MTV, where he'd revolutionize television as the inaugural host of *Yo! MTV Raps*.

Then there's these, in 1983, a post–hardcore punk band from New York called the Beastie Boys decided to switch their sound from punk to rap after attending a party thrown by Fab 5 Freddy, and while hosting *Yo!* in 1988, Fab would be given a demo tape of a song called "Princess of the Posse," a tape he'd take to Tommy Boy Records, introducing them to an unknown rapper named Queen Latifah. And like they say, the rest is his-story.

* * *

Mel had a verse at the end of "Superrappin'" that kinda went over everyone's heads. It began at the 9:58 mark and ends at the 10:54 mark before he passes the mic to Rahiem. He'd recycle the verse in 1982 on a song he did with Sylvia and Sugar Hill's percussionist and poet, Ed Fletcher, whom we called Duke Bootee. They'd do a song and call it "The Message" and Mel would do the same thing on that song that he did on "Superrappin'"—save that verse for his last. But this time on "The Message" it hit—*and it hit hard.*

That "a child is born with no state of mind" lyric was the one that set Mel apart from everyone else. That was the verse that changed the culture. The intensity of the delivery, the difference in microphones used in the studio during the recording, the slowdown of BPMs from 115 to 101, the storytelling leading up to the final verse, all made the record do for rap music what Stevie Wonder's "Living for the City" did for soul music. "The Message" was our culture's version of that song.

But personally the song had the opposite impact. I constructed a group called Grandmaster Flash and the Furious Five. As a unit we were number one in our era and our category. When records are put together that destroy our formula—our invincible formula—it saddened me. Was "The Message" a hit record? Absolutely. Did it change our lives? Of course it did.

But the Grandmaster Flash and the Furious Five formula was not on that record. I think it would have been a bigger record had our formula as a group been on that record telling that story.

People get angry with me when I say this now, saying "Well Flash you had nothing to do with that record, your name was just on it." My response is this: If it wasn't for me, taking the bad deal I took with Sylvia Robinson at Sugar Hill Records—who by the way came out to Disco Fever every week to watch me, knowing what I do—there never would have been "The Message." My group, their label, my deal. The record was a gift and a curse. Huge song but because it wasn't a Grandmaster Flash and the Furious Five formula is probably one of the reasons why the group slipped away.

Here's the true story of how it really happened: Sylvia and her son would come into my residence multiple Tuesdays. Unlike Bobby Robinson of Enjoy Records, Sylvia's jewelry sparkled, the rocks on her hands were boulders. Sitting at the best seat in the house, sipping on Moët, the best champagne we knew at that time. She would enter my residence like an artist. She played the role like she was a Boss. With Hank and the gang in tow. To complete the appearance: The Rolls was parked downstairs directly in front for all to see. In hindsight, she was this "being" that I could not see through. And she wanted it that way.

A gentleman enters my DJ booth, he introduces himself as Joey Robinson. "JR, Sugar Hill Records." I do a double take. *It's that label with that song that's being heard everywhere. What does he want with me?* He goes on to say, "My mom wants a meet with you." He gives me his business card. It's legit. Later Rahiem and I take a bus out to Teaneck, New Jersey, where their offices are to see what she wants. Neither of us knowing a lot about the record business, what we do know is we are already signed to Enjoy Records. We tell Sylvia this, she says, "We can take care of that." *What does that mean?*

It made no sense to me for her and her son to come to my residence, the Disco Fever all the way in the Bronx on multiple Tuesdays, on a night I was calling "Terrible Tuesday." Sylvia and her son made it a point to be there every Tuesday, and have a seat waiting for her at the bar right below my DJ booth. At the end, it made no sense to me that she acquired the hottest group in the streets to end up with one hot song only to destroy Grandmaster Flash and the Furious Five.

In my opinion, she could have possibly been *the* label. To run postmodern hip-hop *before* the other labels that now run postmodern hip-hop. So the questions are: Did you really win, Sylvia Robinson? Were you the Queen?

"The Message" would be the final song to ever have Grandmaster Flash and the Furious Five on it with Sugar Hill. By that time things were bad; Sylvia had broken up our group, turned us on one another, didn't pay us what she owed, and made the MC the forefront. Eventually I was able to legally fight my way out of my deal with them. I went in wanting to separate from Sugar Hill Records. I originally tried to get the whole group to leave the label. Mel, Cowboy, and Mr. Ness stayed. Creole and Rahiem went with me. My lawyer fought hard, trying to get compensation, and that didn't work. While we were in court, I told him, "I can't lose this case." I couldn't go back to working for Sylvia after suing her.

I remember sitting there and the judge almost speaking in a language that I didn't understand, but it wasn't foreign. Mort looks at me while I'm sitting there and says, "What's the matter with you?"

I say, as I'm thinking I'm still locked in a contract with the label, "I can't go back there."

He said, "You're free! The judge just told you in that encrypted language that they speak that the marriage between Sylvia Robinson and Joseph Saddler, aka Grandmaster Flash, is now severed."

I ran outta that court room to the top of the steps outside and just got down on my knees and looked up at the clouds and said, "Thank God. I got away."

And that still didn't stop them from putting "Grandmaster & Melle Mel" on the twelve-inch "White Lines (Don't Do It)" a year later, in 1983.

The difference in hip-hop and other forms of music is, as future goddess MC Queen Latifah said, "We related to it on a real level, we could see exactly what you all were talking about in these records, and you all are talking about things that we experience, someone was talking about the things that was happening in our neighborhoods. Whereas everybody else was making love songs and talking about love and before that there were songs about revolution, hip-hop was talking about the effects for that revolution." Which is one of the best descriptions of what the "The Message" meant as I've ever heard.

The song changed everything for everybody. For us as a group and for Black music and Black people as a whole. Without it half of the people in this book would have never found hip-hop or become a part of hip-hop. As dark as the song was it became the culture's light.

* * *

In 1981 on radio station WHBI in New York a radio show called the *Rap Attack* came on. The host was a guy named John

Rivas, who went by the air name Mr. Magic. The show became popular before moving to WBLS in New York the next year, where it became the hottest show in the city, and the first actual commercial all-rap radio show.

That student at Adelphi University by the time 1982 arrived was no longer a kid. He'd launched a radio show at WBAU called *The Super Spectrum Mix Hour*, one of the few radio programs in the country and state of New York area dedicated to what had still yet to be labeled hip-hop. The DJ went by the name of Chuck D on air. Carlton Ridenhour was his government name. New York focused on making the musical and oral traditions of Blacks in America understood and accepted beyond just us.

"We followed the footsteps of Grandmaster Flash" is how Chuck D put it. His thing: "To flip radio into the one thing hip hop stood on."

To move radio in a way he believed radio should move. While at Adelphi he connected with Spectrum City DJ Hank Shocklee; partnered with William Drayton, aka Flavor Flav; became friends with André Brown, who would later be known as Doctor Dré, one half of Ed Lover and Doctor Dré who took over the hosting job of *YO! MTV Raps* in 1989 from Fab 5 Freddy; befriended Bill Stepney and future journalist Harry Allen.

Radio was a bigger thing to him. Through radio he and the team he was building could push rap music harder into competition with what was being done with rock and rock 'n' roll music.

Chuck said, "Nobody at that time was servicing hip-hop right (in radio)."

Even though in LA, KDAY 1580AM had hired a new music director, Greg Mack, who would convince the station to go to an all-hip-hop format in 1983, followed by a hip-hop radio show done by Sway and Tech out in the Bay Area called *The Wake Up Show* became nationally syndicated in the mid-'90s.

"We weren't being catered to by record pools, our charts always saturated with rap and hip-hop, we treated rap songs on air the same way a radio DJ in the '60s would treat a song by Gladys Knight and the Pips," was Chuck's description. "Not having the DJs talk about the songs was another slap at hip-hop."

They'd give full introductions and provide full information to songs. "That was Grandmaster Flash and the Furious Five with . . ." "That was Busy B's with another one, he got that 'Funky President' in there . . ." They'd treat rap records with the same respect as other radio stations treated other forms of music.

"We never got in the way of the record, we made you like the record even more," Chuck said during our discussion. "I always felt it was derogatory to throw songs at people. Like all of a sudden they're supposed to hear a song [for the first time or second time], catch it and then figure it out. No. We'd break it down for them. We had influences, like Mr. Magic, *Zulu Beats* on WHBI with Afrika Islam, Hank Love and DNA (on WNWK), the Awesome Two, the World's Famous Supreme Team, who were dynamic, then later what Chuck Chillout and Red Alert were doing on KISS-FM. So what we were doing was taking all of those elements so that we could shape our show and get into syndicated radio."

And the promo era that followed—along with the launch of Ralph McDaniels's WNYC's public access show *Video Music Box* becoming the visual version of it—where NYC radio DJs introduced their audiences to new groups and MCs by playing "promo songs" during their shows. Red Alert, Chuck Chillout, Mr. Magic, and later Funkmaster Flex became somewhat famous for playing promos. Ultramagnetic MCs, KRS-One, D-Nice, and Run-DMC all had promos before they became who they became—they made on-air promos a big deal. For many it was an artist's intro in either getting heard or getting a record deal.

By 1984 WBAU became a gateway for a new record label and artist management company. With Long Island being only five or six miles from Hollis, Queens, where the management company's main artist, Run-DMC, were from, it was easy for the artists to just stop by the radio station. WBAU became the number one station for talent of Rush Artist Management and on the new Def Jam Records label.

"So when the artists were on the road, they didn't take tapes from 'BLS or 'HBI, they took tapes from 'BAU because we played all their stuff—and we were happy to do it because that's what we were trying to build, that's [the sound] we were happy to give to radio," said Chuck.

One thing led to another and their concept of syndicating hip-hop radio or having an all-hip-hop radio station in New York was never going to happen. As Chuck said, "Because radio and all of that was really controlled by gangsters." Even as Bill Stepney had an "in" having a scholarship at WLIR in Long Island and had conversations with the heads of the station, saying, "If you guys at least give us a weekend, you'd be surprised."

Chuck: "But they were afraid that hip-hop and rap, this Black shit, was going to cannibalize their whole thing. And it would have. So they made the business decision, the safe, white business decision, 'Let's not let the spook through the door.'" But at the same time the white half of the co-ownership (Rick Rubin) at the Def Jam label Chuck and team had built a relationship with by promoting their artists, who saw something totally different.

The point is it isn't necessarily Chuck D's contribution to MCing or Public Enemy's advanced technique of sampling that is his and the group's legacy. It isn't how Chuck was the Smokey Robinson to Hank Shocklee's Berry Gordy. It's really Chuck and Hank's radio station inside the Roosevelt University and their impact on pioneering and shaping how radio stations across the country—then the world—accepted hip-hop as a respectable and generational art form and form of music that has to be acknowledged. Yes, years later his group Public Enemy would end up being one of the most important and innovative groups in music history, regardless of genre, but their intentional efforts to change Black radio and force it to accept hip-hop was maybe just as pivotal.

* * *

Lost in the uproar of "The Message"—and the power of "Planet Rock" to be honest—was the song we did called "Scorpio." The futuristic, electro feel of it was the exact opposite of what the message in "The Message" was in both words and sound, but it was also, without having the familiarity of Kraftwerk songs in it, did the same thing that "Planet Rock" was doing as far as showing a new techno side to what rap music could be. It was a sound that may have been having a greater impact in Los Angeles than any other place in the world.

I say that because on the opposite side of the country, Tracy Marrow was trapped. Wrestling with what the fuck to do with his life. At twenty-four years old he'd served time in the army, sold drugs and stolen cars, robbed banks, as he says, was "head of a crime spree," knew what he was doing wouldn't last, learned to spit game and "talk" on the mic. Tracy had to get the fuck out of real shit he was into. Hip-hop literally saved his life.

He's heard the tapes that were circulating from New York while he was in the service stationed in Hawaii. He had to be a part of it. "Hip-hop got in me," is how he likes to say it. Once discharged and returned home to LA, he searched for entry points. But LA's foundation wasn't like ours in New York. They moved differently and moved to a different beat. We were breakdancing, they were pop locking. Our 101 to 110 BPMs was our preferred pace, 120 to 130 BPM was their preference. Our James Brown to their Parliament-Funkadelic. Different vibes.

"The closest thing you can connect to what they were doing in New York to what was happening in LA was *Soul Train*," Tracy Marrow says. "The dancers on *Soul Train*, the funk style. We were dancing off music from the Bar-Kays, the Gap Band, groups of that nature. Parliament was very, very big in California. The Funk Fest we had at the LA Coliseum, was huge. That was the music prior to anything coming from New York. Then for us it merged into an electro/techno sound, based off the Kraftwerk/'Planet Rock' rhythm and beats. And that was our transition."

But somehow the tapes and the style of the music on those tapes, the rawness, all of that, wouldn't leave him. "LA cats wanted to be involved in hip-hop badly," he admits. "Because what NY created was so dope, so magnetic that we wanted to be involved."

The part he wanted to be a part of was not what the rest of LA was into. He speaks of a moment that was a part of LA history, a moment when at one of Uncle Jam's Army's jams, the

DJ Egyptian Lover, held the records in the air and announced on the mic, "Uncle Jam's is now going live!" But the music didn't stop. He had a TR-808 drum machine. And the actual drum machine was playing instead of the records. Egypt got the drum machine from a guy from New York, his name Afrika Islam. Islam put Tracy in the game.

He became good enough on the mic that Uncle Jam's Army, LA's legendary and premiere party throwers, only allowed him to rap during their jams. Partially because he was trying to rap like New York rappers. He wasn't trying to rap heavily over the techno beats. He was on that "boom bap." And he came to the mic with a lot of street credibility. His résumé in LA was official. So when he stepped on the stage the people were like, "That's Ice." He had what KRS-One would later coin "political clout." He stood in front of Crips, some Bloods. They knew him. His clout allowed them to say, "We'll listen to what Ice gotta say. We believe him."

He joined a DJ crew called the NYC Spin Masters. Honduran cats from Brooklyn making a name for themselves in LA. Scratchin' songs and spinnin' breakbeats. Everything Ice was looking for. They put his name on a flyer.

Then after so much time trying to become one with what was happening in New York, like so many others at the time and in the game, Ice had a Russell Simmons moment. At a place in LA called Casa Camino Royale, where he was performing the early records he'd cut trying "to separate myself from my other life." He didn't know you could talk about that life and be an entertainer, even a rapper. They called him on stage, he was rocking, to the detail, a Fila track suit, his perm was pressed, Kangol, and white K-Swiss sneakers. That night on stage he did him. Russell walks up to him and simply says: "That's you! You are not Grandmaster Flash. Dress like an LA playa. This is you, Ice. Be you! Stop being New York. Be you. Talk about your shit! Stop playing a NY rapper, be LA!" And the Ice-T the world got to know was born.

"When I heard Schoolly D's 'PSK' and I did the research and found out he was talking about 'Park Side Killers,' he was talking about *that* life, that's when I was like, 'I'ma talk about who the fuck I am and what I'm coming from.' That's when '6 in the Mornin'' happened."

That was the birth of what they co-opted into calling it gangsta rap. Somebody talking about their life, not trying to act like they were in the entertainment business, someone giving it to them raw.

"I compared it to punk rock," he'd explain to me, reminding me of the exact same feeling Fab 5 Freddy had years before. "Because the punk rock movement was just raw white boys just saying, 'Fuck it! This is who I am. Fuck you!' So I did that with hip-hop. I'm like, 'I'm finna talk like we talk in the streets. I'ma talk about *my* life. The positive and negative shit about it."

Basically his art was his autobiography and some parts of the lives of everyone he knew.

Ice-T said: "The thing of it is when you're in the streets you really thought that your crew was the only crew doing what you do, you don't really know that this is a national thing. That there's cats moving the same way in Detroit, in Chicago, in Miami. But when that hit me, I was like, 'Oh shit! So all I gotta do is say the normal shit I do?' I realized I ain't gotta be nobody else, just be fucking Ice and tell the fuckin' truth. And break it down. I think that's what my key became. I can break shit down so street niggas understand; I can break it down so the white people understand how we see things. But at the same time talk in the lingo of the hustlers so that only certain cats would understand it. That's part of the coolness of music to me, is to talk authentically. Not to break everything down so far that everybody gets it. It has to be encrypted to some degree because the streets are encrypted. I had that ability to do that. And when I found out that my brand was just being honest, the sky opened up for me."

An empire followed. Movies: *Colors*, *New Jack City*. Television: *Law and Order*. Music Corporation: Rhyme Syndicate. Rock Band: Body Count. Governmental hate: "Cop Killer." All fitting the foundation of Ice presenting his version of "keeping it real" in relation to his life.

Ice-T: "In music I call it 'faction.' I created a word for it. It is factual occurrences put into a fictional story. So in other words, you can tell me, 'On the way home the cops jacked us, they pulled us over, they hit my back seat with a box cutter. Opened it up.' Now that really happened, right? To you because you told me that. In an Ice-T song that can happen to me. I'm taking a factual thing, an actual event and putting it into a record. So everything I'm saying is true because it really happened. It's based on what's real."

And he was the one who introduced LA realness to all of us, putting their life on the forefront, no longer on the back burner. Opening the eyes of many to what was going on, opening the door for many in LA to follow.

He breaks it down, "I've been able to live doing the things I like. Look, Stephen King likes writing horror movies. He's made a career writing horror movies and books. I've made a career just saying what I've seen in the streets and reflecting on it in different ways. I've made a career talking my shit."

* * *

Russell Simmons pulled up behind me as I was going to a party, and he opened the trunk of his car. This was sometime in 1984. I can't remember the exact month. He had just started this record label. He said to me, "Flash, I need you to try out this record. It's a new artist that I have. His name is LL Cool J, the song is called 'I Need a Beat.'"

While I listened to it I was like, "This muthafucka is really mad. He's pissed off." You had to stop and listen to *the level* of what he was saying and to listen to his ability to rap. After I listened, I told Russell: "Whoever this little kid is screaming like, that is going to be a star because he's mad as a muthafucka, and he's demanding to be heard."

Only to realize the kid wasn't mad or angry, he was hungry.

The prodigy, James Todd Smith, the one who hid under the stage at the (alleged) shootout at the Armory, would be the one who turned out to be LL Cool J and would be the first artist—along with a group called the Beastie Boys—to have a record released with a catalog number on it from Russell and Rick Rubin's independent record label Def Jam Recordings, a label that started in an NYU dorm room by Rubin while he was a student. The record label that ended up becoming what Sugar Hill Records could have been if Sylvia just treated her artists right.

But Russell and Rick knew what they were doing and knew what they had in LL—the type of artist you could build a whole label around. Like Berry Gordy did with Stevie Wonder and Marvin Gaye. One who allowed everything else to fall into place.

He was sarcastic and nasty (in a good way) and at the same time so fuckin' fly about how he went about delivering his rhymes; it separated him from almost all other rappers. Women gravitated to his songs. A shy kid who wouldn't say anything to girls at the parties but saved everything he wanted to say for when he went into the studio and said, "here it is," to the world. He was his own Cyrano de Bergerac. But inside of him was the same person who'd later deliver the song "To Da Break of Dawn."

It was at eleven years old when he began *leaning into* rapping, wanting to be a DJ with that equipment his grandfather got him was too difficult for him to master. So he started writing.

"I used to literally have garbage bags of notebooks of rhymes," LL told me during our sit down. "I had so many lyrics my papers were on an ironing board, and I'd iron them. I'd have so much shit written and thrown all over the place I had to literally iron my lyrics to keep them."

And then he fell in love. "Then one day, at fourteen [years old], I got inspired. More than I already was. There was this kid in school, little kid with a knapsack, when I was in junior high walking down the hall, the hall was dark even though it was during the day, all of the classroom doors were closed and the kid was signing [the 'This DJ . . .' part of] Jimmy Spicer's song. And I was just walking behind him. Like in a trance, like in slow motion. You remember that Bruce Lee shit from *Fist of Fury* when he does the arm movements and it looks like he has five arms moving at once? Like he's moving so fast that it's slow? I was looking at the kid, and I was getting hypnotized. I said, 'That's what I want to do right there.' Because it made me feel something. And that was when I started working on [my] demos."

Even within the hunger and intensity LL (along with Jay-Z later and at a slower pace) put out in his records, from the perspective of someone who is a DJ, especially in the era when the clubs were strong, in that 96 to 110 beats-per-minute space he was the king. There was no other rapper alive in the beats-per-minute space who could do what he did. Because scientifically when you dance, one foot goes up while the other goes down but it's the lyrics as they sit on top of that beat that makes the marriage very, very important. If they don't match up, the rhythm is lost. The marriage is over. They must be in constant, solid sync. And the songs had to be fun to play in that 96 to 110 BPM range. When we DJs wanted to test a record—it was called the sandwich technique—we'd put on an LL song before and an LL song on after the record we were testing. Because just in case the test record misses and people aren't feeling it, we gotta get the people back on the dance floor. An LL song never failed, he held people on the dance floor; that's what made his songs so powerful.

My belief is that to be able to create something that's a version of something people will love, you have to go through the journey of meticulously rehearsing it, practicing it, timing it, testing it, failing, going back, failing again, trying again and again. That's the one thing I was very hard on "the Five" about and very hard on myself about.

When I came up with the timing thing I stressed to them, "You all *have to* fit the lyric in-between the beat!"

Their words had to mechanically slide right in-between. When people saw and heard us, they were seeing and hearing six people, but they were really only hearing and seeing one person, one sound. And that doesn't happen overnight. The one thing LL always understood was how the rhymes had to meticulously fit into the beat. He recognized the difference between a DJ/producer/conductor and someone who just presses play on a CD to make sound. He recognized the difference between someone who could take average, recognizable music and turn it into something that moves the world and someone who couldn't. He understood the power of people who had the ability to open the aperture, opening the scope of the music, in not being limited or so conservative artistically that the sound being created doesn't have a chance to flourish.

And these are things he would tell you he knew at sixteen years old, things he'd carry with him into his twenties and thirties.

Things which according to him pissed a few people off. One in particular.

UTFO, a rap group out of Brooklyn, paired with a band from Brooklyn called Full Force and produced a song based on a story about an unknown, fictional girl named Roxanne. It was a B-side song to a song called "Hanging Out." Roxanne was so nice in how she played the guys in the song they named her twice calling the song "Roxanne, Roxanne." It became a hit. Radio, streets, clubs, everywhere. WBLS's Mr. Magic's then DJ, another guy from Queen's, Marlon Williams, known as DJ Marley Marl, took a page from the old school book of the soul music/doo-wop era of the late-'50s and repeated what Smokey Robinson and the Matadors' "Got a Job" did with their answer to the Silhouette's song "Get a Job" by responding to UTFO's song with a fourteen-year-old rapper they had on-deck named Lolita Shanté (Gooden) to play the role of Roxanne on a record that Marley would produce.

They'd call the song "Roxanne's Revenge." With Shanté, in full character, taking personal disdain to how she—as Roxanne—was mischaracterized by every member of UTFO in "Roxanne, Roxanne." From this a culture-inside-the-culture was born. And the tentacles from this battle would end up being endless. It would also be something that helped shape LL's career. As LL became Kool Moe Dee's target.

L's answering Moe Dee's "How Ya Like Me Now?" with

"Jack the Ripper" elevated the generation's version of the response record. It literally in 1987 and 1988 created a genre of battle rapping on records that had always been done in the parks and clubs and shows long before those two set the new standard. Their back-and-forth was an energy no one had ever felt or really heard verbally in any genre of music before. It was almost like they gave the culture another dimension. While they didn't create the subculture of battle rap or "diss records" LL and Kool Moe proved more than any two MCs that rap was a verbal combat sport.

CHAPTER 11

"Scratch Dance" is a song out of Los Angeles in 1983 on Carbon Copy Records that is basically the West Coast version of "Wheels of Steel." At the helm, on the turntables, an LA native named Chris Taylor, the engineer Victor Flores. Both were credited as the artists on the record. While I used "Good Times" by Chic and "Rapture" by Blondie and "Another One Bites the Dust" by Queen on "Adventures . . .," their record went further using everything from "Raid" by Lakeside to Whodini's "The Haunted House of Rock" to "Buffalo Gals" by Malcolm McLaren to Herbie Hancock's "Rockit" to obscure songs like Yazoo's "Situation," "When Boys Talk" by Indeep, and "I.O.U." by Freeez. The song made noise out West.

See Taylor, who'd been given the name "The Glove," was in LA very much like me in New York, just about eight to ten years after. He was tearing up his family's stereo equipment, trying to figure out how it all worked. Same hell to pay for messing with the records. Went to Radio Shack just like me to buy things that he thought he needed to build his system and he kept messing with the records. Putting his hands on the records. Breaking the rules. Creating sounds. Quick mixing.

But no one, at least no one he knows of, was "that type of" DJ in LA at the time.

He sang in the church, played organ in the church, learned the keyboard from the great Toussaint McCall, grew to be six feet, six inches, played basketball, was in honors classes at Inglewood High School, went to Cal State Northridge, studied to be an aeronautical engineer, quit school, didn't know what direction to go in life, so one day he just asked God a simple question: "What can I do that I can be the best at?" God's answer: "DJ." So he went through the rest of his life with the producer mentality of: man versus machine.

"And I'm going to win that battle every time," Chris "The Glove" Taylor says as we reflected on his life. "Because machines were meant to serve. We created them to serve. Period."

He asks me: "Hey Flash, you ever see those movies where they take the best fighter in the village up the mountaintop, and there's a dude at the top with a long-ass gray beard who kicks his ass for three weeks? That's us. All these DJs think they're bad and we're like, 'Come here, man. You're fast, huh?' Then we show them and they ask: 'How are you eighty [years old] and so fast?' And we're like, 'Bro, it's not age it's a state of mind.'"

His life would unfold like the Forrest Gump of the earliest part of hip-hop culture in LA. Meeting Egyptian Lover in the backyard of the house of the guy who is the backbone of Uncle Jam's Army, ends up DJing at Radio, at the time the number one club in LA where he's DJing. One time a guy gets on the microphone to tell people to move their cars and shit, that guy happened to be a young Ice-T. Egyptian Lover then took him to the Playpen, Uncle Jam's Army's eighteen-and-over nightclub on Crenshaw, where while spinning there he meets two members of KDAY's Mixmasters. He becomes a member of the

Mixmasters, he's in Uncle Jam's Army, still spinning at Radio when a write-up of the club in *The Los Angeles Times* Calendar section led to movie producers reading the write-up and deciding to do a movie about the club. That movie was called *Breakin'*.

He'd become a reporter for *Billboard*. Would be the DJ in Chaka Khan's "I Feel for You" video. Cross paths, befriend, and work with another pioneering DJ in LA named Andre Young. Was thought of by some as the "Grandmaster Flash of the West Coast." Bookending his contributions to being artist, composer, and producer all in one on the *Breakin'* soundtrack and the master of sound, mixing, and drum programming and producing on *The Chronic*. Was the second producer signed to Death Row Records. In the end, he produced songs for everyone from Ice-T to Snoop Dogg. And ain't nothing more LA than that.

Except in Compton, on Van Wick Street, there was an adolescent being bused to school but saw "everything under the sun" because his one brother and two sisters were eight, nine, and ten years older than him. He was the baby boy but he grew up fast. Like cat years fast, as he watched the scene unfold on the streets around him. Water fights, baseball in the streets, basketball, football, go-carts, bikes, ramps, jumping off house roofs, flipping on mattresses, everything in-between. Dice, cards, dominoes. Drug dealing, gang banging, set claiming, low riding. Young fella had a choice to make as he got older. He'd gone "left for a couple of seconds," came back to his senses, "didn't want to hurt anybody for no reason," was "always strong enough to stand up to peer pressure" because he was "always down to say 'no' to anyone." And because of his father, his brother, and older sisters, he'd "rather thump in the streets than [against them] at the house." Where he knew he'd lose.

Gangs were an option. Selling dope another option. But music grabbed him early. At fourteen he started rapping. "It was 1983 and I was at that age: You gonna be a sports guy, you gonna be a banger, you gonna sell dope or what else? And music came to pull me away from all those other temptations. Thank God," is his memory of how this thing we created probably saved his life.

"Let's go back to the records," Ice Cube says to me about that time of his life. "'The Message' had a profound impact on me, but all of those records were big in our neighborhoods. Huge. Those records showed us, in LA, what professional rap looked and sounded like. We had tapes and stuff off the streets but Kurtis Blow, Grandmaster Flash and the Furious Five, Run DMC, to some degree the Sugarhill Gang. Just-Ice. His song 'Latoya.' Run and DMC's 'It's Like That' and 'Hard Times.' Those were the records that were grabbing our neighborhoods because they captured the same spirit as the funk of 'Flashlight' and 'Knee Deep' to us. We looked up to all the groups and songs coming from New York that was making a lot of noise. But 'The Message' was the one that caused a profound change and it affected us the most."

Because "The Message" allowed Cube and the crew he'd end up assembling, N.W.A, with the inspiration and framework to paint a picture of their lives in Los Angeles, on the West Coast, the same way Mel and Duke Bootee did with life in New York at that time. It allowed them, as I told Cube, to "say shit on the mic that everyone in the game was thinking about saying, but you guys said it out loud."

His response was, "We broke it on down to ourselves and said, 'We're never going to be as famous as the New York cats so let's just rap about what's going on in the neighborhood and at least we'll be neighborhood stars and the people in LA are gonna love us if we talk about what's going on around here.'"

And he was the one who had the mind and the pen to tell those stories. The DJ of the group—well one of them—named Dre convinced Cube to write in that truth storytelling style. They'd call it street knowledge. But Cube never thought they could make a record out of it. Until another cat from around their way bought one of Dre's mixtapes with Cube spittin' street knowledge on it, rappin' on the street about the streets. The guy who brought the tape, name was Eric, knew Dre from high school. They used to DJ together. He listened to what Cube and Dre were doing and told them, "What you all are doing on those tapes, you all should make records out of that."

Eric Wright had his own, small, local, independent record label called Ruthless. He went by the name Eazy. Last letter "E." He convinced Cube and Dre to come his way to do business. Spit rhymes and make music that would be true to the label's name. "Do that hard shit on Ruthless," as Cube put it. But first Eazy and his partner Jerry Heller put out a record on their label by a girl rap group J. J. Fad titled "Supersonic." Their LA-version of Egyptian Lover-meets-Salt-N-Pepa. Forcing Cube to step to Eazy.

"I said, 'Ruthless? I thought we were hardcore?' You gotta record that's going pop right now."

Eazy said, "When you gotta hit you gotta go for it."

So I said, "Okay, let's put us together some hits."

There were lanes in rap music and everyone pretty much stayed in their lane. Your sound and rapping style defined your lane. And there was no "biting" allowed. You could not come into the game sounding like anyone else. That was career suicide. For N.W.A, the way they saw it, in 1987 when the group had fully formed, all the lanes were damn-near filled so there wasn't much room for them to do anything else but what they did. They figured their "underground" style of storytelling was where they were going to live. They figured with their first record they finally had their own little lane on the West Coast and that was going to be it.

"Back then there were records out, comedy records, where there was a lot of cursing and stuff," Cube admitted. "Blowfly, Richard Pryor, Eddie Murphy, even singers like Millie Jackson. They were big in the '80s. And you'd find their records in the blue section of the record store. That's where they kept those types of albums. And we thought that was where our N.W.A record was going to be. Next to Millie Jackson. We never knew our album was ever going to be in the regular section of a record store."

But *Straight Outta Compton* was not only selling millions of records, making Ice Cube, Dr. Dre, and Eazy-E household names across the country, being one of the first records the government decided to put a parental advisory sticker on, laying the groundwork for a whole new sound and category of music—putting an entire coast of the United States on the hip-hop map.

As Cube put it, "The warning sticker we guessed was the compromise the record industry made to at least give parents a warning that, 'Yeah, this record could be hot!'"

* * *

In the November 1985 issue of *Spin*, in a section called "Singles: When Stupid Music Happens to Smart People: The Sounds of Nonsense," John Leland wrote about the song, "The Show." "In the rap battle to make the stoopidest record, Doug E. Fresh is out front. . . . And Slick Rick is the least fly MC this side of the Concept."

I'll let Doug E. Fresh take it from here: "I had an idea that came to me in a dream, it was this idea called 'The Show.' I jumped out of bed and called (Chill) Will and Barry (B.) my DJs and told them about the dream, my idea. I said, 'Barry, I want you to get the Cold Crush record where they go "Oh my God" and cut that part. Will, I want you to take Flash and them's record where it goes "Is it real? Is it real?" and cut that part. I want these two things cut at the same time.' So then I went to Rick (MC Ricky D/the future Slick Rick), told him the idea. He said, 'Can I be honest with you?' I said, 'yeah.' He said, 'I think that idea is so wack.' I said, 'Aight, I got it.' I still thought it was a great idea. So Greg G from the Disco Four used to throw parties at Broadway International, he had me perform there and he owed me some money. When I went to him for the money he said he didn't have it but told me he'd lent Teddy Riley his drum machine and keyboard. Now Teddy, I used to teach about hip-hop because he came from the church. He was more melody driven; I was more beat driven. I would show him rhymes that I had, I would write rhymes for him. I would show him how to make a beat. Greg called him and told him, 'Dougie needs to come over there, he needs to make a beat.' So I go to Teddy's house, Teddy turns the drum machine on. I learned about this thing on the drum called 'swing.' And 'swing' makes the beat move differently. Now I have no technical skill of learning drum machines, I have the skill of *I know what I'm going to do*, when you cut it on. He turned it on, I said, 'No, faster. Right there.' Then I played the beat I had in my head to 'The Show.' This is it. Then I hit the swing, and it changed the way the beat was moving. Teddy and I just stood there, for like a half an hour, just listening to the beat, and he said, 'I've never heard a beat like that.' Me neither. 'This is unbelievable. This beat is crazy. This beat is like . . . hypnotic.' Then I asked him to hit a button on the keyboards to make the 'Uan, uan, uan, uan' sounds. And at the beginning of the song I put the horns sound I heard for the movie *The Wiz*. Then I said I want to do a conversation rhyme instead of doing just one whole rhyme. Like me having a conversation. 'Ayo, Doug?' 'What?' 'Put your Bally's on.' 'I was about to, but I need a shoehorn.' I wanted a different style, like we're talking but we're rhyming. Nobody was doing that. So when I put these things together, and I got Rick to come in there, I got Chill Will in the booth and had him get on the mic and say, 'Ladies and gentlemen, the most exciting . . .' he didn't even like his voice, but his voice fit like a glove, and I was working on the drum roll and Teddy changed it, like doubled a part of it up to make it better and I was like 'That's it! That's it right there.' It all came together."

Doug E. Fresh continued, "But the real story is before this I had been doing shows, local shows, because my name was getting out there. I was walking the walk. I'd do a show for $1,000 here, $900 here, $1,500 there, and I took the money and started stacking it. Same as I did when I was nine years old bagging groceries at the supermarket. I'd gotten to up to around $10,000. So when it came time to go into the studio to record 'The Show,' Teddy's mother didn't let him come and his boy had already told him, 'Yo, that idea from Dougie ain't gonna work.' So my manager, who was a music teacher at Truman High School, since Teddy couldn't come, played the music based on what we created on the demo tape we did at Teddy's crib. So I had to get on the phone with Teddy, while we're in the studio, to tell the music teacher the notes to hit so that it can accurately be what we wanted. Now remember Flash, I took my $10,000. See with you all, when you all went to the studio Sylvia Robinson paid for it, Bobby Robinson paid for it, and I knew because I watched how they did you all, I said, 'No, I'm going to pay for it because they're going to try and tell me how to make it and I can't listen to them right now.' *They don't know what something is telling me to do*. And I'm going to be arguing with them all day. I'm just going to spend my $10,000, and I'm going to make this happen. So I went down to Daily Planet Studio on 30th Street to record. It came down to the last hour. And we finished the song. I took all the money that I had, no one gave me anything, I put it all on the line, and I rolled the dice. So now, I'm the first guy in hip-hop to own my own masters."

And the B-Side: "The school teacher from Truman, since he was acting as my manager asked me, 'Hey what's that thing all the kids be talking about at school that you and Rick doing? This 'la di da' thing?' I said, 'Oh, you mean 'la di da di.' He said, 'Yeah, let's do that.'

"We did that song in the studio in five minutes, one take. Because Rick and I were doing it all the time. See, I was the guy walking down the street as a kid doing the beatbox for the rapper, for the MC, because I could MC and beatbox, I served two purposes. I had an extra dynamic to my skills than he did. He wanted to rap and I wanted him to rap well and I knew how to make the beat so that his rap would be good. So when Rick would say something, I'd drop the beat out on the punchline—then bring it back in. You know Flash, like you did. Like I've seen you do with an MC when you DJ. You're the inspiration. They can't understand the depth of what you did Flash in setting all of that up from the beginning. They don't understand if the beat to that rhyme is not dropped out at the exact right time they're not going to get the full accent and total impact of that rhyme. And that's what I did in the studio with Rick on the song."

At that time, not many did understand the dynamic between the beat and the rhyme, the DJ and the rapper, the sound and the voice, and how for it to really work the depth of everything Doug said I'd set up had to be in harmony. Dougie got it. He understood.

"The other thing I did on 'La Di Da Di'—and I'm only telling you this Flash because you are a scientist, so I know you appreciate this—the first beat was my version of 'Impeach the President.' Then I switched it and did my version of 'Action.' 'It's all because of you . . .' Then I switched it to doing my version of Davy DMX's 'One for the Treble.' Then I switched the beat again and came back to 'Impeach the President.' That was the whole science of 'La Di Da Di' and the simplicity of it.

"When I went in there and spent my money—twelve grand in total because I had to borrow two grand from my manager and had to give him that two back after I did my next show—and both songs were done, I went and found a distributor. Once I found a distributor, I made a deal with them. And here's the twist of the whole story, the crazy part: I always say I can never thank the Creator enough for making a dream, an idea of mine turn into a reality. The name of the label 'La Di Da Di' and 'The Show' came out on is Reality Records."

Doug is more than just two songs, he's probably more of a walking spirit than he is one of the most talented people to come through this culture. He's the one who brought God into mainstream hip-hop. He is a student; he is a servant. Like me, we both believe musically what we do is to serve and we're put on this earth to share. He believes in the balance between mathematics, science, and spirituality—in life and music—and how they can "tri-exist." More than anything he believes in the "It" theory: "If we allow 'it' to do what 'it' does, 'it' will take care of 'itself.'" And "it" can represent both anything and everything.

But "The Show" and "La Di Da Di" are more than just two songs. They were like standalone movements all into themselves. Sounding unlike anything else in hip-hop in 1985; sounding nothing like anything else in music. Evidenced by Ghostface's "Beat Box" "tribute" forty years later. And the stories behind them are more than just the stories of what could easily be the single greatest A-side/B-side twelve-inch in the history of the culture. They're the stories of the culture as a whole and how one man cultivated his gifts and bet on himself and what the results of that belief-in-self turned into. Not too different than just about everyone who's had a hand in bringing life to and shaping this culture has done. Doug just followed the path that we laid down and created his own path. The definition of entrepreneurship, the definition of empowerment, the definition of this culture.

The beatbox thing with Doug E. has always been a thing. While I used the beatbox often as an additional sound source during our park jams, someone actually recorded a jam from the Bronx River Community Center in 1979 and released it as "Flash to the Beat (Live)"—not the version that was put on Sugar Hill—which became an underground tape and was really the first time people outside of seeing us live had heard what a beatbox actually did. And this is before Bam and Arthur Baker did "Planet Rock"; this is before Marvin Gaye used it on "Sexual Healing."

The TR-808 is a drum machine (or a rhythm device) that was built originally to replace the drummer in bands or help musicians compose music from another instrument besides piano, keyboards, or guitar. I have a little bit of a different opinion. They say it was not designed to replace the DJ, but that's what it helped do. More respectfully it changed the role of the DJ in hip-hop. Pushed us from the back of the stage to almost off the stage. Turned all of us into producers first, DJs second, third, and fourth.

It was the drum machine the company Roland built to replace or as their upgrade to the CR-78, their first drum machine created in 1978. And what made the 808 so popular and the thing in hip-hop was the analog synthesis they used in the machine to recreate sound. It gave us the ability to make the crazy beats and sounds going on in our heads that we wanted to use to produce songs come to life. It had the ability to play thirty-two different percussion rhythms and add different sounds as well as putting accents on those sounds. Damn near every concept and idea I had in building the Quik Mix Theory using Technics 1200 turntables, the 808 was programmed to do with the "Rhythm Composer" built into the machine.

Bam used it for "Planet Rock," Rick Rubin used it on T La Rock's "It's Yours," in the very beginning, Arabian Prince on J. J. Fad's "Supersonic," Man Parrish on "Hip Hop, Be Bop (Don't Stop)" and "Boogie Down (Bronx)," Newcleus on "Jam on It." But after that there weren't too many hip-hop songs made without the 808 being somehow a part of rap songs' structures. From Egyptian Lover's "Egypt, Egypt" in 1984 to "Throw the D" by the 2 Live Crew and Dynamix II's "Purple Beats" down in Miami to Missy Elliott's "Lose Control" and Outkast's "The Way You Move," T.I.'s *Trap Muzik*, and Migos' "Bad and Boujee" to Kanye West's 2008 revolutionary *808s & Heartbreak.*

For Doug and me, it was something I introduced to the culture, something copied from, and something he literally humanized. "Everybody knew Flash was on the beatbox," Doug E. references the origin. "Anybody who was really doing this came after you. There was nobody else doing it. Master Don started with the beatbox *after* you! Master Don was on the funk box, the funk box is him on the 808. Before that he was playing on another beatbox but the thought of using the beatbox originated with you. Nobody had heard it before you."

For me the beatbox was a secret weapon for us; me and the Furious. I could say the same for Doug E. that his ability to beatbox—on top of rhyming—was his secret weapon. It made him unique to every other MC out there. He described it as being "one of one." Then he turned around and referred to me as "*the* one."

"I'm a one of one. No matter how many people tell the story and want to confuse the story and twist it up, you know you're the One," is how he put it. Telling me that it was his DJ Barry B who told him when he first heard Doug do with his mouth what I was doing with a machine, "You should call that 'The Human Beatbox.'" And Doug E. simply took it from there.

* * *

Not to be overlooked is near the end of 1984, October to be exact, Def Jam signed a distribution deal with Columbia/CBS Records. No longer independent. Again, I'll put it this way: If Sylvia had treated us right—or hell, just not sent LL Cool J a rejection letter—there probably never would have been a Def Jam.

Chapter 12

It seemed between 1985 and 1988 the DJ was slowly morphing into a producer. Not so much scratching on records but instead more the stacking of songs to make records. James Brown's "Funky President (People It's Bad)" and "The Funky Drummer," the six-second drum break of The Winstons' "Amen, Brother," "The Grunt" and "Blow Your Head" or anything else by The J.B.'s, all became the go-to for every producer building records off the drums and drum breaks of preexisting songs. If the DJ thing was one kind of explosion, then the producer thing was another kind of explosion. And a lot of that explosion happened because of the new birth and use of a piece of equipment that was programmed to do the exact concept I'd started with the Quik Mix Theory and extending drum breaks years ago.

It's believed the first modern day sample used in a song happened in 1971. It's either a song by a South African musician named John Kongos, who apparently used a sample of a recorded African drumming track, or one by a French composer named Michel Bernholc on a song called "Burundi Black" where he added keyboards and guitars on top of looping the drumming pattern of twenty-five drummers from the Ingoma Tribe to create the rhythm and make the song. No one knows which came first, like the chicken or the egg, or "Rapper's Delight" and "King Tim III." It's an ongoing argument.

I struggle with this sampling thing. Is it an advancement or is it something that's going to push me further out? But as Ice Cube said, with sampling you can "reinvent greatness into something new." But in the world of hip-hop, *I am the original human sampler*. What I did on the turntables emulated a seamless loop, essentially what became modern-day sampling.

Another type of sampling is when the producer samples the parts, e.g., just the bass drum or a snare, the hi-hat, a groove. So there are producers who do loop sampling and those who do parts sampling. For me, those are the two different types of sampling.

A short list of the producers whose works fall under these categories would be: Parts: Pete Rock, Easy Mo Bee, Just Blaze. Loop: Marley Marl, Hurby Luv Bug, J Dilla.

Then there is the third type: those producers who've mastered doing both. Examples: Dr. Dre, DJ Premier, Q-Tip, D-Dot, Pharrell Williams, Timbaland, The Bomb Squad, RZA, DJ Quik, Battlecat, DJ Toomp, Organized Noize, Jermaine Dupri.

When you break it down, in my opinion, with looping being actually taking an existing piece of a composition with a rapper speaking on it, it should start with Cowboy and me. If all of the producers are a part of the postmodern era of sampling, I'm premodern. Without me breaking down breaks and repeating small pieces of records, there would have been no template for looping or any other method of building songs of parts of already popular and recorded songs.

Then there are the, what I call, "unsung" producers: Larry Smith, Nile Rodgers, Rick Rubin, Prince, Jimmy Jam and Terry

Lewis, Teddy Riley, Large Professor, Hit-Boy, DJ Kay Gee. They too are like heroes to me.

Whether it was us on turntables extending breakbeats in the beginning or the new DJs using drum and sampling machines to make records, it all came back to James Brown. More specifically, his drummer Clyde Stubblefield. Who really is the blueprint. But James Brown had kinetic energy. Hank Shocklee called it a vibration whenever he talked about Mr. Brown's creation of sound and music. He'd hear James Brown's live Apollo Theater record "Revolution of the Mind" and never be the same. He'd carry that sound and image on the cover with him for decades and use them both to shape his contribution and homage to Black music. Go look at the cover and then listen (again) to Public Enemy's "It Takes a Nation of Millions to Hold Us Back" and you will see and hear the connection.

"The reason I'll always say James Brown is pivotal is because he took the vibration, he took the heat musically, and turned it up to eleven," is Hank's belief. "Everybody else back then was at a seven or an eight, and sometimes they'd hit a nine, and once in a while on very few occasions someone would hit a ten. But James took it to an eleven."

And it's that "eleven" energy on which Hank and I vibe. Everything amplified. The passion of both of our connections through music come through during our entire conversation. But more so do our commonalities and sensibilities. He cuts me off making a point, I cut him off making a point. Both of us making the same points. It's kinetic. It's like two musical savants sitting alone at a Black family barbecue at a picnic table agreeing over who invented funk music but debating over who used James Brown's music best in a sample.

The rare beauty of talking over each other, at each other, and to each other all at the same time. There's less than a handful of people I've met in life I've shared moments with like that. Hank's one. Vibe is short for vibration, right?

To understand how James Brown did what he did, both sonically and frequency-wise, you have to first understand the fact that he not only had the greatest band in the world, but he was the one out front talking about Black greatness and how the political scene was fucked up for Black people. The baddest band playing the baddest grooves with the baddest sound saying the most important things about Black life. Always Black empowerment.

And on top of that, as Hank would attest, "James Brown was the only one who let the music breathe. He never got in the way of the music. He would let his records breathe. And he'd do one thing that I always wanted to hear every time I'd buy a James Brown record: I wanted to hear him scream. Because the scream represented the frequency of him going up! See, James Brown never just screamed to just be screaming, he'd scream when the groove was at the apex. Letting you know that we're at the height, at the zenith. When he went to the scream the band would take everything up a notch. That high point is what caught my attention. It's the one thing I wanted to dive into. Because my thing was, 'Why can't this high point be in the beginning of the song too?'"

Very much the same beef I've always had about why can't the drum break, especially if it's the part of songs people like the best, be in the front? Or be more of a song instead of the singing and orchestration? All the records Hank would listen to that led him to become cofounder of the Bomb Squad, arguably one of the most influential production teams of this generation, if not in music history, would be records that had deep messages of inspiration about people. That was his backdrop, that was his thread. Gil Scott-Heron, Bob Marley. They became the fabric that made him.

He'd call seeing us, the Furious Five, as a kid in Long Island "life changing." Not an "eleven" but life changing was good enough. It helped him see music and not just hear it. Also life altering was him coming to the parks when there would be four DJs spinning on all four different corners of the parks at the same time and standing in the middle of the park, so he could hear all four DJs at once, and he'd wait for that one or two seconds when the beats of whatever the different songs the DJs were playing would sync up and align.

Hank said, "It was all a part of the chaos. Instead of hearing the sounds separated for that one instant they are all one big mush, like a harmonious mesh. So the combination of those elements is what gave the inspiration for the PE sound."

Add on top of that, Hank was a big Beatles fan. And he was up on everything they did sonically from the sixties that no one else was doing recording-wise. The usage of their vocals, running John Lennon's vocals and George Harrison's guitar solos through Leslie speakers and amps, the magic of their EQing (equalization) from Geoff Emerick, gave their music a psychedelic vibration to him. Which helped him *see* sound differently. And when he heard Umar Bin Hassen say "the one thing about niggers I do not love is niggers are scared of revolution" at the end of the Last Poets' "Niggers Are Scared of Revolution," with only congas and a saxophone as the instruments on the entire album, that became Hank's other backdrop, his foundation.

His connection with Chuck D was—there's no other word for it—destiny. Chuck being someone deeply into the technical aspects, the math and science of DJing along with the instrumentation of early '70's music, and Hank being one who was deeply into the technical aspects of sound; both into graphic art; both DJs, one a radio DJ, the other spinning on the ones and twos; both from the same town in Long Island; it only seemed like their collaboration at some point beyond Chuck doing the flyers for Hank's parties on campus and Professor Griff DJing with Hank at those parties at Adelphi University, and, of course, building the Spectrum radio programming format together, their bond was bound to happen.

When Rick Ruben at Def Jam approached them about forming a group based off of "Public Enemy No. 1" promo tapes Chuck would do to get people to listen to WBAU (even though Chuck was reluctant to be an artist or frontman for a group), according to Chuck, "Rick felt that [the sound] is weird enough but also distinct enough to bring into our fold as a representative of the direction that we'd like to go with different, phrase-type rap records."

The story goes, while at Def Jam the group "wrote a song for Run-DMC called 'God Bless the US' but Russell [Simmons] didn't like it. It was too political. So we thought, *why don't we try to do it?*" according to Hank from an interview he did speaking with the Grammy Awards organization. Rick apparently called Public Enemy and said he'd turn the song into a twelve-inch, and the group said, "We want to do a whole album."

Hank in that interview explained: "We needed a full album to tell a full story. We did the whole album for about $10,000, and that record got us attention. I wanted to show what PE [Public Enemy] represented." Which actually changed the concept of modern-day sampling and looping in hip-hop production. "Other groups were hybrids of musicians and drum machines, so we said let's ditch all the musicians and just use records and take samples. That got us notoriety."

To me, it's the sampling part that distinguishes Public Enemy. But in order to make what they did make sense, it's essential to know that beyond the group's upliftment of Black people in their lyrics and on records speaking about corporations and business and talking about things that are really bad within our communities and in the world that need to be fixed, and to make a whole movement of that—Hank Shocklee being an audio engineering revolutionary is of equal importance. And also very much like me, Hank Shocklee—and I'm sure he'd 100 percent agree with this—is a weirdo. In the best way. But sometimes you have to be the one to introduce and implement change.

* * *

Which is directly related to one of the other most important tentacles that came from the "Roxanne Wars." The mind and creativity of the guy who produced the response from Shanté. Marley Marl, a great DJ, took to the use of sampling in a way that not many—if any—had ever done. Taking (I'm sure) some of the techniques applied by Gary Pozner, in-house producer at Select Records in his use of the E-mu Emulator sampling synthesizer on "Roxanne, Roxanne," Marley applied innovation to his knowledge of breaks and spinning and scratching breakbeats. It could be said that in hip-hop he was one of the first to put on display for the world how sampling could really be considered a form of art. Pulling the snare from Art of Noises' "Beat Box" to build an entire song around and doing in a much different way then Peter Collins did on Jermaine Stewart's "The Word Is Out," using James Brown's "Funky Drummer" on "It's a Demo" and Fonda Rae's "Over Like a Fat Rat" on "Eric B. Is President," but not just using them but how he used them along with his drum programming created something completely different.

"Marley was the first [producer] to actually go in and truncate actual kicks and snares and then re-sequence them," music historian JayQuan said in an interview for a minidocumentary for the National Hip-Hop Museum. "All of the hip-hop records I have at home that I use when I DJ that get reaction, I could start sampling those records," Marley said. "It made me realize that if I add these sounds to hip-hop that get reaction, the next songs are going to get reactions. Nobody was thinking like that. *Nobody* was thinking like that."

For lack of a more accurate term, he became recognized in hip-hop as the original "The Godfather of Sampling." A DJ by creation and trade, Marley almost single-handedly put Queens on the map as an incubator of young, Black hip-hop talent that would one day transform the culture. If they labeled Run "Son of Kurtis Blow," they should have coined Marley "Son of Larry Smith" or "The Next of Larry Smith." It's a Queens thing. Because if Larry was considered a pioneer then Marley is the descendant. The one who took that Queens sound—if there is such a thing—and gave it to the world in many different forms to make what was being done a more complete and complex art form.

His later use of Sly and the Family Stone's "Trip to Your Heart" in LL Cool J's "Mama Said Knock You Out" will remain one of the benchmarks for sampling and truncating prerecorded music. Because as important as Marley was to sampling and producing, he was just as important for crew—not group—forming. His Juice Crew was really like the culture's first real all-star team. D.I.T.C., Tha Dogg Pound, G-Unit, Cash Money Millionaires, Roc-A-Fella, Terror Squad, the Dungeon Family, the Hit Squad,

Young Money, Black Hippy, Griselda—all formed *after* Marley's Juice Crew showed everyone how it's done.

While Marley was building on those sampling and drum programming technics, Hurby Azor, a music student at the Center of Media Arts in Manhattan, was trying to do the same but a kinda different thing with his girlfriend and her best friend while working at Sears. They called themselves Super Nature, and Hurby introduced them to the game the same way Marley did Shanté. But their diss record was targeting Doug E. Fresh and Slick Rick, and their two songs "The Show" and "La Di Da Di." Their song was called "The Show Stoppa." Hurby literally took the song once it was done to Marley at WBLS to play. Marley promised him he would and Marley kept his promise.

That Marley assist led to Super Nature changing the group's name to Salt-N-Pepa, adding a DJ, releasing their Hurby "Luv Bug" Azor–produced first album and having that album go platinum thanks to the hugeness of not just "Push It" but from "My Mic Sounds Nice," "I'll Take Your Man," and "Tramp" that put on full display Hurby's early ability to utilize well-known samples of songs give them new life based on the identity of his group. And turning Salt-N-Pepa into the female equivalent to Run-DMC.

Then there was Dana Dane, Antoinette, Kwamé, Sweet Tee, and Kid 'n Play. Hurby, like Marley, started roster building. Dropping hit song by one artist, after hit song by another, followed by hit album by another. He became a force that was hard to deny or fuck with for a stretch. A producer a lot of those other producers tried to emulate but couldn't because they didn't have his talent, ear, or ability to sample the ways that he did. Especially when he would add those go-go sounds from DC to his songs. "Hurby was always really good at finding out what that blend is," Kid said about him. He sure as hell was.

And things like Hurby using Otis Redding and Carla Thomas's "Tramp" for Salt-N-Pepa's version of the song by the same name, and Marly sampling Otis Redding's "Hard to Handle" later for his trailblazing song "The Symphony," only made their interconnection as innovational producers—"The Godfather and the Godson of Sampling"—make more sense.

* * *

Immediately following in Marley's Queens shadow was this intuitive teenager in Jamaica, Queens, trying to test into schools that his older sister was getting accepted into. They called him "Q-Tip" because . . . "I had a high top [fade, haircut] in high school, and I was pretty rail thin, and they used to look at me and say, 'Ay yo, this nigga look like a Q-Tip.' And I'd be like, 'Fuck you. Your mother.' But then on the trains going home, the girls would be like, 'Bye, Q-Tip.' 'See you tomorrow, Q-Tip.' 'Yo, Q-Tip, Hey, Q-Tip . . .' So when the girls started saying it I was like, 'We'll . . . aight.'"

At fourteen he wrote "Bonita." It was a deep, contemplating, lyrically unique love song coming from the mind of a fourteen-year-old who wanted to be "put on." He'd build a crew among friends he grew up with. And in 1985 he'd take his "little 1, 2 money," and he and his five-man crew would come to Giant Studios on 14th Street between 7th and 8th, pay the guys running the studio with money from his shoebox to get into the studio to rehearse. They did this every weekend. Once they finally had two songs structured enough to record—keep in mind "Bonita" was not one of them, and keep in mind they're in the tenth grade—they went in the booth and went for it.

Jazzy Jay, Bam's former DJ and of "Jazzy Sensation" fame, who would also be the one rumored to introduce Russell Simmons to Rick Rubin, who had just built his own studio in the Bronx up the block from the Disco Fever, came to hear the session because at the time his engineer, Skeff Anselm, was dating Q-Tip's sister, and Tip would bug the shit outta Jazzy to "put them on" in a totally different way than he'd written about with Bonita. So as a courtesy Jazzy went to hear them the first time Tip, Jarobi, Phife, DJ Ali Shaheed, and A-Boogie on the drums, recorded at Giant.

Jazzy's response after hearing them: "Uh . . ." Pause. "You know . . ." Pause. "You all gotta lot of imagination."

Tip would often find himself in this basement in New Jersey hanging out with an unknown and underground collective of like-minded talent where they'd share stories, thoughts, and ideas and test out their latest rhymes and freestyles on one another. There was a turnstile to get into the basement. Tip would sit on the turnstile. He'd bounce from that family of MCs to another family of MCs at his high school, Murry Bergtraum in Lower Manhattan, where he'd share homeroom with Afrika Baby Bam, who would later form a group with classmates Mike Gee and Sammy B called the Jungle Brothers; it was also where a future MC by the name of Brother J from a another soon-to-be formed group called X Clan was also a student who Tip met along with his DJ Ali Shaheed both on their first day of school.

They'd call the name of their group Quest because, basically, that's what they all were on. Tip would build with Afrika from Jungle Brothers, hunting in bins at record stores, catching beats to cultivate the Jungle's first album. With Phife away at boarding school, Tip—thanks to Mike Gee from Jungle randomly telling him that DJ Red Alert was his uncle—did a promo, one called "The Promo," one he built off an Average White Band song he'd found and sampled. Red played Tip's promo on his radio show on KISS-FM every night at 11 p.m. Prime time for NY hip-hop. Which led to Quest going into the studio to cut their own album and during an early, early session on a song Tip had written called "Black Is Black" while recording the intro Tip said: "I'm Q-Tip from Quest." Afrika stopped him: "Naw. If we're Jungle then y'all gotta be a Tribe." And A Tribe Called Quest announced themselves.

Together the five of them, even as over the years they were reduced to four, then three, they'd form one of the most important groups in the culture's entire history. Q-Tip functioned as both artist and producer on a rare frequency. While A Tribe Called Quest singularly changed the course of hip-hop with their first three albums and beyond, and with their role and position in one of the most meaningful collectives, Native Tongues, the culture had seen up until then, it was Tip's rare gifts of rhyme and production and over all aura that remained at the center.

ATCQ's second album changed the EQ dynamics of how an album is finished, particularly the low end. For me, being a scientist masked as a DJ, it's unfortunate when I hear a song on an album that everybody likes I can no longer like the song or album—without knowing *why* everyone likes it. *Is it the sugar? Is it the flour? Is it the milk? Is it the eggs?* What makes this song do what it do? Why does what happens happen when people hear it? For Tribe, it was their *The Low End Theory* album in 1991. In the clubs when I played anything off that album I could feel the low end, the speakers would want to cry, they'd want to die because the low end was like 40Hz or below—but it was really 60Hz because you could hear it. Now there have been some amazingly produced and engineered songs and albums up until then, and all frequencies were in-check, but with *The Low End Theory*, for some reason, they paid very serious attention to the low-end frequencies. They changed the sonics.

"When we were doing the album I'd tell our engineer, Bob Powers, how I wanted it to sound. It was he and I. And he's telling me shit, educating me a bit, because I'm still only nineteen [years old] at the time and only have one album under my belt. But I was hearing shit," Q-Tip explains. "We were doing a concert in LA with KRS-One two years before, and Ali and I bought the cassette and the vinyl of a group whose music we kept hearing out there that they weren't playing in New York. We had the group's first album, but their second album sounded totally different. We brought that album back with us to New York. It was NWA's *Straight Outta Compton* album. We went to Battery Studios and threw the album on in there and just listened. It sounded crazy! That's when we knew we had to change shit up."

I don't know what it is about these Queens dudes when it comes to producing and hearing, hiding and layering sounds but they're a little different. Similar to how we were different in the Bronx in our hearing, finding, and playing breakbeats in songs. Other DJs in other boroughs may have been doing it too, but in the Bronx we heard and did it differently. Larry Smith heard things differently, Marley Marl heard things differently, now Q-Tip. When I ask him what made him, a great MC, want to be a part of the production process, his answer takes me back to my own childhood and gave me a clearer understanding of how much alike we really are: "I guess because I never got the chance to finish taking apart my mother and father's television when I was a kid. I was still on a mission, you know what I'm sayin'. If I didn't get it done when I was five, I was going to get it done by nineteen. I had to deconstruct something, Flash."

* * *

Miles Davis spoke about the power of the "silence" in a note: "It's not the notes you play, it's the notes you don't play." And, "the real music is the silence and all of the notes are only framing this silence." James Brown invented an invisible "One" note that all funk music became based on, explaining the One as "the downbeat at the beginning of every bar." For Andre Young, it was Quincy Jones's "thirteenth note" that was his genius. A word he doesn't attach to self.

"I learned that from Quincy," Andre told me, "if you can get away with the space in the thirteenth note, if you can make that space, that silence, work . . ." Which only validated what I already knew by listening to the songs he produces. The space he takes advantage of when he's sampling, where there is no sound, to me is where his true brilliance is. I can tell he's very slow and very methodical in his approach to building songs, whether it's for him, his group, or someone he's producing, it's always an event. Which tells me that he's very meticulous in everything from the strings to the hi-hats of the drums to the timing. If you listen to a Dr. Dre song, it's not when things are happening where his gift is, it's in the spaces when things are not happening. In that thirteenth note.

He believes in this heart that he was bred to, as he says "do this shit"; bred to become who and what he'd become. "They got a picture of me DJing at my mother's parties like when I was four years old. In a onesie, putting the needle on the turntable. Before I could read, I would know how everybody was going to respond to certain music, certain songs when they were being played. I knew my colors, I knew what a James Brown 45" cover looked like, so I'd look at the labels on the records, and I'd know what records to play."

He'd grow into taking music classes, learning to play the trumpet, studying jazz theory. At twelve years old someone took him to his first ever concert: Funk Fest in the LA Coliseum on June 4, 1977. The same tour that became mythical for the live *P-Funk Earth Tour* double album was put out literally a month before the concert he went to. A concert that was blowing grown folks' minds, let alone what it had to do to a little kid. Fucked his head up.

Then "Adventures" finds him. Or as he puts it to me, "Then your ass shows up!" He's sixteen. "What the fuck is that? *What the fuck is that?* Everything for me stemmed from that one record. I listened to that record probably a thousand times before I found out how it was actually done. And once I found out, I listened to it probably ten thousand times."

He starts doing mixes first at a club, Eve After Dark, and a skating rink, Skateland (Dre calls it "Du Doe's"), both in Compton, with the skating rink becoming what many people consider "the birthplace of West Coast hip-hop." It held two thousand people, security carried Uzis, and rap acts would also perform there. Then Dre locked down the drive-time shift, 5:00 to 5:30 p.m. on the KDAY radio station in LA, similar to Marley Marl at WBLS. But as Dre was building his skills up as a DJ and his name was getting out all over LA, thanks to him recording, pressing up and selling his mixes at swap meets, with a young Ice Cube rhyming on them, he still had this desire to tap into the engineering side of the game. The ability to produce new sounds kept calling him.

Lee Bailey, a radio legend at KUTE-FM in LA, started a

voice-over production company in the garage of his home in 1979. From there he created Bailey Broadcasting Service and the syndicated radio show *RadioScope* in 1983. After meeting Bailey a few years afterward, Dre would take the bus to Bailey's house to learn the mixing board while making tapes in Bailey's garage where the Bailey's kept their small studio. This afforded Dre to not be intimidated once he elevated to a full mixing board, once he transitioned from DJ to full producer and engineer.

"If you're only using two tracks [on the board] you aren't orchestrating. You're just getting the volume and the EQ right with somebody else's work," is how he explained it. "I need to spread everything out. That's where the fun comes in. It's just like a painting. I'm adding colors. I need the canvas blank. I need to start with the EQ flat and all of the levers down. That's how I have to start."

And he started in 1985 with songs that became underground West Coast jams like "Surgery" as producer for and member of the World Class Wreckin' Cru until he got with Cube, who was actually in another group, C.I.A. (Criminals in Action/Cru' in Action), and a year later produced a song with Cube out front called "My Posse," which led to him bringing Cube with him when he left WCWC to start that new group with that local, independent Ruthless Records label owner Eric Wright to be, again, both member and producer of a group they'd agree to call exactly who they were at the time: Niggaz Wit Attitudes.

The rest we know.

Dr. Dre: "There were no thoughts when it came to us [N.W.A] recording our first album. You're talking about kids that are eighteen to twenty years old, coming out of the hood, really reckless, saying some really fucking foul shit, who'd make records and then go play them in the parks. Because they're gonna let you know. If it was wack, 'Turn that bullshit off!' That was our damage control, the basketball courts in the parks. We knew what we were saying was different and it was going to ruffle some feathers and we were really trying to take it extra. Really trying to take it there. These were the stories we were hearing. It was all we knew at the time so it was all we knew what to write about. This was our reality. And all of a sudden, to our surprise, it broke through, and all we were trying to do was be the shit in Los Angeles."

And it—and they—became the shit around the world. Street knowledge again was its name. Not gangster or gangsta rap or G-Funk. Dre has no idea where those other descriptions of what they were doing came from. Just like the street artists getting the term "graffiti" attached to them. Giving birth to LA's version of the culture that was in spirit and built very much like ours in New York but totally its own in sound and essence. With everything after N.W.A's first album—and a whole West Coast sound—hinging on what Dre was going to do or come up with next.

* * *

In 1984 Grandfather Bill's grandson graduated from high school. Around 1988, while Dre was shaping the West Coast sound and an eighteen-year-old producer Anthony Banks went from producing and selling mixtapes out of the trunk of his car in Oakland with his partners MC Ant and DJ Terry-T, to recording their first album *The Great*, Grandfather Bill's grandson, who was going by the DJ name Waxmaster C was 1,500 miles southeast of LA, 1,900 miles from Oakland shipping off beat tapes to record labels.

Waxmaster C would eventually change his name upon his

mother's advice (mom is from Brooklyn) to DJ Premier. She'd tell him to drop the "e" at the end so that he'd stand out. That would happen later. "I used to go vinyl shopping with my moms," DJ Premier explained. "My mother and I were vinyl freaks. Every time she'd go record shopping, I'd go with her because she'd go pick up vinyl. And I had top billing at Prairie View [A&M] University where I went to college from doing all the fraternity and sorority parties. I had all the latest records."

Then, the MC he'd start his first group in college with, Theodore Campbell, aka Topski, while they were sending demos out to get a deal, joined the navy, leaving Wax "dolo." Wild Pitch Records had an MC from Boston named Guru who was the MC of this group on the label called Gang Starr, who at the time was looking for a DJ. They'd heard one of Wax and Top's demos. They were interested in signing Waxmaster C without Topski. But once Theodore joined the navy, Chris Martin called Stuart Fine, founder of the label to ask if the offer to be the DJ for Gang Starr was still on the table. They said, "Meet us at Tudor City Place" just steps from the United Nations headquarters in New York. Wax showed up, they shook hands, he met Keith Edward Elam, he was in Gang Starr.

"Guru and I in the studio, we were just . . ." he paused to try to explain the tightness of the two by holding up two joined fingers. "You could shoot a bullet between these two fingers, and they wouldn't pop open. They would still stay together. That's how tight we were. And we were just excited to be accepted by New York because at that time it was still New York or nothing. I was up on N.W.A and Ice Cube and Too Short because I was in Texas going to school, and those records were coming to the record stores and you could ask anyone, 'What's poppin' now?' And they'd say, 'Oh, Too Short or the LA Dream Team,' then because [Texas] it's the South we were getting MC Shy D and all of the Luke Skyywalker records. But still those records during that time had the New York influence. From the 808 'Planet rock'–style beats to the just the regular 'Microphone check, one, two . . .' shit. Things were starting to go into the early sampling stages, but it didn't matter where you were from everybody wanted to sound like New York to get accepted. And Gang Starr was."

By the time I met him, he was on the WBLS doing the radio mixes from 8 to 10 p.m. before Funkmaster Flex's 10 p.m. to midnight show. He was able to edit out the curse words in the records by back spinning the part of the song where the words would come up. I needed to know how he did that. "Dude, when you asked me," Preemo says to me over a Zoom call at Dizzy Gillespie's old house, which is now his home, "how at the station how I did the clean versions, when you asked me, I'll never forget, 'What's that reverse thing? Show me right now.' And I turned the power switch off on the turntable and rewound the record back on the curse word, and I showed you how I did it and you went, 'Ohhhhhhhh!' I lost it. I was like, 'Oh my God, I just impressed Flash!'"

I knew before, but that's when I *knew* this dude is incredible on the ones and twos.

He took our formula and made it his own. Going from a Technics SL-B1 belt-drive turntable to an E-mu SP-12 to an SP-1200 sampler as his weapons of choice. People would copycat the way that he did things in both DJing and sampling. The way he designed his hooks in his samples, I called it the "TTH" system: the Talking Turntables Hooks. I'm a scientist first, but after that I'm a big Star Trek nerd. The Romulans have this cloaking device where they can make a ship disappear. It's still there, but the electromagnetic spectrum and other sensors or opposition can't see them. Premier had a way of taking the sample culture and doing the same thing in such a manner you didn't even really realize what he did. He put a word in, then a scratch, *word in, then a cut, word in, then a cut*. There are producers and DJs around the world that tried to copy that formula of how he made the turntable talk to make his hooks.

"I had to hear the sample in my head first. I tell people that all of the time," as he explains how in his mind he formulates what he's able to create.

A Miles Davis blast and then he'd take a James Brown grunt and he'd take a Led Zeppelin snare and a Queen melody and a . . . "Even if I don't use that once I'm in the studio, it's still kinda what I'm hearing before I go in looking for something to match what I'm hearing in my head. And it doesn't have to match exactly, but I'm still hearing *something*. The idea, the concept. I would always hear what I wanted to do, but I need to find out how to make it do what I wanted."

He learned looping first from King of Chill, learned how to chop from Showbiz, who taught him how to make samples cut one another off by putting all of the samples into the same output. "Oh," he said remembering how it all unfolded for him. "Put all the outputs on four? Okay, that's what it does? Now step back. Watch what I do."

He has a sonic edge. His ears hear differently, his hands on the decks move differently, his sample selections hit differently. Bottom line: Everyone after him mimicked him. He, much like others but unlike any other, has advanced the culture in a way I'm not sure too many can lay claim. "DWYCK," "Step in the Arena," "Skills," "Code of the Streets," "Ten Crack Commandments," "Unbelievable," "Kick in the Door," "Mathematics," Nas's "N.Y. State of Mind," and "Nas Is Life," *For the Love of*

Hip-Hop, Jeru the Damaja, KRS-One, PE, Group Home, The Lox, Das EFX, Christina Aguilera, Common, Jay-Z. He's left a musical thumbprint.

What's always been funny to me with Preemo is his real name: Christopher Martin. It's like the regular name a superhero would have. The same name as Christopher Martin from Kid 'n Play, the same name as Christopher Martin the lead singer of Coldplay, Christopher Martin the world-class principal trumpet player from the New York Philharmonic, same as the reggae artist Christopher Martin from Jamaica. All large. Just a fly-ass name. But with him it sounds like some James Bond–type shit.

And as I'm talking with him, I keep noticing the tattoo on his left arm for some reason. Trying to figure out the words. Of course, the tattoo reads, "Grandfather Bill."

* * *

It becomes, I'll say, weird and very alarming when you watch something—a concept, an idea, a practice, a love, a theory—that you created evolve in front of your eyes, and you do not get any credit for what that idea has been turned into.

Yeah, sampling was invented in 1971 but what DJs from Queens to Long Island to the South Bronx to Texas to Los Angeles to Oakland did in taking a whole different approach when it came to creating "the art of sampling" is exactly what we did in respect to the record player and turntable. We flipped how it was supposed to be used into a global phenomenon. Our ingenuity, especially in sampling, revolutionized the culture and music. We went from being referred to as vinyl manipulators and song thieves to geniuses. Prince Paul, Ant Banks, Sir Jinx, Shock G., Erick Sermon, Teddy Riley, and a few years later Pete

Rock and Large Professor and Dallas Austin and DJ Quik, then Havoc, Timbaland, and RZA. Following them the next era of sampling geniuses—The Alchemist, Just Blaze, No I.D., Kanye West, and J Dilla—would raise the level of the art form even higher once the 2000s began.

The machines would become their instruments just as the turntable was once a DJ's band. The CompuRhythm CR-78 drum machine was replaced by Roland TR-808 drum machine, which became so big they eventually made an entire documentary on the role it played in hip-hop culture, DJ culture, and pop music culture. The Yamaha DX7, the Moog Grandmother analog synthesizer, the Casio SK-1, digital drum machine, pioneer Roger Linn and his multitimbral LinnDrum machine, the E-mu SP-12 and SP-1200, and Akai's MPC60 all played a role.

Between '85 and '87 we, meaning Creole, Rahiem, and I (with the addition of Mr. Broadway and LaVon Dukes on the mics), released a couple of albums on Elektra Records. First time on a major record label for me, first time the label ever put out a hip-hop album. And it was full circle in the story of the culture because on the second Elektra album, *Ba-Dop-Boom-Bang . . . And Even More*, Larry Smith was one of the producers.

Bob Krasnow, president of Elektra—who'd just taken over as chairman in 1983 and signed groups and artists like Metallica, Anita Baker, Tracy Chapman, Mötley Crüe, and the Cure—brought us into their fold and was the one who put me in a seat of power. Giving me the power to produce records in a way I was never able to do at Sugar Hill. Once I got some money, I bought a bunch of equipment and drum machines. I started making beats.

One of the greatest later summed it up pretty well. He said in an interview, "That's the whole basis of sampling. It's not genre specific. It's kind of like, 'Oh my God, that part in that record really hits me. Finding that part that you consider the magic and looping it over and over again." That person would be DJ Jazzy Jeff.

All of this sampling innovation and experimentation at the time kind of came to a peak when a dance group out of London called Coldcut took Eric B. and Rakim's song "Paid in Full" and remixed it into a song they called "Seven Minutes of Madness"—using samples of everything from Don Pardo, Geoffrey Sumner, and Humphrey Bogart's voices to Ofra Haza's "In Nin'alu" chant to snippets of songs from the Salsoul Orchestra, James Brown, the NYC Peech Boys, Mikey Dread, Lyn Collins, Rick Jones, all on top of the "Ashley's Roachclip" drum and the "Don't Look Any Further" bass line samples of the original—which took what I did on turntablism with "Adventures" and did the same for sampling.

CHAPTER 13

The scientific word for it is *convergence* or *confluence*. The act of merging or flowing together, the development of similar characteristics that become a force. *Concurrent* is used when something or some things occur simultaneously. I'm partial to the term *synergy* scientifically. When the combined effect of two or more substances or occurrences become greater than the sum of their individual selves or the effects they cause individually. That's what we were dealing with in 1988. Not just us, hip-hop, as a culture and a music genre, but what the world had to deal with—the pinnacle we were about to reach based on the synergy of everything that was about to happen.

It felt like 1979 all over again but stronger. A better way of saying it was 1979: the Remix. I don't want to list everything that came out in 1988—because what emerged in 1988 was bigger than just the music—but the same way it seemed like all of the "first" rap records kind of came out "synergistically" at the same time in '79, it seemed like the most important and seminal music in the fifteen or so years since this started all hit again at the same time.

And the beauty of it is that, even with the music that carried over from '87, you heard all of it everywhere. Streets, radio, clubs, malls, events, parties, TVs, bars, on the trains, from boom boxes, from people's apartment windows and houses and living rooms, from cars, in people's backyards, in the parks, through headphones blasting loud. Even when you didn't hear it directly, people were reciting lyrics nonstop in conversations or to themselves.

The 1987 carryover from Eric B. and Rakim's first album and Boogie Down Productions' first album and songs from N.W.A and the Posse's first album and Ice-T's first album and Too Short's fourth album and DJ Jazzy Jeff and the Fresh Prince's second album and Heavy D and the Boyz's first album and Audio Two's "Top Billin'" were heard and felt as the confluence of '88 began to take shape. Which saw, in twelve months, Rob Base and EZ Rock drop "It Takes Two," and Eric B. and Rakim drop "Microphone Fiend" to introduce their second album, Public Enemy release *It Takes a Nation of Millions to Hold Us Back*, N.W.A drop *Straight Outta Compton*, EPMD drop their first album, *Strictly Business*, Big Daddy Kane releases *Long Live the Kane*, Slick Rick gives us *The Great Adventures of Slick Rick*, MC Lyte erased stereotypes with *Lyte as a Rock*, Ice-T releases *Power* and the album cover became as big as the album, DJ Jazzy Jeff and the Fresh Prince entered the game with *He's the DJ, I'm the Rapper*, Biz Markie comes with *Goin' Off*, BDP unleashes *By All Means Necessary*, Too Short does the same with *Life Is . . .* , Salt-N-Pepa drops the follow-up to their platinum-selling *Hot, Cool and Vicious* with *A Salt with a Deadly Pepa*, Stetsasonic and producer Prince Paul came with *In Full Gear*, Ultramagnetic MC's came with *Critical Beatdown*, the legends Run-DMC had *Tougher Than Leather*, both album and movie, and MC Hammer became a national phenomenon with his second album *Let's*

Get It Started. Also, that same year, the world was introduced to Kid 'n Play, the Jungle Brothers, Eazy-E as a solo artist, Marley's "The Symphony," and De La Soul.

Not only that, Bobby Brown went solo with *Don't Be Cruel* and Teddy Riley, already having his hand in producing two of the songs on Bobby Brown's album, would officially introduce the world to his group, Guy.

Quietly that same year, inspired by what Russell and Rick had done with Def Jam, in Houston, James " J." Prince came to New York with a record label he and a business partner started the year prior. It was in '88 that Prince, after apparently meeting with the executives at Def Jam, moved himself and his label back to Houston and signed their first act, the Geto Boys. His label Rap-A-Lot was built to offset the music and styles coming from both the East and West coasts—setting the Geto Boys up to shock the world and bring the entire South into the conversation. And this after Luther Campbell opened business in Miami, Florida, with Luke Skyywalker Records (now Luke Records) and bringing the 2 Live Crew from California in 1986 to indoctrinate bass music into hip-hop.

The Public Enemy effect was real. The N.W.A effect was real. The KRS-One/BDP effect was real. The EPMD effect, real. And not just in hip-hop. The music had transcended itself and gotten into the fabric of America in a way that caught Americans by surprise. This thing we were doing that was supposed to be a fad and gone by now was doing the exact opposite. We were becoming a voice but we were also becoming a problem.

* * *

The Dana Elaine Owens "her story" in relation to the Fab 5 Freddy "his story" that followed his getting her demo tape to

Monica Lynch and Dante Ross at Tommy Boy records, which ended up launching Latifah's career, is way beyond the simple story of discovery, good looking out, and good fortune. Because if anyone in hip-hop was destined to become what they became, it was she.

"She told my brother and I," she says of her mother and the "whole life" she had before she was Queen Latifah, "that the world is not fair. That we're going to have to work twice as hard to achieve the same things, just because. And that was a cold lesson to get when I was probably eight years old. One I didn't want to hear because I felt that it was terrible. 'Wait, you mean because of my skin-color I'm going to have to work harder? And because I'm a girl I'm going to have to work *even harder*? That's not fair.' Which took us right back to her telling us the world is not fair. But this was the reality. But my mother reinforced that lesson with so much love and creativity and strength that we never stayed stuck in that."

Her father never raised her to be a girl, in the sense that if her brother Winki could do something, so could she. Her father didn't have a "guys only" mentality with things. He taught Dana and Lance (aka: Winki, who unfortunately passed away in a motorcycle accident when he was only twenty-three years old in 1993) karate, put weapons in both of their hands, teaching them both how to use them, teaching both how to change a car battery. Separate but equal.

But it was in the basement of Mark James, aka "The 45 King," in Jersey where Dana would become Latifah. Same basement where Q-Tip would sit on the turnstile. "He had lights and different things from outside, he had stop signs and gadgets and all kind of gear. Technique turntables, mixers, and beat machines. He was a producer and that's where we would just go and hang out and it became like the spot. At some point because all of us thought we have flavor we started calling ourselves "The Flavor Unit" and we would just sit around and freestyle and critique each other's rhymes and talk about what we wanted to do in life and smoke and chill and drink and do all of the things that teenagers and young people did. That's kinda where it all began."

And in that basement over that period with her: Apache, Latee, Lakim Shabazz, Chill Rob G, Markey Fresh, Shakim, Lord Alibaski, Jerome Jenkins (Double J), and the guy who introduced Latifah to all of them, Ramsey, who eventually took his rent money and used it for Latifah and Apache to go into the studio to make demos. One of them ended up in Fab 5 Freddy's hands and the rest is her-story.

The MC SHA-ROCKS* and Lady Pinks and Lady Bs, Cookies and Annas and Tinas, Sweet Tees and Salt-N-Pepas, Lytes and Latifahs survived the impossibilities. During eras where and when so many talented female artists fell victim to fear and exploitation as they fought for the respect they'd earned while at the same time had to fight misogyny, lyrical abuse from male rappers, and stereotypes in this culture that often turned against them.

But Dana Owens stood out. Postured and positioned. "When your mother puts a book on your head . . ." she said while laughing but dead-ass serious. "Look, you had to have book on your head at my mom's house and you had to walk down the hall and walk without it falling. It wasn't so much about dropping the book, it was about your posture. There's something about raising your posture higher that raises your head up that makes you feel that you are worth more, that you are more valuable, that you should be seen." It made her magnetic; it exudes confidence, letting people know, "She's here."

She put out two songs to begin the journey, "Wrath of My

Madness" and "Princess of the Posse." They caught on, she was getting national play. Then show promoter/writer Dave "Funken" Klein started booking shows for her. While doing that he connected her with the Jungle Brothers and Red Alert. And once she met them, "It was over. That connection birthed a whole different tree," according to Queen.

What followed, like many others in this book, was culture changing. Latifah became as critical to hip-hop as Janet Jackson did to R&B. Song after song. Album after album. She spoke for herself, never needing anyone to speak for her. And took the lead, with Shakim, to establish a hip-hop rooted empire in the form of a company called, what else, Flavor Unit Entertainment, entering the land of the sharks in LA, to leave the same imprint in Hollywood they left in New Jersey.

"I didn't have a manager for the first couple of years of my career," she tells me, "just my mom, my crew, me and the family. That's all. All the meetings I'd take would be me, my mother, Ramsey might come along to a few, Mark might come to a few, but mostly it was me making my own decisions. And then Shakim started to come to the meetings. He would sit in every meeting and not say anything, and we would talk about everything afterward. We'd talk about what we thought. How to market things, how to promote the things or projects we just had a meeting about, how to get it out there. Really learning game at the same time we're trying to teach people what we're doing and how to sell it because they might not get it. Shakim had a very good business acumen, very interested in the business side of things, never was he trying to be the star."

He became her second set of eyes in the room. That person every artist in this business of music needs. Especially with what they were trying to do and the moves they were trying to make. Shakim and Latifah were as hungry and determined to be entrepreneurs as they both were for her to be a successful artist. And wanting to do it without ever leaving hip-hop behind.

Queen: "I don't really know life without hip-hop. Everything I've been blessed with comes from God but also comes through hip-hop. When I got nominated for an Academy Award and my publicist called me to tell me, I just ran through my house screaming 'Thank God for hip-hop! Thank God for hip-hop!' That's the first thing I said because if it weren't for this music, this girl in this male-dominated society, period, may not have had these opportunities. Hip-hop gave us the opportunity because we were creating it. It allowed us to become entrepreneurs, to become creators in what we were gifted in, to get out of the hood, to get out of the economic situations so many of us were in, to see a future for ourselves that did not involve drugs or jail, see something different than what the world was pushing on us in our neighborhoods."

Their company ending up having impact on music, film, television, management, record label, brands, products, artists—hell, they were the ones who introduced Naughty by Nature to the world. Them learning to own rather than someone else owning them.

It's all full circle, her circle of life. "It goes back to the basement, because when we were in the basement all the things we ended up doing were all of the things we talked about down there. It was a culture in the basement, it was a gathering place for thoughts and ideas. We'd talk for hours about different artists from the past who had gone through things, artists who had their whole publishing taken away, artists who made these big records that everyone knew but they didn't own anything, how people were tricked in certain ways with contracts, these were the conversations we'd have and we'd talk for hours and hours. So when we became a crew, part of the identity of the Flavor Unit was, to first, buy our mothers houses instead of renting, to put our families in better economic situations. For us this wasn't about music, no more than people being hustlers on the streets is all about just hustling. No. It's about changing your economic status."

And second? There is no second. As she said, "If I can buy the damn house myself, fuck the bank."

* * *

The eighties were rough. At least for me. When that whole thing went down against Sylvia and Sugar Hill in court, that was one of the roughest times personally and professionally. I was still, to me, an innocent—more naïve—child. What the fuck did I know about the record business and the legalities and the publishing? I knew nothing about any of that. I was too young. So, for me, being a part of the invention of this culture, that kind of gave me something to come back to. And I came back with nothing. Went through depression, went through drugs, went through trying to end it, not once but twice, until my sister and my girlfriend grabbed a hold of me and took care of me. I didn't have to go into rehab, but they took care of me enough for me to come back in the game.

Coco said he once read someplace—something he now holds to be true—that your "gut feelings are your ancestors talking to you." I wonder what are my ancestors telling me?

All the time I put into taking things that did one thing and creating something else—something more—that no one thought of before witnessing my creation has been the greatest gift. The sublimation, this example of a phase change, like what occurs in a chemical reaction, like when carbon dioxide undergoes a sublimation from CO_2(s) solid to CO_2(g) gas. This is about sound from one element to another. A musical scientific and mathematic balance.

I'm God-fearing, always have been. I don't like the idea of walking into any room with any kind of braggadocio's attitude. But the new technical and electronic equipment they are developing—to make things easier and more advanced for DJs and music producers—are all based off of my thinking. But I'm no longer in the mix. The '90s were about to arrive. Things in the business and the culture have gotten so out of control over the last ten years I have to leave my creation. Or is it being taken from me?

Part V

The Business (Level 4: 1990–'Til Infinity)

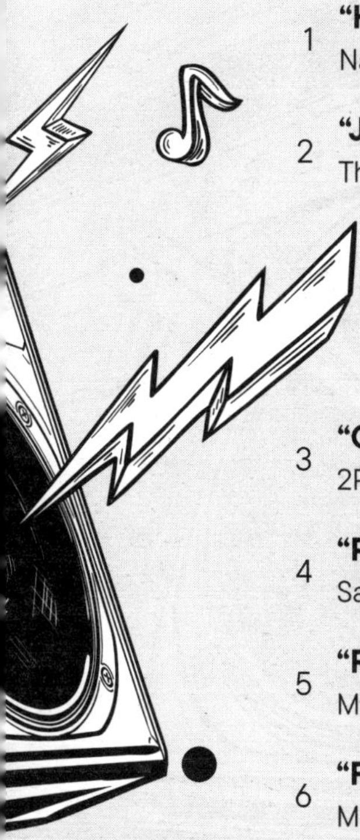

1. **"Hip Hop Hooray"**
Naughty by Nature (1992)
2. **"Juicy"**
The Notorious B.I.G. (1994)
3. **"California Love"**
2Pac ft. Dr. Dre (1995)
4. **"Push It"**
Salt-N-Pepa (1986)
5. **"Real Love"**
Mary J. Blige (1992)
6. **"Fantasy"**
Mariah Carey (1995)
7. **"Son of Scorpio"**
Dennis Coffey (2000)
8. **"Cavern"**
Liquid Liquid (1997)
9. **"C.R.E.A.M."**
Wu-Tang Clan (1993)
10. **"Fight the Power"**
Public Enemy (1989)
11. **"Creep"**
TLC (1994)
12. **"Gold Digger"**
Kanye West ft. Jamie Foxx (2005)
13. **"In Da Club"**
50 Cent (2003)
14. **"Lose Yourself"**
Eminem (2002)
15. **"Not Like Us"**
Kendrick Lamar (2024)

Chapter 14

The culture's born. Exploded. Been bought and sold. Commodified and commercialized. No longer in our hands.

By 1989 Basquiat had died. Drug overdose. Freddy aligns his death so young with the deaths of Jimi Hendrix and Janis Joplin. Coco feels the art world is responsible.

When reminiscing about Basquiat, Coco shared: "The pressure of the art world and his addiction contributed to his death. It can be a complicated industry. I just feel strongly that Basquiat was one of those special people who had a vision—someone who never considered himself a graffiti artist but instead an 'artist.' You know there are people who when you meet them you just *know*, just their demeanor lets you know that this person is on some other shit. You see how smart they are. Basquiat, dude was beyond brilliant. He was genius. I just feel like they took him."

I feel, creative people, we're all born with gifts, but then there are those that take the risks of taking their thinking to make it public and on our paths of doing that we will even do things that are stupid. I think with Basquiat, he went from doing this style that no one was really doing like he was to falling into this world with Andy Warhol and from there he went down a rabbit hole and said, "Oh shit, how did I get here?" One that he was never able to escape or save himself from. But he still *wanted* to do his art. He had love, but he needed *genuine love* to help save him.

When speaking of him, Lady Pink said something I thought was very interesting: "He was more of an artsy guy, definitely not a graffiti writer. He is one of the original, like, street artists. Like a Keith Haring and other artists who work in different mediums, different styles. Basquiat did not learn style (from a master), he was not a study of fonts or anything like that. He was more upscale and not down with the riffraff, the rest of the hood, not, nope, nope, he was totally artsy. Just because he wrote the word 'SAMO' on a wall didn't make him a part of (what we were doing). He did not subscribe to style or to pieces, he was not down with any crew, he didn't chill with anybody. He only chilled with other artsy dudes. His style to me, then, at that time, was very primitive and rather crude. But now, I appreciate his work, his style. I appreciate the rawness of it and all of the stuff that he ended up representing."

Do the Right Thing, a movie centered around Public Enemy's song "Fight the Power," in the summer of '89 would put hip-hop and all of its attitude, angst, and anger on display on film in a movie so powerful that it began a hip-hop centered public conversation. America's comfort with how Blacks are seen carried over into the 1990 Academy Awards as *Driving Miss Daisy*, a movie about a Black chauffeur for a white woman in the South won the award for Best Picture; while *Do the Right Thing* was not even nominated. It also put the film's director Spike Lee, even three years after his first feature film (seven years after he directed the video for "White Lines" while he was still an NYU grad student), into the spotlight and microscope as culture's first true non-MC storyteller and filmmaker.

The beginning of the '90s seemed to serve up warnings from day one.

Ice Cube came to New York in January 1990. Stayed locked in the studio for three months with Hank and Chuck and the entire Bomb Squad crew working on an album that would redirect the course of hip-hop music. N.W.A's voice meets Public Enemy's sound. The birth of *AmeriKKKa's Most Wanted* merged the coastal eliteness of the East and West. And at that moment Cube's pen was curating and pushing culture forward, like what was done eight years ago with "The Message."

"People who weren't from the streets were learning the knowledge of what was going on," Cube expressed about the convergence. "Then people who were in the streets through our music may have been learning what the government is doing to you and what angle you can maneuver in. It was always the mission of delivering street knowledge. There was no way to see whether or not the culture was going to appropriate any of it or take any of what we were saying and run with it. But my vision for that came once I became successful as a solo artist."

And the May release of *AmeriKKKa's Most* . . . set a tone for the '90s that would become the best of the two worlds hip-hop would soon split itself into.

On May 19, 1990, *Newsweek* finally decided to acknowledge the existence of hip-hop by putting a rapper on its cover. The rapper, LA's Tone Lōc. Above his cut-in-half head shot: "Rap Rage: Yo! Street rhyme has gone big time. But are those sounds out of bounds?" To which Ice-T replied in an *LA Times* interview less than a week later: "It was totally biased. I can't believe they got so worked up about sexism and bad language,

[Jerry Adler's] story is really a reflection of White parents who are freaked out that their kids are all into rap. More than half my fans are White kids now. That's what's scary about rap to the people who're in power—it breaks down barriers between the races."

In July 1990, a rapid-fire, 216 words-per-50-seconds delivery of one of two MCs on a song called "The Originators" hit the streets. While having some notoriety from his appearance and few words in "Hawaiian Sophie" the year before and his microphone debut on the record "H. P. Gets Busy" in 1986, this second verse on "The Originators" would be the true introduction of the fresh-faced kid from Marcy Projects in Brooklyn, Shawn Corey Carter's gift. This would be the beginning of his ascent.

That same year, back in Los Angeles, two black fashion designers, Carl Jones and Carl Williams, would separately launch hip-hop fashion brands, Cross Colours and Karl Kani, and back in New York a twenty-year-old from Harlem would leave Howard University and begin his entrepreneurial path at Andre Harrell's new Uptown Records label. The intern's name was Sean. Everyone called him Puffy.

* * *

On September 17, 1990, in episode 2 of a new NBC sitcom called *The Fresh Prince of Bel-Air* a young dude straight outta Philly appeared on everyone's television screen. Shades on, fade fresh, boom box in hand. His on-screen introduction became legendary, his first words of "You got that right!" along with his disrespectful but accurately appropriate dap to Uncle Phil as he entered and awed at the Banks' crib, was straight authentic. The culture—the non-Theo Huxtable/Eddie Winslow/Dwayne Wayne character-type—had arrived on American network TV.

But what made the scene so dope was the fact that the audience loudly applauded the second he appeared in the scene. Because by then the hip-hop world was familiar with who DJ Jazzy Jeff was, even in Hollywood. They knew because a year and a half prior, on February 22, 1989, Jeff Townes was already two albums deep into his partnership with Will Smith and on that night they'd just been awarded the first ever Grammy for a rap music artist or rap music period. It was an award Jeff would accept at the ceremony himself as Will—along with other rap artists—boycotted the ceremony because the award show wasn't going to put the rap award segment on television. While Will and Jeff's "Parents Just Don't Understand" was the song that won them the Grammy, it was the first song released from their second album, "Brand New Funk,"—his use of Donald Byrd's "Dominoes" and James Brown's "My Thang" and Pleasure's "Bounce Lady" along with his "turn it all around" slow speed backspin as the break before Will's final verse was masterful—that let everyone know Jazzy Jeff and the Fresh Prince was a group of equals. That when it came to turntablism and production Jazzy Jeff was no one's sidekick.

"I said 'No' to Will about doing the TV show. I was like, 'Nope that ain't me. I don't do that. I do music.' Typical young ignorance. Sticking to my morals. 'I can only do one thing and I can't let you stop me from doing the one thing.' If it wasn't music I didn't want to do it. I fought Will like hell, but he kept twisting my arm," is how Jeff begins the story of how he got to that day in 1990 when he became Jazz.

"Now one of the biggest inspirations I've had in my life is Mr. Kenny Gamble. Yes Flash, *the* Philadelphia International Records *Kenny Gamble*. From the beginning of everything that Will and I did, Gamble has always been in my life. Always giving me advice. And this was one of those times that I reached out to him right before the show. And I'm telling him, 'They want me to go out and do this TV show . . .' and I'm saying all of this shit because I'm expecting him to be like, 'Don't do it! Stick to your guns and do your shit!' And as I'm saying all of this I look over at him, he has a frown on his face. And I'm not used to him with a frown. And he looked at me and he said, 'Do you know what the fuck this is all called?' And I said, 'No.' He said, 'It's called success! Who the fuck told you that success was going to go the way that you wanted or be as easy as you thought?'"

Jeff agreed with Will to only do three shows; he ended up being on the show for six seasons.

And all that time, through all of the success his partner was amassing, Jeff never ever stopped DJing. Never stopped being a DJ. He functioned as if it was his sole responsibility to keep the art form alive so that people wouldn't forget the role few play in this, still. Of our importance. Raising the culture's bar on what a human being can do with two records, two turntables, and a mixer. And a different level of success found him in 1990, it was his Bruce Lee *Game of Death*-like performance at the New Music Seminar DJ Battle in 1986 where Jeff became famous. Taking what I'd created to, let's just say, an unseen-before and unheard-before level. He went from dope young kid in Philly to getting national acclaim.

"By all intent and purposes, I'm the nicest guy on the planet," Jeff tells me going back to that battle that put him on the map. "I am nonconfrontational, I never wanted to be on the battle circuit, I never gave a fuck about who's the best. I just like spinning records, doing what I do. And I'm only in the competition to show everyone what I can do. That's it. So when we get there, because I'm from Philadelphia, they put me up against the reigning world champion in the first round. And I'm not dumb, I knew what they were doing. They were trying to get me out of there. Saying, 'You all got "Girls Ain't Nothing but Trouble" out, but . . .' A song that did not let anybody know what kind of DJ I was. So they put me up against DJ Cheese, and I walked up to Cheese, stuck my hand out to shake his and said, 'Good luck.' Cheese looked at my hand and walked away. Now I gotta bit of a mean spot, a mean streak in me. So now it's like, 'Aight. Ok. Bet.' There were two sets of turntables. Everybody who had spun in that first round on the left turntables won, everybody who spun on the right turntables lost because the needles were jumping. And this is where it goes back into the technical aspect of this all. The shit we all learned from you, Flash. Because Cheese didn't shake my hand I deliberately walked to the turntables that everybody lost on."

He goes on, "Will was in the crowd and he lost it! Screaming at me, 'What the fuck are you doin'?' But I was like, 'Nope, I'm going to do this my way.' The one thing that nobody did that I did was, I put some slip mats on the turntables, and I reached in my bag and I put my own needles on the tonearms. Also in my bag was WD-40. I took that WD-40 and shot it in the crossfader to make the crossfader loose. Now everyone knows if you put WD-40 on or in an electrical content it's going to attract dirt which is going to make it short out eventually. But that muthafucka was not going to short out during the seminar. So I tested the fader, it was loose. I put my headphones on. I tested both tables and the needles didn't jump on either. I looked out in the crowd, looked at Will, and gave him the thumbs up and he knew. And I put my muthafuckin' foot in Cheese's ass."

Jeff said, "What you have to understand is, LL was a judge.

Mantronix was a judge. Duke Bootee was a judge. Lady B was a judge. Bambaataa was there. I'm doing this on the New York stage. So after I win and get to the finals, because everyone was complaining about the problems with the equipment, they put everybody who lost back in. So I had to beat all of them again and then beat the champion—again. Now I'm getting booked at the Latin Quarters and Union Square in New York. Yeah, 'Girls Ain't Nothing but Trouble' was out but now everyone is like 'We want to see who this DJ is who they say beat everybody from New York.'"

And that's how the universe worked for Jeff Townes. A kid who at eight years old started making tapes, whose father was a real MC, Masters of Ceremony, for Count Basie, whose older brother was a bass player for the Intruders, whose mother for years of his childhood and in high school gave him five dollars every day for lunch money, and he'd never buy lunch. Instead, he'd take the money and go to the record store to take advantage of the three 45s-for-99-cents deals. He and I had a parallel yearning. He knew music was calling him.

The reincarnation. The torch carrier. Someone had to save the DJ as we were slowly disappearing. We came from two different eras. Two different classrooms. I say classrooms because there were other students in our neighborhoods who were able to do what we did, but for some reason we both surpassed the restrictions and expectations. Jeff's still here. I'm still here. I asked him how? What's *his* secret?

"I don't care what accolades I get, I'm still learning something every day," falling perfectly into the student metaphor. "If you start getting to the point that you are smelling your own shit and you start believing that you are the greatest thing in the world, that is the end. You need to be a student, always a student. Lemme tell you something, for forty-years I've been thinking this is going to end. For forty years, I think I've been lucky. For forty years it's not the skill or the talent level, I've just been in the right places at the right times. *For forty years.*"

We have this conversation. One that only he and I can have, but one I'm sure many can relate to. Jeff starts: "I used to do things, DJ events, shows, that type stuff. And I'd come back to my neighborhood and sit on the mailbox while all the fellas would be drinking forty-ounces. And it would be weird because everybody'd be like, 'Yeah, we went to whoever's house party this weekend' and such and such and such. And they'd be like, 'What did you do this weekend, Jeff?' And in truth, I'd been in LA doing something with Magic Johnson. So in my head, in answering their question, I'd be like, 'Nope.' I'm not saying that. Nope."

I stop Jeff, only because what he's saying hits too close to home. "I used to come home, and the guys would be like, 'Flash, where were you for the past three weeks? We ain't seen you.' And I used to tell them, 'Yeah, I was playing in this club in Germany' or 'I was DJing in Paris.' These are my homeboys, I'm thinking they'll get it. They'd be like, 'With two turntables and you were just DJing? Wait, wait, wait. So you're trying to tell us that we ain't seen you in three weeks because you were in Germany, Japan, Paris?' Just the looks on their faces. After a while I just started saying, 'I was with my kids.' Or I'd say, 'I probably was sick.' I wanted to share my experiences with somebody, with my homeboys, but I couldn't."

Jeff says they simply couldn't comprehend it. But he takes it one step deeper. "For me, when all the shit falls apart—and it can all fall apart—I can end up back on that mailbox. So to this day, I need to keep my ass humble and need to stay a student. Trust me, I've seen a lot of people back on the mailbox. That's always been my fear. One of the things that I've realized, Flash, is that sometimes it's hard to accept that we're different. Most of the entertainers, most of the athletes, most of the artists are different. We think differently, we react differently, we have a different purpose. And that can be a very lonely existence if you don't find a way to surround yourself with like-minded people. Because as a DJ our jobs are to walk into a place, assess the people, assess the vibe, and make sure we deliver what we are supposed to deliver for those people. That's what I've realized my life is about."

Parallel yearnings, parallel journeys, parallel purposes.

* * *

November 1993. *The Source* from the time it began in 1988 had worked itself up to be the hip-hop bible of magazines. It was like the culture's *Rolling Stone*. It told *our* stories. When I got the call somewhere around the middle of 1993 about them doing a special anniversary cover for their November issue, I asked who was going to be on it? They told me they were attempting to get Bam and Herc and myself. I told them, "Um, good luck with that one." I didn't think it would be possible because we were always beefing with one another. And they're trying to get all three of us in a room? For an interview and photo shoot? How's that shit gonna happen? But they pulled it off. They pulled off the impossible in my opinion.

It was an honor to be on that cover and be honored as the culture's Founding Fathers. They understood that hip-hop was not created by one person. That it was the seedling of our three minds and talents with the watering of the people who came after that helped this to grow.

And that watering took generational shape in a thirteen-month period between November 1991 and December 1992, when Los Angeles would lay claim to the culture's crown with the release of two albums that gave the culture new definition: 1991's *2Pacalypse Now* by Tupac Shakur and a year later Dr. Dre's *The Chronic*. That was then followed by a ten-month span between November 1993 and September 1994 when three others would follow having that same impact and reclaiming the crown in New York and individually reshaping the lyrical and musical direction of the culture: Wu *Enter* (11.9.1993), Nas *Illmatic* (4.19.1994), Biggie *Ready to Die* (9.13.1994).

And just one week after the release of *Illmatic*, something else happened to happen: Down South, in Atlanta, André Benjamin and Antwan Patton released *Southernplayalisticadillacmuzik*, the album that really introduced OutKast to everyone outside of the ATL. These six albums, especially being released so close to one another and in such a short period of time, became the culture's future by setting a new stage for what would happen and what the culture would eventually become.

* * *

He came in the door . . .

That was 1987. As the sound evolved, so too did the lyricism. Rakim welcomed himself to the world in 1986 on "Eric B. Is President" and "My Melody." Only to have that followed up by the full album *Paid in Full* which literally initiated the third seismic cultural-altering shift in hip-hop's history. If "Rapper's Delight" and "King Tim III" were the first and "Adventures on the Wheels of Steel" was second, then *Paid in Full* might be respected as the third.

By 1994 to 1995 it was a whole different story.

"I got caught up man, I was tired of the business," Rakim says to me as we sat for what felt like a therapy session that the both of us needed from each other. "I drove all the way from Connecticut to New York to see my accountant, Bert Padell. So I had a good hour ride to get my game plan together, so that I'm concrete on my shit, because Bert ain't no joke. I'ma let him know how I'm feeling. '*Yeah, this is what it is! This is what I'm doing. I don't give a fuck about this shit no more.*' So I get up in his office, sit down, sticking to my guns. I'm like, 'Bert, I'm done with this bullshit man. I'm tired of this shit, na'mean? I don't wanna be . . .' I sat there for a good twenty minutes and poured it all out. Burt just sat there and looked at me, didn't say a word until I was finished. Then he said, 'So let me get this straight, get this clear: You're ready to quit rapping and everything because of what you just told me?' I was like, 'Yeah, no doubt.' He said, 'So what you are saying is because the business side of this is fucked up you don't love it anymore?' I sat there for a minute. Then I said, 'Well I ain't say *that*. I just said I don't want to do it anymore.' He was like, 'Well, how are you gonna let something prevent *you* from doing something you love?' It was like before he even finished his sentence that shit already set in. And then I got mad. Mad at the muthafuckas I was mad at."

Rakim continued, "It's almost like if you're on the block and muthafuckas are chasing you off the block and you say, 'You know what, fuck that block. I ain't going back no more.' But at this point for me it was, 'You know what, I'm going back to the block, and I'm clearing that muthafucka out! I dare one of them niggas to be on that block when I get back up there.' Burt's sentence, just that quick, by his mannerism, his calmness, his straight-to-the-point-ness, that shit made me, in that moment, reverse my shit to 'How can I get these muthafuckas back?' How could I look at what I felt was stagnating the game for me and look down on that shit? There were a few different things I wound up doing when I left his office, but the most important was me leaving saying to myself, 'I ain't gonna let this shit pimp me.'"

The scary part to me is how the game almost lost Rakim, but also how I knew exactly how he felt because I'd gone through those exact same feelings. Of how the business of music can fuck you over. I know his pain, the business of this game can bring you to that moment. The beauty of Ra though is when he could have walked into the sun and called it, ended it, he didn't. But just imagine if he did.

I've kinda always felt that Rakim and I have lived very similar and related circumstances in the history of hip-hop, yet very separate lives. My contribution to the culture came musically, his verbally. Yet we're connected in experiences and the vulnerability we share with what we've done. He knows, I know. Not too many others walking the earth do. He did a lot of things the way that I did. I call it being an empath, looking at life and looking at things that can help you create the things that you are trying to create. I'm a strong believer that thought is the ancestor to everything that is manifested. You have to think about it first—and then make it happen. Rakim's way of thinking I believe is to get the assignment and go to it and become one with it so that he can do things with language (me with music) that's considered abnormal to everyone else but normal to him.

His, "seven MC's" adding up to twenty-one MC's "ate up at the same time" line was math to my science. His, "I drop science like a scientist" line was science to my math.

For him it's both scientific and mathematical. Like the five-eight timing on Dave Brubeck's "Take Five." That same intricate timing in jazz while "still trying to find the One" was built into his words and flow. "If I felt that I wasn't digital enough on a certain word . . ." he says in our session, ". . . look, I'll take a four- or five-syllable word, and where you would normally place the emphasis of the rhyme, I'd place it just before or just after. And if the syllable ain't dropping exactly where I want it, it's like naw, I gotta do that over." Very much how I've been and am when either constructing a song or during a mix. The calmness and openness between us is like therapy while we talk to each other. A deeper understanding. "When you hear something and you try to do it and it doesn't translate exactly how you want it—it's dope to *them*—but it might have been one small unnoticeable piece that missed or that small thing that's slightly off that only you heard, and you're like 'Naw, gotta do it again.' And I can tell myself that it's alright, but if I let that shit slide, every time I hear that song or that verse the only part I'm going to hear is where I didn't make it perfect."

It yells at you. For people like us, it haunts you. And for one of the greatest MC's who ever lived there still remained fear for what he was giving to the world. That search for self-perfection. Rakim was empathetic to his own creation and creativity. Everything after *Paid in Full*. Even after he and Eric B. split. He overly cared. Maybe too much.

Ra continued. "You sit in a room and you create and then you send that shit out and that's it? Nah, it's deeper than that. When you know that you are writing for a world, when you are creating for a world . . . I'ma say it like this: The day I knew my record got played on the radio it made me feel real different. Immediately. It made me feel like I was under a microscope. In an instant I was wondering what was being said. Do they like the work? Is it good? When I started feeling what was going on and how what I was doing was resonating with people, I kind of played it like it wasn't really happening. That was the best way for me to handle it, to not let it get to me too much. You could feel people pulling at you, I thought that feeling was just because that was my first record. Naw. Every fucking time I dropped a record it was that same feeling. I was so conscious of people critiquing my work that I was kind of out of myself for a moment. The shit affects us more than we understand."

But with Rakim, I do understand. The kid who started out as Kid Wizard gave the world *him*. And *him* was nothing we'd ever experienced or heard in music before. He took the culture to a level no one ever thought it could go. For me, I lose touch sometimes with what I contributed to the culture. Sometimes when people remind me or tell me it overwhelms me and causes me to feel a certain way. It's a degree of love and appreciation from people that almost makes you feel nervous, sometimes even scared. I'm sure Rakim probably feels the same. So I asked. I was wrong.

"Naw, I'm the exact opposite. That feeling's what keeps me going. It gives me confidence knowing how the people feel about what I've done. But it took a while to set in." People kept explaining to him how his writing, his lyrics were over their heads, so he tried dumbing himself down, writing and having to erase a lot of shit to appease others. Asking, "Are they going to understand this shit?" While his humbleness kept him grounded, he realized that the complaints of him being over people's heads was his confirmation. "That was when I knew I was taking it somewhere," he said. "The people were actually letting me know that I was onto something."

Turntablism. Lyricism. Intellectualism? Like Jay-Z said, "Rakim chose words because they rhymed, but it was his genius to combine them in a way that made it feel like those words were *always* meant to be connected."

"It's Been a Long Time," not the classic intro from "I Know You Got Soul," instead I'm talking to him about the song he and Premier did for *The 18th Letter* in 1997. The song that never would have been born had he not taken that drive from Connecticut to New York to Bert Padell's office that day.

Me: "That there mathematically and knowledge-wise, that was one of your best works. Where you went, to me, you just said, 'Fuck it, I'm going to go to the tenth power with what I'm talking about. (Muammar) Gaddafi and all off those things? A lotta people can't relate, but I think you spread your wings on that record just to let people know that you have the capability to spread your wings that far if you need to. To me you said, 'I know how to fly, I know how to land, I know how to land next to you, and I know how to fly ten thousand feet in front of you but still see you. I don't care if you all don't understand the pockets, if you can't hang you just need to let go and fall to the ground and let me fly over you because that's where I'm going.'"

Him: "In the beginning when I used to write rhymes I could take inspiration from anywhere. For instance, I was a Muhammad Ali fan, I was a Bruce Lee fan. Just thinking about what they did and how they did it would give me instant inspiration. As you go on you start realizing that it's not that easy to inspire yourself. With me, I couldn't just think of Ali anymore, I did that a million times. So after a while I'm like, 'Where am I going to get this inspiration from today?' So I remember one day I was sitting there just looking for somebody, man, to inspire me. You know, to think of their story to get me to that, 'Well if he can do that, then I can do this' type place. And I'm just sitting there. Thinking. Nothing. Then I'm like, 'Well shit, I'ma have to inspire myself today.' Na'mean? Because at this time, if I can't inspire myself then what the fuck am I doin'?"

* * *

"Remember through the '90s everybody who was into hip-hop they wanted to find every breakbeat ever used. They were after that whole late-'70s/early-'80s sound, how we recorded shit, all of the old equipment with the tubes in the board. That whole period in the '90s nerdy DJs tracked down every single thing that was ever sampled. They loved that era of hip hop."

—Fab 5 Freddy

The Sample Era, as Cube said, began to end with *The Chronic*. Then there's the argument that the '90s was the culture's greatest and most influential decade/era. For me it wasn't until I got out of the Sugar Hill deal and on to my deal with Elektra that I developed a true appreciation and fondness for production and sampling. Using the sampling drum machines, not being the greatest keyboard player but being able to just peck the keys to get the melody that you want. You don't have to be a virtuoso keyboard player, you need to know what you want as far as sound is concerned. I had fun doing it. Plus I had Gavin Christopher as one of the producers working with me at Elektra. Working with Gavin and Larry Smith taught me so much about how to start and finish a record. But has that era ended?

Look, what Dr. Dre would end up doing for the next twenty years would change music and the business of hip-hop. An example of what the culture and some of the people from it are capable of. Some do believe his *The Chronic* album—and the high rise in the cost of clearing samples—began the end of the era. But Dre's discography and résumé themselves are so much bigger than sampling. The D.O.C., Snoop Dogg, Tupac and "California Love," Nate Dogg, the Game, Eminem, 50 Cent, Aftermath Entertainment, partnering with Jimmy Iovine, creating and the selling Beats Electronics, starting USC's Iovine and Young Academy, which offers a Bachelor of Science degree in Arts, Technology and Business of Innovation, again *The Chronic*, *2001*, *Compton*, the 2022 Super Bowl halftime show. Even though he'll never refer to or see himself as a genius, he is responsible for providing LA with a sound. But probably more important, from 1990 'til now he's given the West Coast—through his music—a cultural identity and also given hip-hop commercial relevance without selling hip-hop music out. And he's stepped into the business side that has probably been equally as impactful.

The impact and elevations of LL and Cube can be looked at the same way. Both becoming two of the greatest MCs ever but both breaking into Hollywood and becoming major players, both becoming major business leaders, Cube founding and being CEO of the Big3 basketball league, LL purchasing and launching Rock the Bells Radio. The same can be said about Jay-Z and what he's built. And despite the legal drama and the dark things exposed in the documentary, it's hard to ignore what Sean "Diddy" Combs's overall contributions to the culture have been. Same with: Will Smith, Queen Latifah, Ice-T, Eminem, Pharrell, Kanye West, 50 Cent, Kendrick Lamar. And those are just some of the artists, all kids who started off being somehow influenced and impacted by what we started in the '70s by them either b-boying or b-girling, tagging a wall, getting behind a turntable, or grabbing a microphone. It's what Steve Stoute said he and Jay-Z asked each other when they met in

1996: "How do you take this thing and turn it from just selling records into something that's much more of an enterprise?"

They say there are four core elements of this culture: graffiti, breaking, MCing, and DJing. Over the years, people like Bam and KRS have included a fifth: knowledge. Some call them the pillars: visual, physical, oral, aural, and mental. It's interesting how business has not been included. The business side of hip-hop is just as important and, to me, is why it's been around more than fifty years. Many of us have had a hand in that part of the culture's growth. Maybe it's time for us to start thinking that way, especially looking at how much of the culture has been taken from us.

There's a difference in birthing the culture and keeping the culture alive. I can't say one is more important than the other. It's like choosing between the tree or the roots. The DJ or the sound system. Both must be recognized.

CHAPTER 15

The "Why this? Why now?" part. Okay.

One person can say that they did this. They'd be wrong, but someone would believe them. There's nothing documented to really challenge what that one person is being told to believe. With possibly that *Source* magazine "Founding Fathers" issue with Herc, Bam, and myself maybe being one of the exceptions. This has been the problem for fifty-three years. This culture, its origins, is the combination of so many different minds. I spoke to DMC about his "voilà moment" and how he brought rock music into this. I talked to Hank Shocklee, and his shit was scientific about what he brought to this. In speaking to LL, his shit is about how home life was rough for him coming up and how he went into his own world and how he came out with what he gave to the culture. This is why this kind of book must be written.

If you grew up in rock music, you knew who Mick Jagger was, you knew who Elvis was, Little Richard, Bill Haley and the rock guys and what they did to build rock 'n' roll. If you grew up in jazz, you knew who Cab Calloway was and what he did, you knew who Miles Davis was and what he did. With hip-hop the shit is too cloudy! Who did what? What went where? When was what done? Chronologically. This book here has to be one of the books that clears up the fog. These stories. I couldn't tell these stories by myself, and that's why I spent months chasing these people so they could tell their stories. In the beginning this thing was a seedling and now it's a California redwood. And I needed to get some of the voices of the women and men who did this shit.

Because no one—and I mean literally no one I spoke to sacrificed larger parts of their lives to make this culture—had any clue this was going to blow up like it did. Especially not when we were doing it. Which is part of the reason I believe the history is so convoluted. So many things that are not true and told by people who were not there have been told. I talk to a lot of people outside of the first generation and first generation of DJs in the culture and a lot of what they say is maybe somewhere around 40 percent incomplete. But they'll embellish the other 60 percent because they weren't there. (Having lived it, I can do the math.)

Which answers the "why this, why now" of it all. From a factual standpoint it all has to connect so that it makes sense to whoever's reading about it. For them to have that "Oh, that was there and that was why this happened there and that happened then and that happened like this and that happened like that" moment.

The people I'm surrounded by and have been for years always tell me I'm too humble. When I disappear before an event is over or when I separate myself from the crowd to let the light shine on someone else, my peers will tell me, "Yeah, Flash, we already know how you roll." But in private conversations over the years every one of them that I've had talks with have told me it's time to speak up and speak out. I'm always concerned about hurting other people's feelings, but before I leave this earth a large part of my responsibility, I believe, is to make sure that an accurate account of how this culture was born be put on record. Not by one person, by those who both lived it and sacrificed to give it life.

In my conversation with Ice Cube for this book, we ventured off into talking about that sacrifice. I was telling him how my sons complained about me not being around when they were kids. I said to Cube, "I told them back then, 'Listen I won't be able to get you the things that you want if I'm sitting here.' And I didn't want a regular job, I had a belief in something bigger. I had two jobs as a messenger boy twice when I was very young, and I was like, 'I ain't fuckin' doing this! Not if I can get something else going.' Then when I got something else going . . ."

It was here where Cube cut me off and said something very profound: "You were busy changing the world, man. It's like telling Martin Luther King Jr. to go out and get a job. You were changing the world."

And that sacrifice led to dark times.

But I was able to come out of it. Grandfather Bill's grandson gave me that reminder. "Everything in the '90s got advanced to the 'Jeep Beat mix.' You had jeep mixes too, Flash. When you were doing 'You Know What Time It Is?' 'Larry,' way after Sugar Hill, this was so way later, and you were still doing things that amazed us. The little nuances on the producing were so in the right spot. We were still studying."

So was I.

Studying this thing called life—the reasons, my purpose, without answers. Knowing through it all, while still discovering, that God has a way of choosing his favorite people and inventors. And that is when the long road of discovery begins. The journey is lonely and frustrating. I believe every true inventor goes thru a "fuck it" period, when we are saying to ourselves, "Why is it not working?" That's usually when the curveball comes and takes away the picture in your mind. That's when God steps in to say, "Ugh, not so fast!" And you're trapped, without a choice. You must complete the task, the invention, with nothing. That's why when I hear anyone call themselves an inventor, I look forward to their SOS, their "Story of Struggle." I'm immediately intrigued because I know what I believe they've gone through based on what I went through.

In this book I found inventors just like me. We yelled at each other as I interviewed them. We compared notes with each other. True inventors don't talk about inventing; you get happily dragged into it, then you go through years of squeezing a square peg into a round hole. You go through emotional swings like anger, joy, confusion, hurt, pain, then *voilà*, you show it to the world and they don't say "no." Instead they respond with, "How is he doing that?" And the people know you're an inventor—no mention needed by the inventor. The world knows and they follow your invention for decades. And you get lost in it all. I sometimes become afraid when I'm called a legend because they all die or disappear. But as EZ Mike always says to me, "You're not done yet." Hopefully the universe hears me.

* * *

So a call came to my office, "There's a Baz Luhrmann looking for you." Baz Luhrmann? Sounded like some shit from *Dracula*. I had no idea who this person was. I called around to a few people of power. All I got back was, 'Motherfucker, you better call that man back! Tell him that you will meet with him!" I asked "Why?" I was told to just research him. Movie director. *Moulin Rouge! The Great Gatsby*. Oh, shit. I made the call back.

I went down to the hidden place in Lower Manhattan where he lives. Gorgeous place. A skinny white man with an Australian accent comes to greet my manager and me at the door. As we walk inside his place he goes over to a picture, a piece of paper placed in a frame, it's a circular drawing someone did of the Quik Mix Theory. And he says to me, "I idolize what you did."

It had been eight years since 2008 when the six of us, as Grandmaster Flash and the Furious Five, were inducted into the Rock and Roll Hall of Fame. Now Netflix with Baz as the director wants to do a series telling the origin story of hip-hop. The series was to be called *The Get Down*. Based on what we called the break of the songs we'd spin in the parks. The "get down" part.

And they did. For one season.

I will say this: There were mixed emotions about *The Get Down* when it came out. A lot of people who saw *The Get Down* who grew up in this weren't really happy with the way it was constructed. I'll say that if it wasn't for Baz searching for not just me but Nas, Lady Pink, Kurtis Blow, Rahiem, Herc, and others and at least putting as much of the Bronx story in his production as possible, no one gave a fuck about talking about the Bronx, I applaud him. Let's start there. Was it clear on-the-mark historically? It wasn't. It was a mythical story; it was pieces of truth around glorified flaws. That's the way he works. This story may be too singular in focus to get the real, full story of everything we were doing and what was happening back then right. The truth of the birth of this culture may be too multilayered for anyone to capture on film. Hell, it's hard to do in this book, so I know! Baz is a filmmaker who can take a pen top and make it the most glamorous looking thing ever. That is his style. That is how he tells stories. All I can do is thank him because the last white person with power who came to the Bronx to tell our story was Charlie Ahern.

Chapter 16

There's always been an applied science to this, it's just not scientific or mathematical in a way people were used to seeing it. The way I see it, if it wasn't for the DJ hip-hop wouldn't be here. That is an absolute fact. That, as I said, is "the what." My contributions—the Quik Mix Theory and everything that came from it—that's "the how."

The one thing I've learned while writing is how similar a lot of our life experiences and thoughts really are. How Doug E. Fresh's life and mine line up. Same with Rakim. Same with Jazzy Jeff. Same with Preemo.

I do a lot of edits on records now. And in the middle of an edit, if it's not hitting, like the kick and the snare, I'll get mad at it and walk away from it for like a day. That's that "walk away theory" that I talked about. What I've learned over the course of doing this for so many years is that the natural science comes in and doesn't allow the brain to hear things, especially if it's the same thing, after hearing it a certain number of hours. The brain can no longer compute. So I have to leave the edit. And then I come back and play what I've done. And I'll listen to it and think, "Damn, that sounds awful." But I'll go, "Okay, I gotta move this here and move this there." It's not numerically perfect, but it feels in the pocket. And that's what we're all trying to find. I shared this with Preemo. And of the conversations I had with everyone for this book, this may have hit the hardest.

"You know what's fucking me up? Now we have never had this discussion ever in all of the years I've known you," Preemo said. "You are saying the things I actually do. Same things. Things I don't ever talk to people about, but you're saying them in our conversation." But I'm saying them about me, about how I do things and have been for fifty years. Things he didn't know I did, was never taught to do, but still doing them to this day.

In Hank Shocklee I found someone who can go down the rabbit hole with me and walk on the lava and not be scared. We can go to different celestial systems of sound. I found a nerd just as nerdy as I.

Q-Tip in the middle of an hour-long conversation about his journey into this and his contributions in this, asks about "Larry." I tell him, "'Larry' was the last song on the album because we'd finished the album but Elektra wanted us to put one more cut on the record. A filler record. And this is when the PPG Wave machine came out where you could stutter the vocals and the 'Bub, Bub, Bub, Bubba-bub' I used as the bass line. Rahiem and I went into the studio, SSL Studio I think, and we did it, I programmed the beat on a DMX drum machine. We were exhausted because we stayed in that room for hours just trying to figure out what else we could do. I fell asleep on the console. The album was completed. And it just so happened that that song was *the* song of the album." Like "King Tim III" how that was the last song they did for that album and look what it ended up becoming. You never know. My point is, I would never know of all the songs I've done and been a part of that would be the one Q-Tip would ask me about.

Comparatively, and I'm just speaking to the music that is being produced, the tracks today—not the MCing or the lyrics—cannot compete with a sample-based track because in sampling we're taking fragments from some of the greatest bands in the world and remixing them into new compositions. So when we sample a groove that groove probably has the greatest keyboardist or the greatest bassist or the greatest drummer or the greatest guitarist—all in those few seconds! I'm not hating, but that's why most of the music coming out of the culture now doesn't have the depth of what we musically built the culture on. Shocklee would say the "experimentation" is the difference. Hard to argue, because experimentation is what started this whole thing from the beginning. The destiny of it all.

* * *

Word had gotten around that about a year before they began celebrating the fiftieth anniversary of hip-hop that Herc had gotten sick, that he wasn't doing too well. I heard that he might be passing away soon. I started calling people, saying 'I need to see him. They say he might not be here too much longer.' Herc's had several strokes over the years. Then I heard that he was going to be at the fiftieth anniversary at Yankee Stadium. That they were somehow going to honor him. I didn't go to the event for the event or to see those acts, I knew and have seen most of those people performing, I went there to see Herc. I walked backstage to where they told me he was. I asked, "Where's Kool Herc's room?" So I get to the room and there's a guy standing there, security, and I said, "I need you to stand aside my name is Grandmaster Flash." He stands aside, I push my way in, Herc had maybe twenty to twenty-five people in the room, everybody just froze. I look at Herc, he looks at me, there was a chair next to him, I sat next to him.

I said "Herc, we're warriors, I came to see you, we've been warriors for many and many of decades, I'm not here to fight you. I heard in the streets that you were not well. I heard you almost went to God." Even then when he saw me there was tension. Basically I'm like, "I come in peace." We all did something to help this culture. After a while the fighting's got to stop. I just wanted to see him to pay him his respects. He started talking about records that I had that he didn't know what they were. Then I start telling him, "Man that sound system you had was amazing." He started talking about how dope he was, I started talking about how dope I was. We joked with each other in that moment. I remember him saying to me, "I love the fact of playing the record and letting it play through" and he laughed. And I said, "Naw, I only played part of it." And we both laughed. For the first time in probably forever. I wished him well. Stood up, bent down, gave him a hug. Then left.

When we were doing it, we didn't know. We just didn't know. As Bam likes to say James Brown says, we were just "doin' the do." We didn't take pictures, we didn't take videos, we didn't do any of that. But here we are. And if I had to do it all over again, I'd probably do it the same way. Because it was for the love. It wasn't like "Ah-ha! I got something that's going to make me a million dollars!" I wasn't even thinking like that. None of us thought like that. We were just doing what we were doing in our own little area. And when I wasn't DJing I would go visit Bam, or I'd visit Breakout, go see Herc. That's how it was. And this is the thing that's so fucked up about how it is now, the people telling our story are not coming to us to ask—and we're still alive to ask! We're still here! But they keep walking over us, reframing our story, keep giving the pioneers peanuts. Or, like I said earlier, as Bam likes to call us, "architects."

MC SHA-ROCK* is the one who continues to put Herc's and my relationship to each other, not *with* each other, into perspective: "Herc didn't create an avenue for the MC to rhyme. Yes he had Coke La Rock and Timmy Tim, but they didn't do long-bar rhymes, long-winded rhymes. That was a different era. When you came in Flash, you came up and started a new wave of DJs creating a new wave of MCs. You provided that avenue. You were the catalyst. That's the difference. When we put Herc up against Flash, there was never really a discussion of who did what. [Flash] changed the dynamics. All Herc knew was that you were this new DJ coming in taking some of his crowd because you were providing more than what was out there. What DJ's were saying was, 'I need to be like Grandmaster Flash. I need to learn that technique.' No one was saying, 'Let me learn the technique of DJ Kool Herc.' No DJ said that. They may have said, 'What record did Herc have? I gotta find that record.' Or 'What record did Bambaataa have?' Because it was a record no one else had. But the MCs, the DJs, b-boys, and b-girls would come to hear Flash because all of the elements would be represented. That's the mechanism of the culture, we were celebrating all of the elements because you brought all of the elements together. No other DJ did that."

I read someone say in *Rolling Stone* in an article about Herc for the fiftieth anniversary of hip-hop that, "If Aug. 11 [1973] is the first of anything, it's not the birth of the hip-hop genre or hip-hop culture per se. It's the birth of the hip-hop religion—the sainthood, the anointments, the sacraments, and the debates." I find that interesting.

Not long ago, Clark Kent shared with me a conversation he'd recently had with Herc. Expressing to Herc how blessed of a man he was. Telling him: "Martin Luther King Jr. started a movement, and he died, he couldn't see the fruits of his labor. Malcolm X started a movement, he's dead. He can't see the fruits of his labor. What you started, along with us and many other people, you got to see it. Now I'm going to give you your props, you planted seeds and a lot of branches came from that tree, but you planted the seed, and you are still here to see it."

A lot of people now want to characterize hip-hop as just the rapper. I'm not hating, but I do know they didn't have better music to speak on until I did what I did. I would not have had people to play for out in the streets if Bam hadn't done what he did, and the music wouldn't have sounded like it did if Herc hadn't done what he did. It was a combination of three people. Three counterparts of three people to give this thing its birth. I know for a fact that before the rapper came in we were playing the music on which this entire thing was built. And this is what I want to make clear. Whether or not Herc and I ever speak again.

* * *

I honestly feel looking back that I didn't put enough into production. At a certain point there was a fight between who was "Grandmaster?" I had to tour and at the same time I had to get Joseph Saddler/Grandmaster Flash ownership back. When Sylvia lost in court to the rights to use "Grandmaster Flash" because it belonged to me, she was able to use the name "Grandmaster" because of its definitive term of what it means. So that allowed Melle Mel and Sugar Hill to use "Grandmaster Melle Mel" as his stage name. So the problem came with promoters, which "Grandmaster" are we booking? The dark-skinned one with no hair or the light-skinned one with the long hair? That became a problem. That's when I had to really get into good company with lawyers. And between my agent and my attorney at the time and me having to play for less money for people to see me for a year or two during that period was a tough time.

Then a good friend of mine, white guy, Greg Cannon, he says to me, "Flash, I have a way where you can capture Grandmaster Flash and Joseph Saddler in a way that can break up the confusion. But here's the key: You have to tell people about your life. What you eat for breakfast, tell them how you are feeling on a certain day, you have to let people into your personal life." And like with Ray Chandler and to some degree Bobby Robinson, I told him "Fuck you, my personal life is my personal life." He kept saying, "Flash, if you follow through with this I promise you people are going to be able to separate who is who and who was what." He was telling me about this thing called the internet and how he could build a virtual home called a website where I could post everything that would inform people who the real "Grandmaster" Flash was.

And it worked. I was able to get Grandmaster Flash back and Joseph Saddler back online to the point that promoters could say, "Oh, we know who we're getting now." Which allowed me to stop doing tours for shitty money just so people could see me on the turntables doing what I do. Going into the early '90s this was my way of separating myself from the "other" Grandmaster who came after me. Who was literally still my friend.

At some point the three original guys of the five who decided to stay with Sugar Hill Records were calling me, saying, "We're tired of being there." Now I've got two, three new guys, I have a new group but my original guys are calling me. What did KRS say: "Tell me what the fuck am I supposed to do?" This became a tough period. I love the new guys, had a lotta headaches and bullshit with the three original guys, but they are my legacy. But at the end of the day, the new three had to go, and I had to bring the old three back and get them signed with me over at Elektra.

I told them: "I have a situation here that's very peaceful, very businesslike. We cannot approach this business deal the way we did it over there [at Sugar Hill in 1980]. It's a big business, they're owned by Warner Bros., huge; they're downtown [New York], meetings have to be scheduled. A&R, legal, everything here is official."

So I went to the president/chairman of Elektra, Bob Krasnow and said, "Bob, three of the guys from the original group want to come back."

It happened. And we were able to sign a publishing deal. And where I brought my BMW, once the deal was signed, I say, "Let's all go down to my BMW dealer in Long Island, and let's go get some cars." While there, I can remember Mel saying, "Let's drive through the Bronx following each other, jump out of the cars so that people can see that we're back together again."

So now we're set, but only for so long. A few things happened, our records didn't sell the way we hoped they would, and after a few years and a few albums we were dropped by the label.

* * *

I never saw it coming. The Pete Rocks, the DJ Premiers, the Dr. Dres, I never anticipated what our role would become, never anticipated the role of "producer" would evolve into us curating what hip-hop musically became. Even while believing the DJ is the reason all of this exists. Can't lie, there was a point where I felt we, the DJs, were really going to be left behind and forgotten. I'm happy that didn't totally happen. What was really cool was to watch other DJs make records knowing that these records would not only be big but fun to play because they were based on DJing or they were based on their experience as DJs on how to rock a crowd. So when they went into the studio they knew how to put together a record that would be killer on the dance floor. Which is probably why the records have the staying power even today.

If I ever wanted to get a true feel or give myself a true reminder of my direct contribution to the world of DJing, all I have to do is look at the list of champions of the DMC World DJ Championships. Since 1985, when their first champion was RJ Scratch from the UK, there have been winners from Germany, France, Denmark, Japan, Canada, New Zealand, and the US. And that's just places of those who won. What's the Notorious B.I.G.'s line: "I never thought that hip-hop would take it this far."

The Quik Mix Theory turned a DJ into an artist.

I believe everyone is programmed a little differently. I call myself "7:30" often. It's a reference to the bit of "crazy" I know lives inside of me. That's just who I am. In talking to DJ Premier I realized how much we think alike. How our minds work when it comes to music and what we've done with music differently than most people. It's how we project what we are thinking to the masses. Same with Jazzy Jeff.

People today take putting their fingertips on a record and controlling it for granted. No one really considered that before this, before I allowed my curiosity to get the very best of me, everyone was just picking up the tonearm and putting it down on the record and using the turntable in a proper way. People say that they "invented this" and they "invented that." They don't know. It took me three years to figure out that if I could put my hand on the platter that's going clockwise so that I can go counterclockwise and re-arrive at the top of the break and rhythmically keep the beat on time or rub the record to make interesting sounds . . . they, just, don't, know. Millions of people think that I "just" put my fingertips on the vinyl and moved it back and forth. I wish it was "just" that simple. Some would call me a prodigy, but they didn't—still don't—know what to call me a prodigy of.

I started working on the QMT in 1971, I perfected it in 1973, 1974. It, just like the culture, is more than fifty years old now—and still not totally understood.

Did I know that in doing what I was doing I was going to jump-start what would become one of the most important cultural, musical, racial, artistic, economic, social, and societal contributions in American history that became a global phenomenon in all walks of life? No. Have I been given credit for exactly what I did, what I created and contributed, and gotten full credit for what that culture turned into and the impact it has today? No. The genius wasn't in what I created—the genius was in the reasoning behind it. It's in the math; it's in the science. It was in my curiosity. It was at Samuel Gompers High School where they prepared my mind and gave me the skills to extend my creativity into something that could actually work. It's in being poor and coming up in poverty and that being motivators. Michael "RIP" Dunham Jr., my good friend of the Spin Firm calls it "the beautiful genius." My economic disadvantages triggered my arithmetic advantage.

He reminds me of that when I talk about and explain "Clock Theory," the "Quik Mix Theory," when I start talking math, the six counterclockwise rotations continuous counts within four bars, the 33-1/3 recording speed, modern day sampling, post-modern DJing, and how I did all that I did, of how most of that goes over people's heads. They don't look at me and realize how I used math, English, history, science, sound and how I was using so many educational things to help develop the things I was developing. And how close to completely impossible to do what I did was because it didn't exist. It goes back to the Einstein thing and why EZ Mike and Rip always associate with people the world looks at as some of the greatest inventors and thinkers of our times. The equations that were going on in my head that wasn't going on in any other DJs head at that time and how it took me years to master something that was not only driving me crazy inside but something no one else in the whole world at the time was doing.

Reminds me that I can't today look at almost any nonviolent existing aspect of hip-hop without seeing something I touched to get it to where it is. A guy one time online wrote this: IN THE BEGINNING THERE WAS LIGHT THEN CAME GRANDMASTER FLASH (@dagmonrabal7547). That means a lot.

I did a set for Pioneer in 2023 in Southern California at NAMM, the National Association of Music Merchants, to celebrate the fifty-year anniversary of hip-hop. The crowd was totally different from the crowds I used to spin for when I started with this whole thing. I told a part of my story that night. I thought the moment was appropriate.

"I come from a time when the music had no charts, when the dopest record came from a black band, a white band, or a foreign band, American band. Being one of the youngest in my family, I wasn't allowed to touch the stereo. Depending which sister was on the stereo or whether it was Mom or Dad, that's my inspiration. My dad was a collector of vinyl and my mom was a seamstress, so I got to learn two things very early: the importance of vinyl—getting my ass kicked every time my father would say 'Stop touching my records'—and I got to understand the importance of a needle. . . . But here we are fifty years later and then producers took my hands on the vinyl technique and put it into a sampler and they've given birth to a record business. This thing that I did with duplicate copies of a record became the music bed for human beings to speak on. Today they call it rap, and I am the inventor."

Then I pressed the button on the deck, and I let the music speak for me.

* * *

My calling? To serve. At the same time, to paraphrase A.G. from Showbiz and A.G.: To show all these corny motherfuckers what hip-hop is supposed to sound like. I get asked all of the time to do "hip-hop sets" when I DJ. And I'll include in those sets, Bob James, Thin Lizzy, James Brown, Sly and the Family Stone, throw a couple of rap songs in there. They'll say: "That's not a hip-hop set." I say, "You asked me to do a hip-hop set, correct? Someone who is part of the ingredients of what this is. I'm going to play Billy Squier, I'm going to play Michael Henderson, all of this music that this culture was built on. Because that's hip-hop." People look at me like, "Uh-uh. No it isn't." To me that's the bigger picture of people trying to bury what this thing really, really was. And actually is.

For me, it all comes back to the Bronx. There was no place else where this entire culture could have started. No disrespect to another place or borough, but this thing was created under strife when it was born. And no other place had strife at the time like the Bronx. Not even Harlem. It's why this culture, even as wide as it's spread, is enjoyed by whites, blacks, foreigners, Americans, the rich, the poor. The beauty in what we put out from the inception has in many ways been returned. As I've said, I'm a person of service. And service is a currency. And currency flows circular. What you put out comes back to you. Mostly in ways you'd never know or appreciate if you don't pay attention.

If Herc, Bam, and I could imaginarily one day sit on a park bench, in the Bronx, with some peanuts to feed the pigeons, and just talk, it would be bigger than this book I'm writing. But because that probably will never happen, it doesn't stop me from going back to a time when there were songs made that were underground songs, songs that talked about important things in the world, the variations of things musically and lyrically that used to be in the culture but are no longer here. I personally think hip-hop is shrinking and those pockets have to be refilled again. That might not happen in my lifetime, but we need to have people as slick as Rakim, as important as Chuck D, as great as Melle Mel, as demanding as Latifah, as clever as Biz Markie. We need that diversification all over again. Which is something we don't really have anymore, and hip-hop was built on diversification—musically and lyrically and artistically. To me, I see the tree leaning. It has to be upright, vertical again. Because that is when hip-hop is at its most powerful, when it is at its best.

The road traveled for this has been lots of highs, lots of lows. Didn't know the things I was doing would be appreciated and loved by so many people. I was always in the moment. And being in the now means I'm paying attention to the moment I'm in. Yesterday and tomorrow, we have no control over. So when I was building the whole thing it was in *the now*. I can't remember a moment when I said, "This is going to be *this* tomorrow." Everything had to be done in the moment because what I was hearing in my mind was not happening in the world. I had to get it out. And mostly I had to do it alone. That can be scary when you are trying and always doing somethings no one else is doing—alone, by yourself. You don't know if you're crazy or not. Ain't nobody there to tell you either way. I was in my own world for a very long time. And it's when you come out on the other side that you realize, God is good. And I lived long enough to see the results.

Look, I can't speak for Herc, I can't speak for Bam, I can't speak for Breakout, I can only speak for Flash. So when God takes me, I want to be able to say that I told the story along with the people who were there to help me write the story. With the ones who built the story.

ACKNOWLEDGMENTS

First and foremost, I want to thank my mom, Regina Saddler, and my dad, Joseph Saddler Sr. They were my first inspiration that led me on the path to become this DJ, artist, and producer that I am. Mom, thank you for being an amazing seamstress who gave me a chance to see what the needle does in a format other than the turntable. Dad, although you reprimanded me multiple times, in a weird kind of way, you taught me that these things—these black circles that would later be called vinyl—are very, very special. (I didn't understand as a toddler, but as I grew into adolescence the picture became abundantly clear, and this is when I implemented math and science which allowed me to invent my DJ technique. Mom and Dad, you're no longer with us, but you are here in spirit.)

To my sisters Violet, Carmetta, Penny, and Lilly: Being the only boy in the family sometimes made me feel lonely, but most of the time I felt special. Without knowing it you all made me understand that music should be put in genres, locations, language, and dopeness, not categories. I listened very carefully as you guys took turns putting the 45s and 33s on the stereo in the living room. You helped me to understand that dope music is just dope music.

To my best friends: EZ Mike, Truman, OJ, and George (who we were so wrong in doing back then, affectionately as best friends do, called "Monkey George" because he looked like Curious George from the children's book). Some of the craziest shit went down in our "club" on Faile Street. Yeah, the early seventies in the Hunts Point area of the South Bronx, wild times, good times. Thanks for helping make me who I became.

Thanks to these old friends: Gordon Upshaw and younger brother Gregory Upshaw. We became really cool, and a big thing on the block of Fox Street was running from one end of the block to the other. One day Gordon said to me, "Dang man, you run faster than me. I'm going to call you Flash." His name was Gordon, and my name became "Flash." Flash Gordon for life. And Octavius Glenn, we called him OG2. He and I would go to other neighborhoods and blocks, which was big on the gangs, and we used to navigate the other areas without getting ourselves hurt or possibly killed. There were times when OG2 had to protect me and I had to protect OG2. We became extremely close. We still talk today—and laugh—about our history.

To my cousins, the Bronson brothers (and their sister Armel) that I used to hang with. Korduannii, Kyel, and Boyd. I've never seen so many people fear three brothers so much. If I ever wanted to get in some trouble, oh my goodness. . . . Here's what we used to do all day long: We would get on the elevator and jump real hard until the elevator stopped and got stuck between floors. Then we'd climb out of the escape hatch in the ceiling of the elevator and just ride up and down on the top of the elevator shaft for hours. That was the scariest shit ever. But I loved it and loved them. They probably were my closest cousins. Although Korduannii and Boyd are no longer with us, rest in peace, we still have Armel and Kyel. I love them all.

I want to say a huge thank-you to the Jeffrey sisters: Judy, Wanda, and Paulette. I remember going to their house almost every Sunday and eating dinner. Their mom was no joke. I remember Ms. Jeffrey grabbed me by my collar and said you had better make sure my girls get home safe from the parties. Thank you for treating me like family.

To the great Sylvia Rhone. A huge executive now with Sony Records, but I must tell you the music business could be a little crazy. Before Sylvia Rhone became the giant that she is at Sony, she used to work for Electra records, and that's where my escape from Sugar Hill Records was—to Electra Records. She was in A&R. One of the few that was very caring about me as a person and as an artist with a group, she had great patience, would always ask how do y'all want to do it, how do you want to work it out? She's just the same way today, so Sylvia Rhone, in the business that can really be quite crazy and evil, thank you for caring.

Lyor Cohen and Russell Simmons and Def Jam Records. Also, shout out to Rick Rubin, the three of these people took this thing from streets and made it big business. And Rob Love. He was one of the biggest dogs at Def Jam Records in the promotion area. He made sure that all the biggest DJs got the records hot off the press.

Raymond Chandler: What can I say? I remember my completion of the Quik Mix Theory. These were the early years and the big thing in the culture was breakdancing. I was good at it for like five minutes. You telling me as I was DJing in the park: "I have a way where you can make money doing that" changed my life. Ray Chandler created this kind of corporation-type thing for us. From the security, how the door was handled, how the flyers were handled, how the promotion was done, how women felt very comfortable coming to our parties, how we were probably number one in New York. So Ray Chandler, thank you for harassing me, thank you for annoying me, thank you for looking at me and scaring the shit out of me, and making me say "yes" to your offer because the rest became history. Rest in peace, my friend.

Disco Bee: I met Disco Bee through a friend. Upon getting to know him, I saw that he was one of the nicest, coolest, most helpful people and did I need help at this time. Bee's family, the Hayward's, lived in a house, most of us lived in the projects. He was kind enough to say, "Flash, you could leave the sound system [which was called the 'Gladiator'] in my father's garage." His father was not the happiest about that, but said, "Okay." Disco Bee was one of my DJ partners along with EZ Mike, but equally important. Disco Bee, I will never forget you. Thank you and the Hayward family, I love you.

I talked in the book about Cowboy (Keith Wiggins), but I will say this in addition: While everybody else was loose talking on the mic, Cowboy came up with a rhythm that would work in between the rhythm of the Quik Mix Theory—my brand-new style of DJing that nobody was doing and Cowboy's rhyme style that nobody was doing started to shake up the Bronx. Cowboy's no longer with us. I miss you, man. I miss the times we had together. When you passed away, I kind of lost faith because the group went into disarray. You were a good rapper but also kind of like the police for us. When one of us was getting out of line you would say, "Put your hands up." And once knuckles were up you'd knock a person out in ten seconds. Like, first there's a circle of people standing ready to fight and then there's not; somebody's laying down there, and it was never Cowboy.

I thank the Furious Five, all of you—Cowboy, Creole, Mel, Scorp, Rahiem. Thank you for figuring out a style that could intertwine with my style of DJing. I personally think that during that era we were number one. Not just in New York, but in the world because no one else in the world could do what we were doing. Everybody was gunning for me or my MCs. And we took them all on—and took 'em all out! So, thank you Furious Five.

Thanks to my childhood best friend from the Throggs Neck Projects in the Bronx. Thank you for all of the baby years, Calvin Jackson.

Hey Jackie Tucker, thank you for finding some of the early Black Door fans. I shed some tears hearing their stories and their undying loyalty to me, so wonderful. Thanks for everything. And Michael "Rip" Dunham, thank you for your time and for those long nights. I appreciate it.

As a lot of my acknowledgments are of people, this particular one is a place. The recreation center of the neighborhood in the Bronx, around the corner from 927 Fox Street. The name of this place was Casita Maria. Today there's the YMCA, back then we had the Casita Maria. I want to give high praise to the counselors and to all the people that handled us, that came and went inside the gymnasium. We played kickball, basketball, and swam; we had a safe place for kids. At that time the gangs were running the streets, and whenever I wasn't flying kites or taking apart some electrical device that I found in the junkyard, I would be around the corner at Casita Maria. I want to thank all the staff and all the people for providing us kids in the Bronx with a safe place so that we could grow.